THE MOVING FORCE

The Moving Force

HENRY I. MEYER

A Division of American Management Associations

Library of Congress Cataloging in Publication Data

Meyer, Henry I., 1921-
  The moving force.

  Includes index.
  1. Business enterprises—United States.   I. Title.
HF5343.M5   338.6′44′0973   81-66231
ISBN 0-8144-5712-6   AACR2

First Printing

To Carol

PREFACE

ONE GOOD BOOK deserves another. After writing an introspective and slightly nostalgic book about big business, I decided the world needed a sequel: a study of how the business establishment fits in with other aspects of modern society.

There are two equally valid ways to analyze a polyhedron or a cut diamond: one is to carefully describe each face; the other is to concentrate on the lines of intersection. I follow the second approach. I look at the interfaces between big business and the other facets of our civilization.

This is not a scholarly book. I am not academically qualified to make a definitive study. There is nothing original in my data or in my sources (a disclaimer which should be made for 99 percent of all undergraduate and 95 percent of all graduate texts). Still, I think the book should be read. It should be read by anyone who wants to understand and to preserve the free enterprise system. My interfaces are the front lines of the battle for business survival.

Unless a writer is producing a manual on something like tax accounting, it is impossible to write a book without having one's ideas, prejudices, and conclusions come through—these are what make a book worth reading. My inferences are based on 25 years' experience in the business world and on the better part of a lifetime reading about, observing, and sometimes crying over the passing parade. My interpretations are likely to be different from those of the reader. We are all different. My objective is not to make converts to my basically conservative position (I'll take all I can get) but to present a reasonably well-documented story that readers are free to accept or reject. Some may like it as a "let me do your reading for you" sort of book; others may marvel at my distortions. No matter. The only criticism that hurts is the charge that the book is dull.

If I ramble on anymore, I will be writing an introduction to the introduction—to the first chapter. The real reason for writing a preface is to thank anyone who might possibly have helped the author—and then to announce that none of them can be held at all responsible.

I have had help. Dr. John Ryan, a practicing economist, served as a consultant in economics (some of his opinions had to be cleaned up for family reading). Jeffrey Simon was my guide into the unknown territory of anthropology. Dr. Peter Baur of the London School of Economics was a helpful correspondent. John Kirkland, executive, gave me the benefit of his experience. The Reverend Dr. Donald Webb, president of Centenary College, and Rabbi David Lefkowitz contributed to my chapter on the interface between business and religion. Donald MacRoberts, sometime almost everything, gave me practical advice and encouragement.

Library help is appreciated in the piney woods of northern Louisiana. The local Louisiana State University library gave me the run of its stacks and a lot of the time of Bill McCleary, research librarian. Connie Bihon, librarian of the Pennzoil Research Laboratory, kindly obtained books for me on interlibrary loans.

My greatest debt may be to those who had to put up with me during the gestation period and who read the emerging manuscript. These include my wife and my daughters and their friends when they could be pressed into service.

Any complaints by irate readers will be forwarded to the appropriate consultants.

Henry I. Meyer

CONTENTS

1

INTRODUCTION

THE MOVING FORCE considers the role of the business community in the Western world. This short statement introduces two terms, "business community" and "Western world," for which we need at least working definitions.

I use the term "Western world" broadly to include Churchill's "Great Democracies"; the nations of Western Europe; countries like Australia and South Africa, which have a Western heritage; and other nations like Japan, Taiwan, and Israel, which have derivative Western economic institutions. Although it is no longer possible to say that these are the "have" nations of the world—not with the OPEC countries in the wings—they are the principal actors on the world stage, the ones that have produced the material for our history books and that seem likely to be the movers and shakers for

1

years. Although I have tried to be even-handed, the text is slanted to the American scene. This may seem unfair to any foreign reader, but with my background and experience it could not be any other way.

I use the term "business community" in a rather restricted sense to include only "big business" and its leaders. I am tempted here to refer to my earlier book[1] for a definition, but this raises the "Bertie Wooster dilemma":

> A thing I never know is how much explanation to bung in at the outset . . . those publicans who weren't hanging on my lips the first time are apt to be fogged. Whereas . . . other bimboes, who were so hanging, will stifle yawns and murmur "Old stuff. Get on with it."[2]

My earlier book is not required reading. The definitive points, at least for starters, are that business is big business, is conducted for profit (which eliminates, for example, government departments and philanthropic trusts), has structural units, and is managed by a hierarchy of salaried executives.[3] Business and its managers (businessmen) cannot be separated; they support and define each other. For typical corporate examples, draw a line through AT&T, General Motors, and Texaco. If you are a small business person, remember the last speaker you heard at a Rotary Club meeting, and you have the typical businessman pretty well pegged.

The critical word in the preceding definition is "profit"—the idea that at least a portion of the income generated by a corporation may be retained by that corporation for reinvestment or distributed to its shareholders. It is this concept that separates what I consider the true business community from its look-alikes in government, in

[1] H. I. Meyer, *The Face of Business*, New York: AMACOM, 1980. Hereafter referred to as *HIM*.

[2] P. G. Wodehouse, *The Code of the Woosters*, London: Penguin reprint, 1965, p. 11.

[3] See A. D. Chandler, *The Visible Hand*, Cambridge, Mass.: Harvard University Press, 1977.

education, and in communist countries. Profit—the profit motive—is the moving force, the Holy Spirit, of what is called free enterprise, capitalism, the market economy. Profit is a provocative term like "sex," "abortion," or "original sin." It tends to divide its users, hearers, and readers, into two camps—fur and agin.

The battle between those who believe in profits and those who despise them has been going on for a long time; it is still being fought. It is the crux of the relationship between business and society; it is the story of this book.

BUSINESS AND THE COMMUNITY

The business establishment affects our lives both through the actions of corporations and through the behavior of the businessmen[4] who run them. In the Western world businessmen are still powerful and respected. In Japan they are at the top of the social pecking order; in the United States the business executive is the adult incarnation of the All-American boy. "Executive" has become a prestige adjective: executive-length socks, Executive Inns, executive pocket knives. Whether we like it or not, businessmen do set a standard of behavior and dress—even off-duty linebackers may look like (better paid) junior executives. (There are other people, of course, who pride themselves on *not* looking like businessmen.) A lot of our business leaders could do without this emulation: all they ask is to be left alone; to be allowed to do their own thing; to provide goods and services; to "make" money. Considering the threats to business (we'll get to them later), this may be a dangerous attitude.

It is social status that separates our businessmen from their opposite numbers in other countries. Even in communist countries

---

[4] I use the term "businessman" in this book in the neuter sense to include both sexes. There are women business leaders but, unfortunately, they are still a small minority.

there are managers, salesmen, and staff people who look embarrassingly capitalistic to their own countrymen. The analogy breaks down in the respective respectability of these people. In communist and doctrinaire socialist countries, "business" is part of the state: if its representatives have to dress and act like the despised capitalists when competing in the open market, it is only role playing. When they return home they had better revert to type—like the Southern senator I watched get on a plane in Washington looking like a fashion plate and get off at home with his tie loose, his hair ruffled, and wearing galluses. In less-developed countries the "business" community is an elite group, too small and too far removed from the masses to affect their lives (except occasionally to steal them blind).

The normal relationship between established communities and local industry is one of love/hate. Communities woo industry by all legal (and sometimes extralegal) means: tax breaks, free real estate, access roads, and so on. Once the plant is established the honeymoon is over and aroused groups will protest everything from pollution and waste disposal to the life style of the workers and management.[5] Community leaders know that the way to increase local prosperity, provide new jobs, and inflate real estate values is to encourage new industry and to learn to live with the consequences.

Business influences our society most directly through the goods and services it provides, which are the fabric of modern life. In Western nations this sort of thing is taken for granted. If we need, or want, something and have the money to pay for it, we can buy it and it will be at least reasonably satisfactory. This situation is not true everywhere. In some countries even blue jeans are scarce.

The role of advertising in modern life is curious. Most of us have grown up with a background noise of advertising. We *know* that one brand of soap flakes or beer is much like another; and if we

[5]It is difficult to exaggerate the hatred of business by elements of our society. A singer, Helen Reddy, performed benefit concerts to support Dennis Kucinich (probably the worst mayor Cleveland has ever had) because "I admire anybody who has the courage to stand up against big business."

are considering a "big ticket" item like a car, we resort to consulting friends and a mechanic. Yet advertising campaigns do work. It may be that we are so indifferent to brand names that we tend to buy that which we last heard of. I don't know.

The ultimate impact of business on society is the creation of wealth. Only industry and agriculture can create the money to pay taxes and support the rest of society by the extraction and conversion of natural resources and by the sale of services to *other* countries. Doctors and shopkeepers do provide useful services, but they don't create wealth. Although corporate income taxes are a large source of government revenue, to these must be added an even larger source: the taxes paid by corporate employees and by small operators who depend on the business community. These revenues, plus those paid by independent farmers, are the only real sources of government income. The rest is either confiscation of wealth or printing-press money.

Money is what most businessmen understand best. It is through the money they distribute to the government, to their employees, and to advertising and public relations agencies that they retain their position in society.

BUSINESS AND ITS PEOPLE

For most workers, company policies and benefits are more important to their way of life than are government laws and regulations. It is not even a question of loyalty. Try this experiment. Ask your friends what their children are doing. If they are in my age bracket, their answer will probably be something like "John is with Shell (or IBM or Prudential) and Jane is with GTE (or General Foods or AT&T)"—*not* "John is a research chemist and Jane is an accountant." The tone of voice is what I imagine to be that of a nineteenth-century Englishman saying "Geoffry has gone out to Canada." The corporate name is more important in our thinking than the job itself! This makes sense. To know that a fairly well-educated person is working for EXXON (say) creates a mental picture of the good life, of regular promotions and eventual retirement. The picture is reasonably accurate.[6]

BUSINESS AND NATIONAL PRESTIGE

On the international scene, the business community, through the quality of its exported goods and services, is the defender of the integrity and prestige of the nation—and of its balance of trade. The way business deals with its foreign customers may, in the long run, be more important on the world stage than the doings of a state department or foreign office.

Western countries, represented by their businessmen and their goods, compete not only with each other but, increasingly, with the "business" apparatus of communist and less-developed countries. An important aspect of this dealing is integrity—not for its own sake but for the purpose of establishing customer confidence. The success of Lloyds of London, and its contribution to the English balance of trade, is founded on faith.

BUSINESS AND GOVERNMENT

In the Western world, business is almost a second government, sometimes working with and sometimes against the elected rulers. Business and government may be like a young couple walking confidently, hand in hand, into the future, or they may be like an old couple, grown weary of each other, condemned to sleep in the same bed. This is not an exaggeration. The attitude of government toward business can vary from paternalistic and supportive (Japan) to critical and destructive (England under a Labour administration).

In the United States the situation is mixed. Some industries exist only because of government subsidy and support; others, like the oil companies, are harassed and piously attacked by populists and leftists to score political Brownie points.

The conflict between business and government is largely

[6]See *HIM*, Chapter 5.

ideological. Business wants (or claims it wants) a market economy with the free operation of the profit motive and competition. Bureaucrats don't like to leave things in the hands of such inanimate forces. They want to control and plan; they mistrust profits (windfalls) but they need the prosperity that only business seems able to provide. As we shall see, the natural leaning of bureaucrats is to the left.

Increasingly, business and government serve mutually exclusive parts of society. Business takes care of the affluent and the ambitious, government of the poor and the failures. Business has the better constituency—the people who "count." It also handles (and owes) a lot more money than the government. Its power base should be solid but it is running scared.

Threats to Business

To this point I have painted a rosy picture of the status of the business community in our society: powerful, respected, affluent. There have been a few disturbing notes perhaps, but nothing serious. This is not an accurate picture. The business establishment today is threatened; it is in real trouble. (A Gallup poll taken in June 1979 showed that 28 percent of Americans consider big business to be the biggest threat to the nation—second only to big government.)

Business leaders feel threatened and insecure. They feel imposed upon by their own governments, which in order to care for their wards and to meet other responsibilities have to go to the business community for money. It is hard to like the rent collector, particularly if he tries to tell you how to run your life. Top management also feels threatened from the inside. The goals of management are often different from, even antithetical to, those of middle management and labor.[7]

Fighting the brushfires of government intervention and rising costs and trying to preserve its own perquisites, top management

[7]See *HIM*, Chapter 8.

can lose sight of the ultimate threat to its dynasty—socialism, creeping and otherwise.

The socialist threat is not only from the outside, carried in the turrets of Russian tanks. In every Western nation there are dedicated, often conscientious people who believe that the market economy has had its day and that it is time for a better, socialist world. They are helped by a host of others who are not declared socialists but just antiestablishment. Business is its own enemy! Every blunder, every excess by business plays into the enemy's hands—a patient enemy that is willing to help capitalism destroy itself.

The business community is running for its life, much as a politician runs for office. Marx (Engels?), no mean phrasemaker, said that all the worker had to lose was his chains. All the top manager has to lose is his power, his perquisites, and possibly his life if the revolution gets untidy.

A fast mull over historical writings or even over current news releases shows that nations can exist without a democratic market economy. The "in" gang in many countries consists of bureaucrats, generals, and even crooks. That old standby, theocracy, is staging a comeback. The business-oriented way of life competes for favor with all these -archies and -isms. Even in the United States, the mother church of capitalism, there are competing life styles. The uprisings of the 1960s were not so much prosocialist as antiestablishment.

A dangerous threat, particularly to American business, is organized crime. Not only does organized crime control vast sums of money, but it threatens the business community by infiltration. When syndicate leaders have made a lot of money in honest crime (dope, gambling, prostitution), they seem to develop an irresistible desire to become "respectable" (remember *The Godfather*)—to buy into the legitimate business community, to disappear into the mainstream, and even to look (pretty much) like respectable businessmen. These people bring their own moral code with them, a code that does not meet the minimum level of morality and credibility that business must maintain to survive. Perhaps the problem will cure itself in a generation or two. After all, some of today's most respected names in business and politics are those of yesterday's robber barons.

THE BATTLE

With these competing trends, the most useful way to discuss the place of business in Western society is to treat it as a battleground.

Part One of this book considers the way things are, or should be, in a market or capitalist economy (defined later). I look at the good things promised by capitalism—prosperity, favorable national image and balance of trade, tender loving care of employees—and at the much misunderstood morality of the business world. I try to distinguish the real soldiers of capitalism from the hangers-on who benefit from it.

Part Two gives equal time to the enemy, which I identify as socialism. Socialism (or communism) may seem like a pretty strong word for all the different forms of collectivism proposed to "fix" the capitalist system, but I don't think this is unfair. Anti-free enterprise fixes may not be compatible with socialist ideology, but they do help its cause. There really is no other civilized alternative economic system—we don't have a legitimate school of despotic economics. The actors in the socialist scenario are an interesting bunch.

Part Three examines the battleground, the social and anthropological fields where the battle is joined: in government, in the media, in church, in school, and most important in casual, off-duty contacts between people.

Part Four is more subjective. Here I consider the stakes in the battle, with a respectful nod in the direction of Friedrich Hayek.[8] Finally I succumb to the occupational disease of writers and professors and play God. I give advice. I tell business what it ought to do to help its cause. Not required reading.

[8]F. A. Hayek, *The Road to Serfdom*, Chicago: University of Chicago Press, 1944.

PART ONE

The Way It Is

2

BUSINESS AND CAPITALISM

My daddy makes book on the corner,
My mother sells synthetic gin,
My sister makes love for a dollar,
My God how the money rolls in!

American folk song, ca. 1930

IF WESTERN BUSINESS is the manifestation of capitalism, our first step had better be to try to define capitalism. What is it anyway? And while we are at it, we will take a look at some other key entries in the Western business lexicon, including free (or individual) enterprise, the competitive system, market pricing, and the profit motive.

OLD IDEAS

As a starting point, I turn to my handy-dandy up-to-date reference: the fourteenth edition of the *Encyclopædia Britannica*. In it J. L. Garvin starts encouragingly, "Capital may be most briefly described as wealth used in producing more wealth: and capitalism as the system directing that process." Then he throws in the towel. "There is no satisfactory definition of the term, though nothing is more evident than the thing." Not much help. He does make the interesting point that "capitalism" was first used by socialists as a term of reproach but was accepted and gloried in by those it was meant to stigmatize. Matching deed to word, Garvin then gets carried away describing the contributions of capitalism to the good life: the provision of goods and services for everybody through the concentration of wealth for its effective utilization; the growth of cities (Marx said this had rescued a considerable part of the population from the idiocy of rural life); the distribution of wealth and learning; the emancipation of the worker. Garvin gives the United States his highest marks, and offers a touching description of American workers going to work in their own motor cars.

Garvin is an early example of a long line of popular speakers at Rotary clubs who define capitalism by its successes rather than by its content. (The fact that he was editor-in-chief of this edition of the encyclopædia may have made it easier to get away with such editorializing.) This attitude is rather like that of the man who said, "Hell, yes, I believe in baptism. I've seen it."

Garvin's article was written in the 1920s, in retrospect a happier and simpler time (at least for businessmen) when the triumph of capitalism seemed sure. Even then there were a few dissenters. About the same time, another Englishman (Irishman), G. B. Shaw, was writing *The Intelligent Woman's Guide to Socialism*. Like most socialist writers, Shaw was shocked by the unequal distribution of wealth. To be fair, Garvin did admit that capitalism had its faults, but he had the happy 1920s concept that they would all be cured by time. Garvin lived to see the Great

Depression and Shaw to see the Labour party take over in England. The gods laughed.

NEW IDEAS

It is fun to play with the past but not always helpful. Let us consider some modern writers: Heilbroner, Galbraith, and Friedman.[1] Unfortunately, all three are economists—I say "unfortunately" because economists always seem to be lecturing to us outsiders. They also lecture to each other, so I guess I shouldn't complain.

Robert L. Heilbroner gets off to a great start in *The Limits of American Capitalism*[2] by completely begging the question: "Capitalism and business are, after all, virtually synonymous—*capitalism* being the historian's term for the system abstractly conceived, *business* the common word for the system in its daily operation." This definition is a vicious circle, like those frustrating dictionary entries where word A is defined by word B, which is defined by word A. Still, Heilbroner's book is a good one, and he probably doesn't *need* a definition for his audience. He is interested in many of the same things that I am: the place of business *in* society and the influence of business *on* society. He doesn't like business very much.

For Heilbroner, business includes General Motors and mom-and-pop stores, whereas I am mostly concerned with big business. There is a warning here for me. He points out that the influence of big business is often exercised through its interpretation by small businessmen. He has some specific bones to pick: he is concerned

---

[1]An arbitrary choice. I have omitted the writer I think does the best job: J. A. Schumpeter, *Capitalism, Socialism, and Democracy*, New York: Harper & Row, 1950. His arguments are too carefully reasoned to paraphrase. I will refer to this book later as *CSD*.

[2]New York: Harper & Row, 1966.

with the change in, and the rate of change of, the role and influence of business in American society and with the evolution of what he calls planned capitalism (more on this later). An interesting writer. In *American Capitalism*[3] John K. Galbraith *uses* the term capitalism rather than defining it. He does say in a footnote that "this term . . . denotes that the men who own the business . . . have a major responsibility for decision. . . ." The remark adds a couple of useful dimensions: ownership (private property or capital) and the freedom to make decisions by businessmen or managers. Free enterprise enters the equation. Galbraith stresses another essential element: competition. "The first requirement of the classical system, as everyone is aware [related to the mathematician's phrase "as one easily sees"], is competition." Like Heilbroner, Galbraith has several bones to pick, preferably from the carcasses of dead and dying businessmen. He says his is a good-humored book—black humor from the business point of view.

Now let us swim in more friendly waters and consider the writings of Milton Friedman. Although he doesn't define capitalism either—any more, I guess, than a writer on laser-induced fusion would stop to define nuclear physics—he does add some fresh slants. Daylight perhaps. Friedman is particularly concerned with freedom[4] and with the influence, or lack of influence, of the central government on the health of the business community, He says, ". . . government must be limited. Its major function must be to protect our freedom, both from the enemies outside our gates and from our fellow citizens, to preserve law and order, to enforce private contracts, to foster competitive markets." Now here is a comment worthy of being framed and hung in any board room. It is a modern restatement of the dogma of Adam Smith and of the sanctity of contracts (private property). Not only must government *allow* competitive goings-on; it should enforce their validity: free enterprise, laissez faire, dog eat dog, *sauve qui peut*, and Katie bar

[3]Boston: Houghton Mifflin, 1952.
[4]In, for example, *Capitalism and Freedom*, Chicago: University of Chicago Press, 1962.

the door. Actually, very few modern businessmen would be comfortable in such an environment. They may be chicken.

Two names keep cropping up: those of the Scotsman Adam Smith and of the German Karl Marx—the good guy and the bad guy. Although these two men lived a hundred years apart—Smith in the eighteenth century and Marx in the nineteenth—both were observers of the growth of industrial society and the concentration of labor for production. Things changed more slowly then. Both were excellent historians in that they examined the present changes in the structure of society as well as the long story behind it. Their researches consolidated current thinking, along with their own, and provided points of departure for further work. They were concerned with future trends as well as with the present; and their writings had, and continue to have, profound influence on political and economic thinking, even though their books are not now widely read by businessmen or by politicians.

ADAM SMITH

Smith looked at the emerging Industrial Revolution and found it good. The pooling of laborers and the division of the tasks of labor increased the effectiveness of the worker and produced more goods for the benefit of society (Smith considered *services* useful but unproductive). He believed in paper money backed by gold and thought that the suppliers of money should be paid for its use (a proposition not completely accepted in his day). Competition, free competition, was the only force required to keep the manufacturing game honest. Smith even supported free trade between nations—a radical position in those days. Like the modern businessman, he did not consider profits to be an ugly word: competition would keep them under control. Like Friedman, he proposed that the proper role of government is to create a climate in which business can freely compete and to provide only those services such as armed forces and roads that are not economically viable for private enterprise. The crowning glory of his inductive analysis was his conclusion that the cumulative result of the individual strivings by entrepreneurs[5] for profit was good—that is was the only way to set fair market prices. The wealth of nations through industrialization could safely be left to the natural working of human greed, to the "invisible hand."

Smith's conclusion was probably right, *in his day*. Certainly no more effective method than free enterprise has been observed for releasing and utilizing the creative and organizational capacities of uncommon men and women. The massive exploitation of the workers by the mill owners, which was to come in the next century, was not yet apparent. The drain of natural resources in those early days amounted only to a scratching of the surface. Besides, there were hordes of itinerant laborers who needed jobs.

KARL MARX

Marx was a giant: philosopher, historian, economist, and writer. One tends to think of him as a wild-eyed reader in the library of the British Museum with a smoking, black, spherical bomb in his hand. Not a true picture. For one thing, the librarians would never have allowed it. Although he is usually regarded as an anti-Christ by businessmen and demagogues, his works, and most of his researches and conclusions, were scholarly and accurate.

Unlike Smith's books, which are largely ignored by the academic community today (except for their convenient conclusion), Marx's works are actively studied. Now that Joseph McCarthy is safely tamped down, there are even self-professed Marxist economists in American universities.

Marx looked at his world and found it bad. The labor concentrations approved of by Smith had turned into dirty, ugly, crowded, unsanitary cities. The English Midlands were shrouded in

[5]The term "capitalists" had yet to be invented.

a pall of black smoke.[6] "Where there's muck there's money." Children toiled from dawn to dark in the mines and at the spindles (often as an alternative to starvation). Exploitation of man by man; cruel, unequal distribution of wealth. All this in the face of rapidly increasing national prosperity in the industrial countries. As a historian, Marx looked for the reason why.

Marx adopted a materialistic interpretation of history: the modes of production in society ultimately determine its social, political, and spiritual character. He accepted the idea of separate, well-defined classes of society striving for domination. Following this approach, he saw the Industrial Revolution as a triumph of the middlemen—the merchants, the artisans, the traders—over the lords of the feudal system. The energy and intelligence of this class, the bourgeoisie, had transformed the Western world. Marx had a tremendous admiration for the bourgeoisie, which

> during its rule of scarce one hundred years, has created more massive and more colossal productive forces than have all the preceding generations together. Subjugation of Nature's forces to man [and] machinery, application of chemistry to industry and agriculture, steam navigation, railways, electric telegraphs, clearing of whole continents for cultivation, canalization of rivers, whole populations conjured out of the ground—what earlier century had even a presentiment that such productive forces slumbered in the lap of social labor?[7]

Marx also realized that *with money goes power* (a good capitalist concept) and that for this reason the new bourgeoisie had taken over control from the old aristocracy. With all these great goings-on, the people at the bottom, the workers, the proletariat, had had a raw deal. It was time for a change.

[6]The scars still show. The American visitor to England has to be impressed by the millions and millions of bricks laid by Victorian bricklayers in railway stations, embankments, and mills. The visitor may be more impressed by the rich, dark patina of these bricks—the result of a hundred years of exposure to coal smoke.

[7]*The Communist Manifesto*.

Dealing always from the position of class consciousness, Marx decided it was time for workers to have a say in their own destiny. There were two alternatives: reform the system from within to be more humane and representative or have the proletariat class do what the bourgeoisie had done—take over. Marx made his fatal decision. The workers must take over and the only route was revolution.

This was not an illogical conclusion. From what he had seen of the leaders of industry and government, he didn't expect much compassion from them. His own situation may have influenced his judgment. One of the greatest thinkers of his time, he lived in grinding poverty. (It is still a good idea to go with the establishment. Marxist economists don't get many lucrative consulting jobs.) Marx could hardly see that amelioration of the worker's lot within the existing system was exactly what was going to happen—that the rise of labor unions with leaders like Keir Hardie, who used universal suffrage to turn union power into political power and the awakening of social conscience, would lead managers to turn from being Scrooges to being Big Brothers.

Actually, there was a third alternative which Marx could not admit with his rigid class distinctions—a blurring of class lines to permit upward (and downward) mobility. To this day Marxism is strongest among workers in countries like England where class distinctions are most clearly drawn.[8]

Marx's attitude toward religion—do away with it—makes him clearly an anti-Christ to modern Western man. Again his position was reasonable. Taking a long historical look, he couldn't see that religion had done much for the little people. In fact, organized religion had been a means of keeping them quiet and under control—"the opiate of the masses."

---

[8]Marxism in England comes in all degrees, from Communist party members (common among shop stewards) to the New Left and assorted other groups.

Marx *had* to reject religion! His humanitarian concept of an eventual man-made utopia on earth directly contradicts the Western religious doctrine of original sin—that people are basically bad. Judging by the unpleasant way people have been treating each other for thousands of years, this seems to me to be the strongest plank in Judeo-Christian theology.

So much for Marx. He may have been wrong but he probably understood capitalism as well as anyone, before or since.

THE CAPITALIST SYSTEM

Having wallowed among economists, ancient and modern, I can understand why Thomas Carlyle called economics "the dismal science." The main theme of modern writers seems to be that we are all going to hell in a plastic–gold–unstructured handbasket. Take your choice. I have to look out of the window occasionally to reassure myself that the sun is still shining, the sky is still blue, and the grass is green. Every modern economist seems to take the position that every *other* economist is sadly misguided. (As my economist consultant said, "Most of them are!")

I don't believe there is any such thing as *capitalism* as a form of government in the Western nations except possibly in an opportunistic hanger-on like Singapore. Such a government would have as its sole raison d'être the welfare of business and industry—the sort of freewheeling thing that Milton Friedman calls for. In an earlier day, perhaps, the American government did approach pure capitalism. It was an American president, Calvin Coolidge, who said, "The business of America is business." Today Western governments have other priorities—social, cultural, and environmental—that compete with the single-minded promotion of business prosperity. The priorities vary from country to country.

What does exist, in my opinion, is a *capitalist system*, a system in which people do things with their own talents and resources to enrich themselves beyond the going subsistence level. This system, free enterprise, is not confined to Western nations. It is an instinct, an inherent striving of mankind. Even in Russia, the peasant sedulously cultivates his allotted garden plot to sell his vegetables on the open (free) market. The more tolerant government is of this basic desire of people to do their own thing, the bigger and more efficient profit-making organizations become. The full flowering is the modern multinational corporation. While the permissiveness of government allows this sort of thing to go on, there will be feedback—big business gains some control of government. With money goes power.

Conditions for Capitalism

The forms of government in the Western nations range from welfarism to something approaching pure capitalism. I don't want to get bogged down in a discussion of political science (another dismal science?), and I don't have to as long as I confine this discussion to the conditions that allow the capitalistic system to function.

Government must leave some room for the profit motive to operate, for a competitive market to set prices, and for risk capital to accumulate. There must be a responsible banking system to make money available at a fair price and to protect its value (and not devalue it by creating more). There must be an institution to spread unacceptable risks—the insurance company. These conditions are sufficiently met even in a nominally socialist country like Sweden to allow the capitalistic system to work. Competition does not have to be fostered by government; it will exist in any society as long as people buy things for a price. Government actions can keep competition parochial or let it be international.

The relationship between democracy and capitalism is subtle (we will get back to it later). The trouble with "democracy" as a useful word or as a condition for capitalism is that it has been debased by being appropriated by Russian satellite nations, by military dictatorships, and by every tribal leader in Africa. Democracy, as we shall see, can be a two-edged sword. The definitive characteristic of *Western* democracy, which seems to be a necessary condition for capitalism to prosper, is not that leaders are elected by popular vote—elected Conservatives tend to behave like Labourites and Democrats like Republicans once they are in office—but that we can elect our leaders *out* of office when we want a change. When John Adams, the first defeated incumbent, quietly left office, he did more for American democracy than most presidents are in a position to do.

The profit motive is the driving force of free enterprise, of the capitalist system. Unless he knows that he can *keep* some of his gains, only an idiot is going to take risks. The profit motive can be dried up in a welfare society by excessive taxation and redistribution of wealth: it does not exist in a doctrinaire socialist system where all the profits (if any) go to the government. Without the profit motive and private property there is still "business." People still make things and provide services, but the spark is gone. The goals of business leaders then become confined to acquiring prestige and perquisites. Short-term satisfaction becomes more important than long-term corporate health. When a corporation has no incentive to stay lean and mean, it quickly becomes cluttered with more or less useless staff departments and executives with important-sounding titles. Innovation is not only discouraged; it is dangerous. "Don't rock the boat" and "Wait for promotion." Corporations start to look and act like government departments. Pure socialism is a good idea that doesn't work.[9]

Any nation that allows its people enough political and economic freedom, that permits its risk takers to keep enough of the profits of their chances, that supports a responsible banking system, and that protects the integrity of its paper money creates the conditions under which the capitalist system can and will prosper. Heilbroner is right: business is the outward, visible sign of capitalism in action.

[9]Apologies to Schumpeter *(CSD)*, who says, "Of course it can."

STOCK MARKETS, BANKS, AND INSURANCE COMPANIES

Stock markets are often pointed to with pride as the essence of the capitalist system in action, as a way to make capitalists out of everybody. Actually, the markets are the servants of the system. They provide a mechanism whereby someone with an idea (one that can pass government scrutiny) can get others to provide capital, share the risk, and join him. He does not have to go to banks to get money and commit himself to pay interest before he knows whether his idea is going to pay off. All he has to do is sell his idea and the promise of shared profits to others. Once the shares are sold and on the open market, they start to lead lives of their own, but this is another story.[10]

Banks are to business what a storage reservoir is to a water distribution system. They soak up excess funds and pay interest on them; they lend funds and charge (higher) interest on them. The bond market serves the same function: in this respect it is a sort of distributed bank. This is an intentional simplification. Bankers do many other things, such as providing channels in international money movements and converting different currencies.

Banks have a good thing going, like gambling houses that provide gamblers with a place to play and take a small cut out of every pot. As long as there is action, and his loans are prudent, the banker makes his modest return on other people's money.

The government is the banker of last resort. The money it collects, prints, lends, and gives away is taxpayers' money. The only recognized alternative to a money system based on gold—which does discipline the money supply but ties up a very useful and beautiful metal for an unnatural purpose—is paper money backed by national prestige. Only if a government behaves in a responsible way to protect the value of its paper money will that money be accepted as something worth saving and as a medium of international exchange. During the days of empire, when England was the

[10]See *HIM*, Chapter 6.

world's great trading nation, the preservation of the integrity of the British pound was an act of faith—more important than mere unemployment or hunger.[11]

Insurance companies do the same thing for a business that they do for a homeowner: they take a risk that an individual does not want to assume alone and spread it among others in the same boat. Knowing that this service is available allows the businessman to take chances. It lubricates the capitalist system. The insurance business is truly international: a nation does not need its own. There are plenty of English, Canadian, or American companies that are eager to distribute reasonable risks in any part of the world. This condition for the smooth operation of the capitalist system is laid on everywhere.

BIGNESS AND BADNESS

Most writers view the increasing concentration of power among corporations with alarm. This phenomenon is apparent in all Western nations: corporations like ICI in England, Mitsubishi in Japan, Citrœn in France, and I. G. Farben in Germany go from strength to strength. It is the trend on the American scene that is easiest for me to document.

Fortune magazine annually publishes its famous list of the 500 biggest industrial corporations in the United States. The *Fortune* 500 leaves out some of the largest (nonindustrial) corporations, but there is a lot of concentration even in this attenuated list. The top 50 of the listed firms have sales as much as the other 450 together. Of this elite group, the top 10 have total sales equal to the other 40. This is "absolute concentration."

Outside the industrial sector there are other giants. In finance,

[11]One of the key points of Dorothy Sayers' mystery *Have His Carcase* is the incredible behavior of the victim, who had changed 300 good English pounds into gold. "Why on earth would anybody want to clutter himself up with all that gold?" says Lord Peter Wimsey.

there are banks like Chase Manhattan and insurance companies like Prudential; in transportation, giants like Santa Fe and United Airlines; in communications, AT&T; in retailing, Sears and Coca-Cola. These are biggies. In fact, a selection of fewer than 200 of the largest corporations of all kinds fairly represents American capitalism in action. It *is* American business.

Is this concentration bad? Most writers and government bureaucrats think so.[12] In my opinion, not always. I want to buy my insurance from a *big* company, corporations must deal with big banks, we have the best telephone system in the world, and shoppers want to take advantage of the low profit margins that only giant retailers can live with.

Absolute concentration is bad when it eliminates competition—the necessary element in a market economy—and allows the manufacturers rather than the buyers to call the tune. (This seems to have happened in the American automobile industry after World War II when manufacturers turned out gaudy monsters with built-in obsolescence. It was *foreign* competition that made them clean up their act.) If you are going to admit competition as an element of healthy capitalism, you have to allow winners! Otherwise business is playing a puerile game, like the noncompetitive sports now advocated for our children. Whether we like it or not, we do have big business and small business. It is big business that shapes our society—with a strong assist from small business, which picks up loose ends and which, with good management and a little bit of luck, may become "big."

---

[12]Not Schumpeter. He argues that oligopoly is the most effective manifestation of the capitalist system. See *CSD*, Chapter 7.

3

GOOD THINGS

THE PROPONENTS of competing economic systems have to at least promise good things to the people. The rallying cry of the French Revolution was *liberté, égalité, fraternité,* This is a useful triad but it is not enough. A group of castaways on a desert island might have complete liberty in the absence of laws and regulations; as far as fraternity is concerned they might enjoy an orgy if they chose; but equality might just be the right to starve together. We need to add some more good things, preferably ones that have been sanctified by having been fought for. The following list is complete enough for our purposes:

- Freedom *(liberté)*
- Equality *(égalité)*

- Quality of life *(fraternité)*
- Security
- Prosperity
- Democracy

None of these items means exactly what it seems, or at least each means something different to different people. The items are not independent: it is quite possible to trade off one for another. They are still the prizes that all leaders and would-be leaders promise, in different degrees, to their subjects and disciples.

Different emphases are due to different priorities, interpretations, and trade-offs. The socialist stresses equality and security, if necessary at the expense of some of the other prizes. The postindustrialist places a higher priority on quality of life than on prosperity or material things. For the capitalist, prosperity is the thing. Not that he despises or rejects the other graces, but he believes that with prosperity all things are possible: without it you have a mean society.

All leaders promise democracy, but they don't mean the same thing by it. I leave this item for Chapter 20. Until then we can just accept democracy as a good thing that everyone talks about but that few have. We can take a closer look here at the other items as they apply to modern society, but since we are now speaking from the free enterprise side of the aisle, let us first consider prosperity.

PROSPERITY, WEALTH, AND POWER

There is individual prosperity, a measure of how citizens are doing, and national prosperity, a more elusive concept only partially defined as cumulative individual prosperity. A nation's prosperity and power depend to some extent on its intrinsic wealth but to an even greater extent on the industry and abilities of its people and on the form of the economic system in which they work. In the Western world it is the business establishment, fettered or encouraged by government, that is the principal agent in mobilizing human efforts to provide a decent life.

I have introduced two concepts in the preceding paragraph that are related to prosperity—"wealth" and "power." Individual wealth is not quite the same thing as individual prosperity. In Western society, where there is private property and ownership, a person's wealth can be determined by an accountant who draws up a statement of assets, debt, and equity or ownership. The critical financial report is the balance sheet, not the income statement, which shows rate of change. The net—what a person owns minus what he owes—is the measure of his wealth. It is the amount of the world's goods that providence has seen fit to put in his hands at this time.

Individual prosperity, on the other hand, is a state of mind. It is a relative concept that shows human nature at its worst. A person is "rich" only if he has more than his visible contemporaries—that the average citizen of a Western nation is much better off than the great mass of humanity doesn't count. Conversely, a person is "poor" if he isn't keeping up. He gets no marks for having more than the starving millions in Calcutta. Only if a significant fraction of a nation's people consider themselves well off, or to have prospects of becoming so, can a nation consider itself to be prosperous and—ultimately—stable.

National wealth is hard to pin down. There is *intrinsic* national wealth—the sum of a nation's agricultural, extractive, and strategic resources. The total can be divided by the population to give a per-person intrinsic wealth figure, but this is not a negotiable asset. Using this criterion, the Japanese and the Swiss would be poor and the Canadians the richest people in the world. Americans in the Great Depression would have been better off than they are now! Intrinsic wealth certainly makes it easier for a nation to become great, but in the short run it doesn't have much to do with individual wealth or prosperity. (In the long run, as Keynes pointed out, we are all dead.)

A better way to figure the wealth of a nation might be to add up the wealth of all its residents. Even this can be misleading. In the Western world, investment and finance are international. Americans own billions of dollars worth of other countries, and other countries are buying up an increasing share of us. We are forced to the conclusion that at least as important as individual wealth are the ability and morale of a nation's people (more on this later), the efficiency of its productive plant and business establishment, the economic climate, and the responsibility of its government. These things are hard to measure.

Power is the outward visible sign of national wealth, preparedness, integrity, and resolve. There are different kinds of national power: military, financial, legal, even moral.

Occasionally, one country is so powerful that it builds up a sort of international police force to make the world safe for commerce and for itself. The British navy took on this job for over a hundred years (during this period, the British army was tiny by continental standards). The United States tried on the policeman's helmet after World War II and found it didn't fit. The world is a more orderly place with a cop on the beat, but there don't seem to be any volunteers. The one nation–one vote concept in the General Assembly makes the United Nations pathetic. By the time the Assembly agrees on the ideological and racial composition of a task force a crisis has to resolve itself one way or another.

The Eastern and Western nations are now armed to the teeth, not because they are anticipating an old-fashioned imperialist aggression but more because they don't trust each other. They are rather like two Mountain families perpetuating an old feud. This is terribly expensive; it drains national resources and limits national prosperity.

Objective Measures—GNP

In order to get some sort of objective handle on national wealth and prosperity, statisticians have devised various yardsticks: gross national product, net national product, national income, personal income, and disposable personal income. Of these, the most famous is the gross national product (GNP), although most people might consider disposable (aftertax) personal income to be more important.

The GNP is defined by the U.S. Department of Commerce as "the market value of the output of goods and services before depreciation charges and other allowances for the consumption of durable and capital goods." In other words, it is total production. Probably the easiest way of computing GNP is the "consumption" method,[1] which entails adding together these four items:

Personal consumption expenditures: durable goods (automobiles, boats); nondurable goods (food, clothing); services (rent, transportation).

Gross private domestic investment: mostly new housing.

Net exports of goods and services: export value minus import value.

Government purchases of goods and services: federal, state, and local (transfer payments excluded).

It may seem curious that production is computed by adding together four *consumption* categories, but this is a valid approach. If a firm makes things and doesn't sell them, it isn't contributing much to national prosperity. The relative sizes of these four items for a particular country are significant. For the United States in 1976, for example, they were:

Personal consumption	$1,094 billion
Domestic investment	$ 243 billion
Net exports	$ 8 billion
Government purchases	$ 361 billion

[1]This is the method used by the U.S. Department of Commerce, Bureau of Economic Analysis, which publishes data in *The Survey of Current Business* and in *Business Statistics*.

Obviously, we were then an inward-looking nation. Before the OPEC oil price rise, our GNP was made up chiefly of things we bought from each other or of goods and services purchased by the government. The export item for a country like Switzerland is a much more important part of GNP. Unfortunately, the Western nations cannot all get rich by taking in each other's laundry.

The last item, government purchases, is understated in terms of money handled. So-called transfer payments are omitted. These include interest on government bonds, veterans' benefits, and welfare payments—all huge items. These transfer payments *should* be omitted from the GNP, as they amount to taking money from some people and giving it to others. *Robar de uno santo para pagar otro.* Transfer payments don't affect the GNP, but they greatly affect individual prosperity.

Government spending for military people and hardware *is* included in the GNP. In peacetime, service people spend their working life in training and on make-work projects. (In wartime, the GNP doesn't matter much.) The salaries of these people might better be treated as transfer payments. Payment for military hardware, even if necessary, buys little of lasting value. In peace, such materiel self-destructs through obsolescence; in war, much of it is abandoned or falls into unfriendly hands. (I saw acres of B-24 bombers staked out and rotting in the jungle after World War II.)

The GNP is a useful figure if only because it can be computed and tracked from quarter to quarter and from year to year. But as a true measure of national prosperity, it leaves something to be desired.

The true measure of the prosperity of a nation lies in the hearts and minds of its people. It can be assayed by some sort of poll: "Are you reasonably content? Do you think things are going to get better? Worse? Remain about the same?" This sort of poll is often taken by an outfit like Gallup or Harris and is published in the media. It is hard to give the results a numerical value.

A lot of comparison or envy is involved in personal satisfaction.

It used to be enough to keep up with the Joneses next door, but with modern communications people in faraway places like Guatemala can compare their own life style with the fatuous style shown on American soap operas. One sure indication of a nation's prosperity or contentment is the direction in which its border guards face: outward, to keep others out; or inward, to keep its own people in. Another clue is the way a citizen defines his own nationality to foreigners: the "-ans" and the "froms." "I am a German or an Englishman," or "I am *from* _____."

For most of us in the Western world, satisfaction is closely related to wealth and opportunity. "Do I have enough money? Is there opportunity for me and for my children?" For us this is number one. In other cultures, different items on our list of goodies may be more important.

EQUALITY

I don't think the old French revolutionaries expected *égalité* in the distribution of wealth. What they did want was equality of status—the end of the class system. ("John is as good as his master.") This is one form of equality; there are others.

Some hard-core communists do look for egalitarian distribution of wealth, but most admit that some income differentials are essential for an orderly society (the commissars, of course, are more equal than others). What they do object to is too much disparity in the distribution of income. They are not alone. In all Western nations there is a trend to income equalization: tax and inheritance laws and union pressures are the movers in this direction.

In Western nations there are two social definitions of equality that are accepted as decent goals. The first is equality of opportunity: the concept that no citizen should be penalized because of situations beyond his control—race, sex, disability, economic status of parents, or habitat. Equal educational, cultural, and employment opportunities should be available to everyone. The fight against prejudice and discrimination goes on. It is far from (and probably never will be) won; but judging from the changes made in my lifetime, the world is now a better place for a lot of people than it ever was.

The second social equality goal is the concept that every citizen (even a resident!) is entitled to at least a minimum standard of living. The minimum is maintained by handouts from government agencies to the poor. As this sort of redistribution of wealth becomes a preoccupation of government, we move toward what is called the welfare society. Welfarism is a preoccupation in many countries and will continue to be as long as the getters have the same voting rights as the givers.

Under the provisions of almost 200 programs, the United States hands out more money than the national budget of most nations: direct payments, rent subsidies, food stamps, and in the near future, I assume, fuel stamps. (Food stamps look a lot like the vouchers we will discuss when we look at socialism.) Bureaucrats like "stamps." The day may come when we have more directed currencies: automobile stamps, mortage stamps, and so on.

Welfarism is not bad. If the alternative is letting people starve or freeze, it is necessary. The legitimate question is the *minimum* level of support that must be paid for by the productive elements of society—by business and its employees. It cannot be so high that it takes away incentive to accept an entry-level job rather than stay on the dole. It should not place an intolerable burden on business competing in the world market. When the minimum support level in one country is higher than the going level for workers in other countries, the labor market becomes unstable. Such situations are now common: England and Pakistan, the United States and the Caribbean nations are examples.

FREEDOM

The proponents of all movements and systems promise freedom, of a sort. The word is so ambiguous that it is usually modified:

freedom from want, freedom of speech, political freedom. The freedom that business needs is economic freedom.

Economic freedom is no more than that a nation's laws permit the market economy, the capitalist system, to function—that they permit competition to set prices, allow the accumulation of risk capital, permit the retention of at least some profit, and allow entry into markets. To leftists and socialists, all this sounds like dangerous exploitation. To a businessman, it is just a statement of basic needs. His claim on society to grant him economic freedom follows this logic:

Given enough economic freedom,

Then business can create national prosperity.

If and only if there is prosperity can the nation afford the other good things that will be largely administered by government.

This is the sequence of thought that created the "economic miracle" in Germany after World War II. It is the sequence that Prime Minister Thatcher is trying to reinstate in England.

To the capitalist, socialists are not necessarily evil; they just have things backward. They want the benefits before they can afford them. The sequence starts with freedom.

QUALITY OF LIFE

Quality of life, as I use the term, refers to nonmaterial values: relaxation, participation in the arts, and (most important from the business point of view) preservation of the environment. As more of their basic needs are filled, people demand quality of life.

Under *pure* capitalism, a business leader cannot afford to be a nice guy and provide these things—competition won't let him. Unless his competitors do so, he can't afford to backfill and landscape the desolation of a strip mine; he can't afford to clean up stack gases. He can't process wastes while his competitors dump theirs in a creek. He has to hire workers as cheaply as possible and work them as hard as he can. This was the situation in the United

States until recently. Check out the strip-mined desolation in southern Illinois, the remains of the Mesabi Range in Minnesota, the pollution of Lake Erie. Read about the big city sweatshops and the Homestake mine. Uncontrolled capitalism does not offer quality of life. Business is not immoral; it is amoral.

Only a higher authority over all corporations can keep the capitalist ship from tearing up the road (to mix a metaphor). Although capitalism is amoral, most businessmen are responsible citizens. They are eager to work with government to help set those operating groundrules that the public is willing to pay for.

SECURITY

Security is the antithesis of the free enterprise system. If freewheeling capitalism rewards the winners, it must destroy the losers. In a truly competitive system, the only security is success. Top management has all the security of a Texas football coach, and middle management all the security of a major-league second baseman. Their jobs are safe only until someone better comes along. Some years ago a group of us (middle managers) were being oriented on our temporary assignment as members of a business task force. We had been relieved of our regular duties; we were uneasy. One of us raised the question of how we would be reassigned when the temporary assignment was over. The president of the company, with what then seemed to me to be a hideous leer, said, "Well, gentlemen, all our jobs are really temporary, aren't they?" He was right. In a few months our company was taken over by a tender offer and we had a new president.

Hold it, Newt! Something has got to be wrong here. In the introduction I brought up the commonly observed point that joining a big corporation makes a person secure and pampered for the rest of his working and natural life (just how secure and pampered we will see later). In the preceding chapter I said that big business is the modern manifestation of the capitalist system. My premise still stands. Those organizations that *do* operate under true free enterprise have to be organized like a baseball team[2]: job security depends on what one has done lately. Advertising agencies and civil engineering firms that bid for jobs come to mind. There are people who thrive in such an environment—people like Tex McCarthy who are either very rich or very poor depending on when you look them up. Big business is the manifestation of free enterprise *only* to the extent that it can stand the heat. Only top executives, people like Lee Iococca, have to face the harsh competitive facts of life (until the company goes broke). The rest of us are willing to let them take all the risks. For everyone to work in a competitive donnybrook would place too much strain on the nerves and the duodenum. In my anecdote, the president lost his job; I didn't lose mine.

The trade-off between risk and security goes on in every board room. Insofar as management opts for security, it may weaken its competitive position; it can weaken the capitalist system.

Security is insidious. It is bought at the price of someone else's or one's own freedom and quality of life. Whenever a union wins more security for its members, whenever a professional group gets protective legislation, the rest of us pay for it. Security is the siren call of the socialist and of the left; it is the *sine qua non* of the civil service. The German people traded the freedom of the Weimar Republic for the "security" of the Third Reich. (They also traded away quality of life, at least for some. The arts, particularly the cinema, blossomed in pre-Hitler Germany, as did the sciences and mathematics.[3] Let us look at a modern example.

In an interview of an East German couple, Dieter and Anneliese Bernhard, Hella Pick found that they were content with their status and with their country.[4] They even approved of the

[2]See *HIM*, Chapter 2.

[3]A whole generation of American mathematicians got their learning from the "yellow books"—the *Mathematischen Wissenshaften* published by Springer in Berlin.

[4]*Manchester Guardian Weekly*, October 14, 1979.

Berlin Wall as a method of preventing the West Germans from "taking away their trained doctors and engineers." Speaking of freedom of dissent, Dieter said, "That is not the kind of freedom I want." The freedom "we enjoy is freedom from unemployment and the freedom of social equality." Two trade-offs in one sentence!

Before sneering too openly at these misguided communists, let us consider a couple of points. Dieter and Anneliese are probably as smart as we are. He is an engineer and she a teacher. They both seem to like and to be good at their work. How much freedom are we willing to compromise in the name of security? Will we quit our jobs, or will we let our employer dictate what kind of ties we may wear? (IBM did.) Will we let our employer tell us how long our hair should be? That we should contribute to a political action committee? That we should take asinine aptitude tests to determine our career path rather than being judged by performance? Security is a corrupting grace.

Of the good things we have talked about, the only one that business takes direct responsibility for, given the right kind of operating climate, is prosperity. Even the security and equality of its employees depend on outside guidelines. There must be some accommodation, willing or unwilling, between business and government to provide the good things for all citizens. This is a big enough subject to deserve a new chapter.

4

GOVERNMENT AND BUSINESS

A Siamese twin from Glen Feather
Said to his girl friend named Heather,
"If it weren't for this dude,
Who's a bit of a prude,
We could make beautiful music together."

BIG BUSINESS and government must work together—at least they have to put up with each other. Business leaders can, and often do, evade this responsibility by looking inward, by dedicating their energies solely to making profits and by treating government agents as a sort of unwelcome army of occupation. This plays into the hands of those politicians and bureaucrats who find it expedient to "serve the public" by treating business as a fractious native population that

---

needs to be kept in line. The jet plane of state flies on, with the pilot and the co-pilot fighting in the cockpit.

GOVERNMENT RESPONSIBILITIES

Whether business likes it or not, government must somehow reconcile social needs with business goals. This makes the job of a responsible government leader delicate and dangerous. Like a physician who is trying to cure a patient of a chronic disease without causing even more serious side effects, he has to try to enact and enforce laws that will keep the capitalist system within civilized bounds without destroying its spirit. Without getting bogged down in ways and means, let us try to list those things that the voters demand of their government.

Redistribution of Wealth

The most controversial activity of government is the redistribution of wealth. A first approach is to insist that corporations pay their workers at least a minimum or "living" wage.[1] If enforced uniformly, the competitive effects cancel out. This would solve the problem if all, or most, people worked for big business. They don't. There are lots of "little" people who run their own establishments; there are public workers, civil and military, who are outside the business system; there are the old, the infirm, and those who are just too incompetent to be worth hiring by a competitive organization. These are God's (or the government's) people too. They also need a living wage or welfare.

Improved Working Conditions

The amelioration of working conditions should be straight-forward: the passage of laws to limit working hours, to set minimum

---

[1]Actually, mandated "minimum" wages have only secondary effect on the salaries paid by big corporations. Large companies have good reasons to pay much more. See Chapter 5.

age requirements for workers, and to ensure safe, humane working conditions. This sort of thing has a long and honorable tradition, dating at least back to the British Labour Laws. The trouble today is that even with the important battles won, government overseers continue to increase their efforts, and their staffs continue to worry more and more about less and less. In the United States bureaucrats are concerned about toilet facilities for cowboys on the open range in New Mexico.

Environmental Protection

Protection of the environment is tricky. It is also a relatively new activity of government in which most Western nations are still feeling their way (developing nations can hardly afford the luxury of such concern). The problem is that it seems to be almost impossible to do *anything* without hurting or endangering something, even if it is only a little fish. The jolly farmer pollutes by fertilizing and spraying. Even if he uses only animal fertilizer and is willing to watch the insects chew up his crops, some killjoy is going to point out that raising cattle is a terrible waste of food. You can't make an omelet without breaking eggs; you can't produce oil without depleting reserves. How clean is clean?

I don't have any good suggestions for solving environmental problems other than the rather weak proposal that they should be handled by a competent group of people who have the confidence of both business and the public—a sort of environmental Supreme Court. But I can't imagine where we are to find such people. The problems are too important to be turned over to economists or environmentalists: the ecologists I have known seem only to want mountains of their own where they can get away from it all.

One thing I am sure of: the best way to preserve the countryside is to make our cities livable. The chances of the urban bureaucrats and the environmental bureaucrats ever working together to this end seem remote.

Promotion of Long-Term Business Planning

A weakness of pure capitalism, not often mentioned, is that cutthroat, unregulated competition inhibits long-range planning by business. In the absence of some regulation, business leaders would be forced to devote most of their energies to putting out short-term competitive fires.

Allowing businessmen to turn their attention to long-term rather than short-term goals can be realized as a corollary to other government constraints. When competitive pressure is moderated, most businessmen can and do look to the future. After all, they are going to retire someday, and they want their stock options to be worth something.

Preservation of Competition

If the capitalist system is worth preserving (in this part of the book we assume it is), government policy must promote, or at least allow for, competition at the same time that it curbs the excesses of laissez-faire capitalism. This is a difficult and delicate task: to leave room for the competitive dynamic to do its thing and still to respect other social goals. The problem is something like that faced by the baseball commissioner, who has to see that the rules of the game are fair enough that skill and teamwork are rewarded, that no team is in a position to dominate its league, and that the players use their bats on the ball rather than on each other. The most visible, and often misdirected, government efforts to promote competition involve the persecution of price fixers and monopolies.

Effective monopolies or cartels are rare on the modern international scene. OPEC is an outstanding exception, but we can't do much about that without reverting to gunboat diplomacy. (See Chapter 11.) Bigness by itself should not be punished. There would be cause for alarm and reason to unlimber such big guns as the Sherman Antitrust Act only if consumers had inferior goods forced down their throats or had to pay an extortionate price for them (as they do for oil).

Modern corporations just don't behave this way. IBM is a case in point—and is under indictment. Although the company has some 70 percent of the American commercial computer pie, it got where it is by providing good (not necessarily the best) hardware and outstanding customer service and, more important, by conducting its business *as if* competition were breathing down its neck. This has proved to be a prudent approach, since IBM could soon face really serious competition from foreign, particularly Japanese, manufacturers. As Satchel Page said, "Don't look back; something may be catching up with you."

By the time the government suit against IBM winds its weary way to some sort of conclusion—hundreds of millions of dollars and thousands of lawyer-hours down the road—the monopoly problem could be academic.

These, then, are the proper concerns of government: distribution of wealth, decent working conditions, environmental protection, responsible business planning, and the preservation of competition. The tools of government for dealing with these things are transfer payments, regulation, and occasionally cooperative efforts with business leaders.

TRANSFER PAYMENTS

The use of transfer payments for income leveling is the Robin Hood thing: taking from the rich and giving to the poor. It deals with the eternal dilemma, "Ye have the poor with you always," but it has some new twists.

The old approach, taken when man emerged from savagery, was to sustain the lives of those who could not take care of themselves in the equivalent of workhouses and orphanages. The new morality claims that all people in a modern nation are entitled to a "decent" standard of living, that they should be supported at a level where they can have personal pride and dignity (and be loyal voters). "To each according to his needs, from each according to his income." It is in the interpretation of the word "decent" and in the determination of just who should be the recipients of this bounty that the battle is joined between the business community and the welfare state.

Let us take the easy cases first. In any society or nation there are people who *can't* take care of themselves: orphans, dependent children, the severely handicapped, the old and sick. In a civilized society, these people must be provided for. There is no argument, even from the most hard-hearted capitalist. The inclusion of old people in this list of public charges is new. Not long ago, people were expected to provide for their own old age or be supported by their children. In today's consuming and inflationary society, a lot of us just don't save this kind of money and the "now" generation refuses to support the last. Thus old people are left to be supported directly by business retirement plans or indirectly by Social Security (an actuarial time bomb in the United States) or by welfare.

Every Western nation strikes a balance between its conscience and its capacity to take care of unfortunates. The United States government is always looking for new deserving wards. We have a long and honorable history of helping those who made sacrifices in our wars. This classification has been extended to include all those who ever wore a military uniform and to their dependents. We also feel it is our duty not only to provide asylum to political refugees but to make sure that they have a shot at the good life. The latest concern is the welfare of aliens, legal and illegal, in the country. If you feel deprived, let us know.

Another class of transfer payments is to the able-bodied unemployed—to those who *could* work but who are unwanted by employers or who refuse to work for the wages people will pay them. (Even with a 7 percent unemployment rate, there are pages of help-wanted advertisements in our newspapers.) If we add to this payments made to people who *do* work but whose incomes the government feels it has to subsidize so that they may have a "decent" life, we have a lot of people taking money out of the system.

The United States has whole island dependencies such as Puerto Rico and Samoa where welfare and food stamps are a way of life. We also have "islands" on the mainland: poor whites in Appalachia, Hispanics in New York City, black ghetto dwellers in big cities. A nation like Sweden with a homogeneous population has an advantage in that it doesn't have such dependencies. The warnings by Enoch Powell against immigration from former colonies to England, so bitterly criticized by liberal organs, are not mindless prejudice.

There have always been supportive relationships between "haves" and "have-nots." Even in the ultimate supportive relationship, slavery, it was to the slaveholder's advantage to see that his people were kept healthy. Despite the horrors of *Roots*, there must have been some American slaves who were treated well, while others rebelled.

The big change is that in the old days the relationship was a face-to-face, one-on-one thing. Today it is handled by a faceless bureaucracy. People used to get something for their money—cheap servants or just someone to hold a horse. The Englishman in India or the American in Manila who had a dozen servants was not necessarily being sybaritic (beyond a certain number, servants are a nuisance). To *not* have hired all these people would have been social injustice. The new system may be better for the dignity of the recipients; on the other hand, it removes them from the sight and hearing of the donors. Society—business—pays a ransom not only to support these people but also to keep them invisible.

In a private enterprise country it is business, the only apparatus that "makes" money, that generates the money for these transfer payments. Public servants pay taxes, but since they are returning money to the outfit that pays them, all this does is effectively reduce their salaries. In a socialist country where everybody works for the state, it is profits (under another name) from nationalized industries that must pick up the tab.

The cost of transfer payments is a cost of doing business and has to be added to the selling price of goods and services. This either promotes inflation or reduces the standard of living, depending on the role you want to give money in the equation.

The inclination of government is to give away more money,[2] to raise people's subsistence level, and to increase bureaucratic empires. (The 1978 budget of the old HEW in the United States was larger than the national budget of any other nation except Russia.) The reasonable desire of business is not to let people starve but to moderate the payments and reduce the number of public wards—to keep from killing the business geese that lay the golden eggs.

REGULATION

Another battle between government and business involves the methods of control or regulation. As we have seen, government regulation is necessary to keep uncontrolled capitalism from polluting the environment, depleting resources, and straining the social fabric. Most businessmen accept this. Their beefs concern the amount of regulation and its method of implementation.

If competition is to be preserved, the rules of the game should be fair and not give one group of corporations an advantage or force one industry to subsidize another. In its zeal to protect the "little man," and with its prejudice against bigness, the government issues regulations that are often self-defeating. A recent example is the entitlement program that forced large American oil refiners to subsidize other refiners to the point where big, efficient plants had to lose money and small ones were rewarded for their inefficiency.[3] The public paid the difference.

Business wants fair rules; it also wants consistency. It is not uncommon for a set of regulations from one government agency to contradict those of another, making a corporation damned if it does

---

[2]According to Morton Paglin in *Policy Review* (Spring, 1979), there has been an 80 percent decline in the number of poor people in the United States, while transfer payments have gone up faster than the GNP. Transfer payments made up 45 percent of President Carter's fiscal 1980 budget.

[3]See *Fortune*, August 14, 1978.

and damned if it doesn't. Rarely does business protest. ("You can't fight city hall.") When Sears filed a suit against the government, protesting the impossibility of complying with mutually incompatable personnel regulations, the worm turned and thousands cheered—the suit was rejected.

On every corporate income statement there should be an item called "regulatory overhead"—the cost of complying with government requests for reports. The cost in the United States is staggering. It would sound like a bad joke if it were not real. The joke is on consumers and shareholders. Murray Weidenbaum, President Reagan's chief economic adviser and head of the Center for the Study of American Business at Washington University in St. Louis, keeps up with this sort of thing. These are the center's figures for 1976:

The paperwork that flowed into federal agencies filled 4.5 million cubic feet of space, the equivalent of ten forms for every person in the United States. The reporting cost to business was over $24 billion. The cost is higher now and it was probably understated anyway, since it could hardly have included corollary costs and those due to impaired effectiveness. This is not regulation; it is harassment. It is regulation gone mad.

There must be government control of business, but not in the monstrous form it now takes in the United States. How did things get this way? The usual answer is that government bureaucracy is to blame: every agency feels compelled to increase its stature and size by demanding more and more reporting by business. There is a lot of truth in this explanation, but the root of the problem may go even deeper. It may stem from the *attitude* of government toward business.

Today's attitude seems to be one of complete mistrust—business cannot be allowed to handle even trivial details without close supervision. No allowance is made for any goodwill on the part of industry.

This adversary attitude may be due to the legal background of most of our legislators, which fosters the concept that the normal posture between men is confrontation. The symbol of law is a set of scales. Many of the most important government–business interfaces are in "hearings." These proceedings have a legal format, complete with judge, witnesses, overpaid expert witnesses, and intervenors. The format seems more appropriate to a hanging than to the resolution of a situation in which both sides presumably want the same thing: to promote the general welfare. It also uses a hell of a lot of lawyers.

The official antagonism does not usually extend to the people who make face-to-face contacts in the workaday world. The IRS people and the regulators who actually deal with American business people usually get on reasonably well with their opposite numbers. Each recognizes that the other is only doing his (possibly distasteful) job. In fact, there is a traffic of employees between government agencies and business positions.

COOPERATION

The way to promote the good things described in the last chapter is not to eliminate government control but to relieve the regulatory burden on business or at least to make the regulations consistent. A reasonable starting point might be for business to be more understanding of government concerns and for government to have more trust in business—to attempt to control by *rules* rather than by *regulations*. There is a difference. In a congenial environment, both sides could work together toward the common goal of making the nation livable today and tomorrow. If reporting procedures were based on consensus rather than on fiat, they could be simplified and data submitted only once instead of 20 times; if business had a recognized voice in the control process, it wouldn't have to employ an army of lobbyists; finally, if federal people would act as referees to see that mutually accepted goals were being met, rather than as nit-picking auditors, control would be both more efficient and more effective.

I particularly like the idea of government agents acting as referees or umpires rather than as bird dogs. Even in a World Series game there are ten times as many players as there are umpires—which is a lot better than the one-to-one ratio that seems to be developing in the regulatory game.

The appropriate agency in the United States to implement such changes, judging by its title and stated mission in the government manual (U.S. Government Printing Office), is the Department of Commerce. Unfortunately, this department doesn't control industry. Most industries have their own special keepers, like DOT and FERC (the verb is "to FERC"), to hold them in line. No agency in its right mind is going to give up its own flogging privileges to another department.

There doesn't seem to be much hope of achieving a cooperative business–government control system. Liberals will never lose their pathological distrust of business, socialists will always fear that someone is making too much money, and free enterprise boosters will object to *any* government regulation.

This is a pity. If governments would *use* the energy of the business community rather than automatically assume an adversary position, we might have more efficient and prosperous nations.

Except in wartime, when cooperation is a condition of survival, modern examples of cooperation fall under the heading "it might have been." In 1969 the British decided to abandon their military base at Aden, at the entrance to the Red Sea. After all, the Iranians could police the area! British Petroleum offered to pick up the cost of maintaining the base. No dice. "Can't have a bunch of bloody amateurs making policy decisions, you know." The priorities of the welfare state triumphed over common sense.

A counterexample of cooperation is the decline of railroad passenger service in the United States—a case in which the railroads and the government combined to screw the public. In the 1950s, railroads were losing money on their passenger service and wanted relief. The ICC would not let them drop a route until it was a disaster area. The railroads *made* disaster areas by discouraging travelers and by letting their equipment deteriorate. Finally, to preserve a faint echo of a once fine passenger system, without which we could hardly have survived World War II, the nationalized AMTRAK passenger system was set up—a makeshift arrangement that provides poor service and costs the taxpayers a lot of money. How much better, and cheaper, for the government and the railroads to have worked as partners in the first place to preserve a necessary service.

This is the point where my socialist friends bring up the superior passenger service provided by state railways in England and on the Continent. True. But the English trains, at least, used to be better under private ownership (I have a long and convenient memory). Then there is the Canadian example. The nationalized railway, Canadian National, has to be subsidized; the private company, Canadian Pacific, which has a parallel operation, makes money and pays dividends and taxes.

Planning

One proposal for change that has a better chance of being adopted than a cooperative system is planned capitalism.[4] As proposed, it sounds a lot like the social democracy of European nations and it scares the hell out of me. A psychologist might say that my fear can be traced to having grown up at a time when the Russians were putting out a new five-year plan every year, but I don't agree. I have had experience with modern long-range-planning models[5] and I have grave doubts—practical, mathematical, and psychological—of their value. I don't object to setting national goals or policies or priorities, but plans have a way of coming unstuck.

[4]See Robert L. Heilbroner, *Beyond Boom and Crash*, New York: Norton, 1978.
[5]Henry I. Meyer, *Corporate Financial Planning Models*, New York: Wiley, 1977.

Planners suffer the occupational disease of believing the outputs of their planning models. And they believe that these outputs show not only what will happen but what *ought* to happen. The next step is automatic: the planner wants to become the implementer—he wants to make sure the plan is followed. To deviate is heresy. The business community usually has enough common sense to say "Down, boy" to its strategic planners, but I am not sure that government bureaucrats will have the wit to do so, particularly if the plan is produced by an impressive computer model. The plan *will* be produced by a computer; that is the way we do things now. Some frightfully bright people from the Wharton School or from MIT will build a model based on econometrics or on systems dynamics.

Planning-model builders confuse mathematical sophistication with reliability: a Box-Jenkins analysis has to give a better prediction than an old-fashioned least-squares fit. This is true only if the input assumptions are valid—and they are *never* all valid for a long-term industry model. The most critical variables are chance events, which cannot be reduced to mathematical form for input into a computer—things like the raising of oil prices, wars and revolutions, fire, flood, and the vagaries of the weather. Econometricians build their models as if nothing traumatic were going to happen for the next five years. Disasters do happen; they happen in a time horizon of far less than five years and will continue to do so as long as nature and human nature are what they are.

The planners are philosophical about it all and go cheerfully back to the drawing board to make a new plan, one that is just as surely doomed. As the draftsman said, "They pay just as much for erasing as for drawing." It costs as much or more to change direction and follow a new plan as it does to shape up the old one in the first place.

I may sound bitter about the prospects of long-range national planning. Consider an attempt not long ago by the United States government. With a deal of fanfare, President Carter set up a new

Department of Energy (DOE) to plan energy policy. The Secretary was a highly respected scholar. He staffed his department with 17,000 people (count 'em: 17,000). It took 18 months to get things organized and to propose an energy bill, a plan. It would be unkind to comment on the quality of the proposal, but even if it had been good it would have been outdated because of the unpredicted (unpredictable) things that happened in the interim. Corporations had quietly gone about converting to coal and to other energy sources without a bill; natural gas supplies, which had been considered a critical shortage, became a "gas glut"; Iran had a revolution and cut off exports. "Man proposes, God disposes."

Way to Go

Government planning would certainly take the initiative away from business. Overregulation tends to smother it. Of the two evils, I favor the latter: business is stuck with a regulatory burden, but it is still in the ring, still trying to make money and to compete. The critical elements in the promotion of prosperity are keeping the free enterprise system alive and allowing competitive forces to operate.

If consumers want to be damn fools, the government should let them, as long as they don't foul the environment or waste resources. If they want to buy electric carving knives or can openers, let them. (I have to say, reluctantly, "If people want to smoke marijuana, let them." The drain on our balance of payments, the promotion of organized crime, and contempt for authority seem to outweigh the social price of smoking the stuff.)

The regulatory people might also consider their own public image and credibility. A department that insists on automobile seat belts (let alone air bags) and at the same time even allows motorcycles on the highway is silly. When one department condemns cigarette smoking while another subsidizes tobacco growers, the system isn't very convincing.

The following diagram is a self-test. It was published by DOE to explain gasoline rationing. The illustration is described in the DOE publication as "a simplified schematic diagram of the major flows of coupons, ration checks, and redemption checks in the rationing program." If you can understand it, you are ready for planned capitalism.

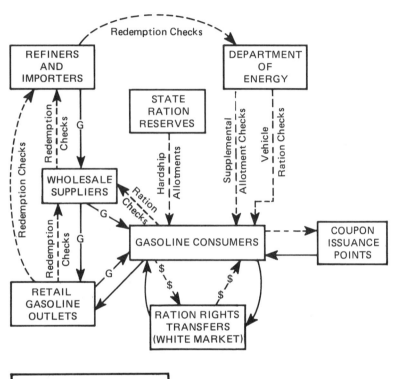

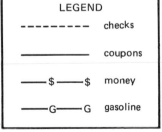

5

NATIONAL GENIUS AND INTERNATIONAL TRADE

A young entrepreneuse from Wilkes Barre
Sold her wares from Bombay to St. Cyr.
When asked why she did so,
She replied, "Oh, I don't know,
I guess it's just good anywhere."

As far as the prosperity of the United States is concerned, the most important slogan is not "In God we trust" (although that is not a bad idea); it is "Made in USA." This is the strange device carried by our products to the far corners of the earth. As it is respected, so are we. The exports of most Western nations carry a similar sign: Made in England, Germany, Israel—in English yet! A few countries insist on using the native tongue—*Hecho en Mexico*—but this is a

54

mistake. "Made in _____" is the language of commerce, and the language of commerce is English.

It is hard to overestimate the importance of these words. They have an impact not only on national prosperity but also on a nation's image and the integrity of its currency. Every exporter who ships shoddy goods is doing his country a disservice; every exporter who ships good goods is a patriot. In many countries, the quality of exports, at least of specific exports, is controlled by law. It may be possible to buy bad Scotch whiskey in Scotland (I haven't tried), but it is impossible to buy it in other countries. The integrity of the label must be preserved.

National images do change. Before World War II, "Made in Japan" was synonymous with trash. After the war, with some American prodding, Japan set about improving its standards, and now the same words have quite a different impact. When a Japanese businessman competes with foreigners in the international market, he is now at an advantage. Buyers want his goods and may even pay a premium to get them. Obviously, this sort of image is a national asset, and it should be. Such recognition is hard won. The basic elements that create product prestige are embedded deep in society: in pride of workmanship, in good education, and in adequate reward for good work. These elements are marshaled by the two great movers in Western society—government and business. Before getting down to specifics, let us take an archaeological detour and look at the ups and downs of national prestige.

INDUSTRIAL JETSAM

Loren Eisley said that the place to look for the secret of life is in a vacant lot in the fall, among the detritus of the seasons of growth and maturity.[1] The place to look for the ebb and flow of industrial influence is in the backwaters of the world: where the artifacts of

[1]Loren Eisley, *The Immense Journey*, New York: Random House, 1946.

industrial society are the tidemarks of civilization. Working as an engineer in the Pacific after World War II, I picked up the scent. In every barrio in the Philippines there was an ancient "Made in USA" Singer sewing machine. (There was also a lucrative black market in needles, sent to soldiers in letters from the States.) Many of the larger towns had an old ice-making machine, often powered by an English Hornby engine built to last a hundred years. I had the job of repairing an old pumping station at the foot of the Taygayti Ridge near Lake Taal—an enchanted spot with a little dam and penstock built by a forgotten engineer: jungle vines, flowers, and rushing water, like something from Kew Gardens. There were two pumps (which the Japanese had taken a bad crack at fixing), an old American triplex mining pump, and a German Pelton wheel (badly designed, nyah, nyah, nyah!)—industrial archaeological shards. A steam launch on the Australian coast had a venerable Scotch triple-expansion engine—an engineer's delight.

How did this industrial hardware wind up in these unlikely places? Who sold it? Who bought it? I don't know. I leave the problem to the professionals. I do know that if I went back today the picture would be quite different: Japanese looms instead of the old English ones, a Sony in every hut, and the howl of the Honda across the land. The rise and fall of industrial nations can be monitored as well in Bataan as in Birmingham or Bavaria.

THANKLESS CUSTOMERS

No nation or business can afford to rest on its laurels, to be smug, to adopt the attitude that anyone who doesn't buy its products is a damn fool. The attitude seems to have originated in England. The English, and the Scotch, were once the world's best engineers. When our archaeologist gets tired of hacking the jungle, he might visit the Royal Scottish Museum in Edinburgh and see the magnificent engines, locomotives, ships, and lighthouses that carried the Union Jack (and "Made in England") around the world.

But these are the models of yesterday; they don't sell goods today. Buyers are a scurvy lot: brand, or national loyalty, lasts only until someone else comes up with something better or cheaper or better promoted or better serviced. English supremacy is over.[2] The days are gone when English ships, almost half the world's merchant fleet, left home with manufactured goods and returned with treasure. The decline was due as much to the failure of the will and daring of British industry as to wars and politics and pushy foreign competition. Nations do go down and do come back. It is impossible to write off the nation that developed the Comet and the Spitfire, radar and penicillin. Britain can come back *if it wants to:* there are penalties that must be paid for industrial leadership and there are competing ways of life and social values. We shall talk about these later.

What makes a nation's goods and services move in the international market? Quality and price, of course. But these are the outward, visible signs of other things: good engineering, good design, research and innovation, good workmanship and quality control, corporate integrity and aftersale support, cost-effectiveness, credit, and, finally, government permissiveness and support. Of these factors, the last is outside business control. One, workmanship, has social roots. There is another social force that completes the picture—the appreciation of quality by the indigenous population. If a nation's own people are not willing to pay for quality, it is unlikely that the country will have premium goods to export.

ENGINEERING AND RESEARCH

Good engineering and design go together: a meeting of esthetics and technology. Sometimes they compete. A good example is the postwar Studebaker. The first model was a classic, with

---

[2]It is an interesting exercise to look for the start of the decline. To do this you must identify the top—the watershed. A reasonable candidate is the Great Durbar of 1903 in Delhi, India, held to celebrate the glories of the British Raj. Other historians suggest the Great Exhibition in the Crystal Palace in 1851, which prompted angry letters to the London *Times* protesting that foreign exhibits outdid the English.

clean design and good engineering—a car ahead of its time. Then the designers got carried away and incorporated a hood that looked like a jet engine pod (and also made the engine hard to service). A successful product became a loser in one easy step.

Engineering excellence in a nation depends on a good education system, a friendly social atmosphere, and a favorable business environment. In countries where engineering is a respected and well-paid profession, it will attract good students who might otherwise go into service and parasitic fields like law, accounting, and business administration. Sweden is a case in point. Engineering is the prestige profession in Sweden and the nation exports and gets premium prices for its fine cameras, automobiles, cash registers, and jet fighters. In the nineteenth century the great British engineers like Brunel, Stephenson, Telford, and Parsons were national heroes.

Engineers need good training (we will talk about the business influence on education later). Engineering training does not export well to other countries unless the foreign student has an industrial base to return to. An engineer or scientist has to work in a supportive environment, usually provided by business or by government. He needs shops, laboratories, and risk capital. Most of all, he needs the support of, and the association with, other professionals. A Cal Tech graduate returning to Zaire is going to have trouble using his training.

Research, basic research, is the lifeblood of a competitive nation. Without new ideas, a nation is playing catch-up. As long as the Japanese were making copies of German cameras ("Ours are just as good, maybe cheaper"), they were not a serious threat. When they applied their own research to make superior optics and mechanisms, they got tough. Basic research—not development, which is often just tinkering—requires money, lots of money. Much of this is "wasted" or nonproductive. Only giant corporations (another argument for bigness), government, and universities supported by government can afford it. After World War II, the

United States started passing out research money like a sailor on shore leave. ("As long as you're up, get me a grant.") Any number could play, both native Americans and "friendly" foreigners. It was hard to find an article in an American learned journal (or even in the Proceedings of the Cambridge Philosophical Society) without a footnote showing government support. Something like this:

> This work was performed under Navy Contracts N0ord 8555 Task F, Bureau of Ordnance, and N5ori 76/XV1 NR 043 046, Office of Naval Research, as report No. 24.

The appended disclaimer was almost a standing joke:

> The ideas expressed in this article represent the views of the author and are not necessarily those of the Bureau of Ordnance or the Office of Naval Research.

The title of the paper might be "The Invariant Metric and the Method of the Minimum Integral."

Ridicule may have helped turn off government spending, but I no longer see the joke. It is better to spend too much, to let the various disciplines monitor their own work, and to accept the inevitable "waste" than it is to spend too little. Thank God for the space program! Not because it gave us rocks from the moon but because it supported and continues to support basic research, even if that research is slanted toward special fields. Without effective basic research even an intrinsically wealthy country like Canada can be second rate. Sound research can make small countries like Switzerland and Holland factors in world trade.

Production and Marketing

Good engineering, design, research, and innovation are not enough. The product has to be manufactured, supported, and sold. Effective manufacturing depends on the organization and efficiency of the shop and on the skill and motivation of the workers. The last item is a cultural thing that goes under many names: craftsmanship, the work ethic, "doing a day's work for a day's pay." Without this spirit business is in trouble; even the best training or apprentice programs are doomed. A dedicated and capable workforce with pride and esprit de corps is an awesome power. Such dedication is common in wartime, but it also exists in favored corporations and countries in normal times: the *Kruppingers* at Krupp, oilfield workers, the carefully cultivated and propagandized IBM employees. Companies with such people have a big competitive advantage at home and abroad. Sometimes whole nations enjoy such an advantage. Why the peoples of some countries are more industrious than those of others I do not know. This is a question for social scientists. The Japanese and the Germans seem to be able to do anything well. American workers vary in effectiveness from highly efficient in making electronic devices to generally sorry in the building trades.

The support and maintenance of products already sold is also a business function. Without good support you don't get repeat orders. For an outstanding counterexample I again reluctantly pick on the English. In the 1950s the British developed and marketed what eventually turned out to be the car of tomorrow: the Morris 1100. It was a highly innovative piece of engineering with cross-mounted engine, front-wheel drive, beautiful suspension geometry, fabulous interior room, good sprung-to-unsprung ratio—the works.[3] Here was a model that could corner the world market for small cars. I owned a couple of the early versions and loved them. But when something trivial went wrong like a door handle falling off (there were some workmanship problems), it took six weeks to get a replacement—presumably by slow boat from Coventry. The Germans, with an inferior design and good service, did corner the market with the Volkswagen "bug." You can still buy an 1100 but under a different name: Rabbit, Horison, or Omni.

[3]Like most important advances, the 1100 was the creation of one man: Sir Alec Issigonis.

There is another aspect to customer service that is not usually taught in business school: consideration and respect for the buyers. When an American or a Frenchman or a German promotes his product in some faraway land, it is not a good idea to come on strong—to tell people what they need rather than listening to their problems. It is better to be considerate, to know the language and the customs of the country. This is not only sound business; it is also good politics. Yesterday's banana republic may be tomorrow's energy source. Our traveling businessmen need training in political science and the humanities as well as in international finance.

It is an exercise in futility to try to sell overpriced manufactured goods and services, even if they are of superior quality. Free international competition is the consumer's best friend: it keeps costs under control. That there is *not* free competition in many products and commodities is often due to government intervention (which we will get to later).

Three factors determine cost: availability of raw materials; basic cost of labor; and productivity. The raw material constraint used to be pretty well defined in old geography books: "Panama is a large grower and exporter of bananas to all parts of the world." The trend today is to ship raw materials and do final processing and fabrication in the consuming countries (where the investment may be safer). The wide dispersal of oil refineries and the very existence of a Japanese steel industry are good examples of this trend. Basic labor costs and production efficiency are now more important than access to raw materials. Typically, labor cost is high in Western countries, where every worker is presumed to have a shot at the good life. Production efficiency, then, becomes the most important controllable element in the cost-of-goods equation. It will ultimately determine whether a nation's goods are competitive or overpriced in the world market.

EFFICIENCY

Production efficiency, or productivity, is in the hands of the business community, and of the government. The fight for improved productivity is waged against the parent government and against organized, and unorganized, labor. The first requirement for better productivity is available money for capital investment. Modern producing hardware is expensive: automated production lines, big trucks, mining equipment. Unless government fiscal (taxing) policy allows the accumulation of funds by business (or provides such funds, as it does in Japan), the cost of improved productivity must be partially financed with expensive borrowed money or, worse, must be postponed while industry struggles on with antiquated plants. An enlightened piece of legislation that recognizes this problem is the Investment Tax Credit allowed in the United States to reward capital expenditure by business.

It doesn't do much good to make large capital expenditures to reduce labor *needs* if labor *costs* remain the same. But this is precisely the position that organized labor takes—based on two spurious arguments. The first argument is that somehow the value of a worker,[4] what he should be paid, is a function of the effectiveness of the machine he operates: he derives vicarious value from the machine's efficiency. The pilot of a 747 is "worth" more than the pilot of a bush plane, even though the latter probably needs more skill to survive; the driver of an automated 200-ton truck is "worth" four times as much as the driver of an old 50-ton truck. The other spurious argument is that workers have a right to keep their jobs—that technologically displaced people should be kept on the payroll even though they are redundant ("featherbedding") or that they should simply be paid for doing useless work. Featherbedding creates bloated workforces, both in the factory and in the office. (We will consider the productivity of white-collar workers in Chapter 7.) Featherbedding also tears up worker morale: most people prefer to do a decent day's work. Paying people not to work, or to do useless work, is common—for example, the reglazing

---

[4]The real value of workers, from ditch diggers to corporation presidents, has never been determined. Economists know this, but it is not a problem they want to tackle. See *HIM*, Chapter 5.

of prefabricated windows; the paying of stevedores to watch containerized goods being swung directly from cargo holds to railroad cars.

Featherbedding and the payment of premium wages for vicarious value is blackmail paid by business to organized labor—a ransom paid to be allowed to keep operating.

How effectively business can cope with labor blackmail depends not only on the determination of management but also on the social climate, on government policy, and even on support by law courts. In a country like Australia, where the labor unions are politically strong and militant, business is in trouble. You don't see many Australian manufactured goods on the international market. Where labor has a strong socialist or communist ideological bent, as it has in England, a "them" and "us" polarization of worker–management relations is created and the chances of effective cooperation are slim. When there *is* cooperation, as there should be under the social democracies of Western Europe, or when there is government paternalism, as in Japan, improved productivity has a better chance. The United States lies somewhere between these positions. Probably the best thing going for American business is class mobility. The production worker whose son is in business school is not totally antimanagement.

QUALITY AND TRADITION

A nation that does not have a tradition of sophisticated and discerning native consumers is not likely to produce high-quality goods. It is unlikely that France would be a large exporter of fine wines if Frenchmen did not drink and appreciate wine. Japanese tourists may look overloaded with optical equipment, but as long as they are, Japan will make good cameras. On the other hand, if a nation's taste gets out of step with the rest of the world, its goods may be unsalable overseas. When Americans demanded powerful, bloated automobiles with tail fins, you didn't see many Buicks in other countries. Taste, and a change of taste, in manufactured goods is easy to observe.

The service industries have more subtle problems. Different peoples put different values on amenities: the whole concept of being willing to pay for gracious living is going out of style, particularly in the United States. There is not much point paying a premium for good food service when the average diner doesn't know a good waiter from a bad one. This may seem trivial but it is not. Industries such as travel, hotel keeping, and dining are big international businesses. Some people even say that the amenities are what make life worthwhile. Because there is a whole generation of readers who may not know what I am talking about, let us go back in time about 30 years and take a little journey.

A Sentimental Journey

We are going to take an overnight train trip. I would rather take a boat trip but this would involve some tedious explanation of the duties of, and the dealings with, stateroom stewards and stewardesses, deck and mess stewards, and the mysterious purser. (Personal service is pleasant only if both parties understand their responsibilities.) We will travel by train.

On our arrival at the station, conveniently located in the center of town, a porter ("red cap") takes charge of the baggage. The depot is a spacious, colorful place in the Railroad Gothic tradition. Beyond the service area—ticket counters, stores, restaurant, and bar—there is a large, open boarding area where the trains are lined up, panting softly in their starting blocks. It is a bit early but we may as well board, since the gate is open. The porter shows us to the room that will be our rolling home—a cabin with bunks (now stowed away), a lavatory, comfortable chairs, and an imposing collection of light and fan switches. The baggage is already there. Soon the train oozes quietly out of the station (in those days trains ran on time). "Let's have a drink before dinner." We just push a button and the porter appears to take our order. The conductor and his retinue drop in later to check tickets—rather like a medical team making ward rounds. We are on our way.

Time for dinner. We leave our room and walk (repeat, walk) to the dining car, which shines with white napery and polished silver. There is a carnation on each table. The steward seats us and gives us menus and an order form. Time for another drink while we make up our minds. The service is good and the food is good, thanks to the now lost art of cooking and serving in the cramped quarters of a moving train.

After dinner it seems only civilized to stroll back to the observation car for an afterdinner drink, a smoke, and a chat with other passengers. Meanwhile, back at the cabin, the bunks have been made up and gear stored for the night. There is no sleeping pill as effective as the soft clicking of car wheels on a good (they used to be good) roadbed. Shoes will be mysteriously shined during the night.

Back to the dining car for an early breakfast. The waiter recognizes us from the night before. If the train is the Twentieth Century Limited, the final treat is a beautiful morning ride down the Hudson Valley to the center of New York City.

This sort of gracious rail travel is no longer available. If it were, Americans would not use it. They would rather save money by going "coach," eating potato chips and dry cheese sandwiches and sleeping on the seat. The accepted dress code for modern travel is blue jeans and T-shirt—all the outward attractiveness of an unmade bed. Americans are not cheap: in fact, more travel today than did then. It is just that comfort is not an item that many of us are willing to pay for. The same economical travelers will hock their dim futures to buy a 100-horsepower water ski rig or to go on a package tour to six countries in seven days. National preferences have a big effect on the goods and services offered in world trade.

NATIONAL IMAGE

All the social customs, skills, and priorities of a country add up to a national image, reflected in that nation's outward, visible products and services. These can change from age to age. The monuments of the Middle Ages are cathedrals (which could hardly be duplicated today). The great heritage from the Renaissance to the end of the eighteenth century is also architectural, more often dwellings and public buildings than churches. Fortunately, the United States caught the end of this tradition, as evidenced by the old buildings and monuments in Washington, D.C. The treasures of the nineteenth and early twentieth centuries may be the works of civil and marine engineers: bridges like that over the Firth of Forth and Oakland Bay, ships like the *Berengaria*, even the Eiffel Tower.

It is too early to predict the triumphs of modern industry, but I am convinced they won't be architectural. They may be those manufactured items where advanced technology and inspired design meet to create masterpieces. Not necessarily big things like the *Viscount* and the *Constellation*. Future museums may display a desk telephone set, a pocket calculator, and a Hasselblad camera.

How does American industry stack up in this bid for immortality? From very, very good to very poor. Watch the construction of a condominium in, say, Houston, Texas. The framing is sloppy (two by fours are not two by fours anymore); the siding is only slightly better than cardboard and is tacked on with staples. All this is covered with a cosmetic single course of "antiqued" brick. The design is "cutie quaint" townhouse. The price tag is $60,000 a unit. But all is not lost! Into these glorified crates go well-designed air-conditioning systems and electrical appliances that are the standard of the world. In our country mass-produced items are usually good; on-the-job craftsmanship is bad and getting worse. There are no finer examples of precision mechanical engineering than IBM line printers and tape drives. Obviously, a nation can export what it grows or builds well: food, airplanes, computers, and weapons systems from the United States; whiskey from Scotland; cabinet work from Denmark.

THE ROLE OF GOVERNMENT

To turn from the sublime to the ridiculous, let us consider the role of government in international trade. From the point of view of the consumer, this is usually bad. The posture of government is to protect home industry and special interests at the expense of the taxpayer and the consumer. There are two approaches: (1) to curtail imports by some means; (2) to subsidize incompetent manufacturers and service industries so they can compete on the world market.

Imports of foreign goods can be controlled in many ways, ranging from total boycott to a gentlemen's agreement. A popular method is to levy a tariff or duty on inconvenient imports. The subject is complex and forms the substance of graduate courses on business and finance. We won't go into details. The justification for such proscriptive measures is always to protect indigenous producers from "cheap" foreign competition. The immediate result is to raise the prices of the protected goods. The long-term result is to protect and encourage inefficient home industries that will eventually fail anyway or that will have to be subsidized indefinitely at public expense. It is dangerous and costly to interfere with the competitive dynamic.

A recent trend that does seem to justify import controls is "dumping." Some nations are so eager to unload their products, usually to get "hard" currency, that they sell them to others at less than incremental production cost. The losses are paid by the taxpayers of the exporting country. The usual defense against this sort of tactic is to set the duty on such imports high enough to raise their selling price up to the going rate. This is a good deal for the importing country. Taxes paid by the taxpayers in the exporting country are collected by the importing country while the imported goods have no cost advantage. The United States defines dumping as selling goods here at less than they sell for in the home market. Such a rule can be hard to enforce. Poland ships a lot of golf carts to the United States. There are no golf courses in Poland.

Subsidies

The subsidizing of indigenous manufacturers—paying them to sell on the home market at what should be a loss—is more pernicious. In picking up the usually deserved losses of inefficient corporations, the government is abetting inefficiency and the consumer pays two penalties. He pays for goods produced without competitive discipline and he pays the subsidy through taxes.

Subsidies just don't seem to work. An industry that needs intravenous feeding of public money is sick and will probably fade away. The U.S. Merchant Marine is a good example. Subsidized and protected by all sorts of "favored nation" rules, it is a tiny parody of the merchant fleet that a maritime nation should have.[5] Another recent example of the futility of subsidies is what the English call the "Polish ships deal." The Poles were in the market for ships. British shipyards got the job by underbidding the more efficient Japanese and Korean yards—a bid of 30 million pounds for work estimated to cost 52 million. The difference, which will be paid by the much-shot-over British taxpayers, is more than the total labor cost of the project. Quite a comedown for England in an industry where "Clyde Built" was once the world standard of excellence and foreigners queued up to have their ships built in English yards.

A more subtle and effective form of subsidy is government financing of private industry to relieve corporations of the expense of raising money from private sources. This is the situation in Japan, where companies can operate at debt-to-equity ratios that would be ruinous in most Western countries. Businessmen complain about competing with "Japan Incorporated," but they can't do much about it.[6]

Overregulation

Excessive ongoing regulatory expense makes it difficult even for efficient unsubsidized corporations to compete on the world market with foreigners who are less burdened. The Pullman

---

[5]The problems are featherbedding and bloated salaries paid to seamen and to shipyard workers. As long ago as World War II, the mess waiters on troop transports made more money than the officers they served.

[6]See, for example, the *Harvard Business Review*, March–April, 1979.

Company in the United States recently stopped making passenger train cars because it couldn't compete with European manufacturers—manufacturers who must add shipment costs and import duties to their selling price and who pay comparable wages! Too much regulatory overhead is a wasting disease. The numerous lawyers in government, and in business, who enforce or fight regulation are just as much dependents of, or parasites on, the business community as are the citizens of our island dependencies where food stamps are a second currency.[7]

If excessive regulatory overhead is a debilitating disease for ongoing operations, it can be fatal for the development of new plants and the implementation of new ideas, which are ultimately the lifeblood of a Western nation. Robert E. Morris, president of the San Diego Gas and Electric Company, reported that in 1972 his company was willing to spend a lot of money and five years to get the 41 permits required to build a new power plant. By 1977 he had only three permits, but the required number had risen to 91! The project was dropped.[8]

WHAT IT TAKES

In spite of overregulation by its own government and the ways and wiles of foreigners, a nation must stay competitive in order to be prosperous, to have a sound currency, and to be respected. No nation today can afford to be an economic island. The keys to success are still innovation, efficiency, and quality, and these are largely the responsibility of the business community (helped by government-supplied research and development). To continue to provide these essential qualities, companies must have the right attitude. They must be combative and daring; they must develop new markets and never give up an old market without a fight.

[7]In competitive Japan, where people try to avoid legal processes to satisfy grievances, there is one lawyer to 10,170 people. The ratio in California is one to 333.
[8]*Oil and Gas Journal,* March 26, 1979, p. 52.

I remember traveling with a self-proclaimed automobile executive back in the 1950s. The question of foreign competition came up. He commented, with a snide grin, "There is a poor profit margin in small cars; let the foreigners have the market." Although he probably wasn't in any position to make such a decision, I considered him to be a traitor then and I do now. Let us examine some simple case studies.

I have on my desk a collection of objects: a pocket knife, a wristwatch, and a camera (put there on purpose; my desk is usually not *this* cluttered). The knife is English. It says on the blade "Stainless, Sheffield, England." I have had similar knives all my life. My grandfather was a director of a Sheffield cutlery company. (He even knew the business—unusual for an outside director—having been a master cutler before turning to music for a living.) He used to send me fine pocket knives on special occasions. Their fate was predictable. Either I lost them or the blade spring broke, since it was made of stainless steel rather than of spring steel. I recently bought myself the knife on my desk. Fine quality, edge like a razor—*but* the spring broke. It is still made of stainless steel.

The watch is American—a Bulova—and this is slightly surprising. Most American manufacturers threw in the towel long ago. They either left the market to the Swiss or imported Swiss movements to put in their own cases. Someone at Bulova had a bright idea. "We can't compete with the Swiss playing by their rules. In any case our mission is not to make a crafted jeweled lever movement; it is to make an accurate timepiece." And make an accurate timepiece they did. Using American electronic technology, they turned out more accurate watches more cheaply than is possible using traditional methods. Switzerland still makes fine escapement watches, but they are now prestige items (check the pre-Christmas issues of *The New Yorker*). If you want accuracy and reliability, get an electronic model.

The camera on my desk is an old Kodak, a prewar Bantam special. It is interesting because it represents one of the last attempts by American makers to compete with the influx of German imports—the Leicas and Contaxes. My camera is now a collector's item.[9] It is well made, very advanced for its day, and designed for professional use. Kodak never tried again. It got out of the professional market. The Japanese were not so chicken. After the war they took on their old ally *mano a mano,* first by emulation and then by innovation, and darn near drove the Germans out of the prestige market. Will the Germans fight back, or will they do a "Kodak"? I think they will fight and, as a consumer, I will cheer for both sides. The working of competition in a free marketplace is the best game in town.

[9]If any collector reads this, the thing is now for sale: I can't get film for it anymore.

6

BIG BROTHER AND SANTA CLAUS

THE BUSINESS WORLD we are concerned with consists of the large corporations based in the Western world. The leaders and employees of these firms form a well-defined social group in each country: the business community. Business competes with other vocational groups—government employees, artists, professionals— to get the best people. It is in the position of a college fraternity trying to pledge freshmen. In order to compete, business plays the roles of Big Brother and Santa Claus to its employees.

The benefactor role of business is something that Marx could not have foreseen: that as alternate life styles became available, the capitalists would have to pamper their employees. The main inducements offered by business are material, mostly monetary. Other possibilities—service to the community, artistic and academic fulfillment—are not usually available as inducements. The attractions of business life are security and money and the things money can buy: the "fur-lined mousetrap." The lure of money may not be as strong as it once was, now that actual starvation is no longer a threat in Western societies and as we move toward what some writers call a postindustrial society. But as far as this chapter is concerned, money is still king and security is the crown prince.

THE BUSINESS ESTABLISHMENT

We have talked about business and capitalism and about business and prosperity, but we haven't really defined what sets big business apart as a recognizable, separate, and important part of the social scene. We have said that business "makes" money, but this is a catchphrase that becomes rather meaningless under analysis. Time to get back to basics.

Moola-Moola

Consider a very simple model of society. The simpler the model, the more meaningful the output (Meyer's modeling law).[1] Consider the development of a remote, populated island—Moola-Moola. No foreign trade or influence to worry about. The island has arable land, minerals, energy—every resource needed to provide a decent life for its inhabitants. In order to use or to exploit these resources, to provide packaged food, housing, and gimmicks, the people have to get organized. Until they do they will continue to lead a hand-to-mouth existence: picking breadfruit and digging clams. Somebody, or some organization, must take charge: to assign duties, invest in the future (build plants), and distribute and ration the output. The obvious person to do these things is the existing tribal chief.

[1]True of economic and behavioral models. The model of a closed technical system, such as a refinery, can be as detailed as necessary. I don't trust monsters like the Wharton econometrics model.

The conversion of resources to provide an acceptable life style would seem to be too important to delegate. But such delegation is precisely what happened in Western countries. In defiance of all logic, the exploitation of resources, the production of goods and services, and the distribution and allocation of output were appropriated by an outside agency—the business community. This remarkable situation sprang up out of the body of the feudal system when capital began to be freed from identification with land, at a time, incidentally, when central governments were weak and distracted with things like war and conquest and religion rather than with economics or politics. The unnatural, improbable arrangement worked! Due to competitive discipline and the profit motive (as Adam Smith observed), the new "second government" did a fantastic job. The business system has existed to this day, not only because it is powerful but because it works. We postulate the rise of a business community on our island.

Moola-Moola is on its way. It even has supermarkets and a Rotary Club. Not everybody, however, gets swept up in the new system: there are still independent artisans and breadfruit pickers and clam diggers. As in our own world, anybody who does not want to join the establishment and who can handle his own capital and labor needs is free to opt out. The most important stronghold of rugged individualism today is family farming, but its days are numbered.

American farmers recently demonstrated in Washington for parity or something like that. They were demonstrating for the wrong reason—people often do demonstrate for the wrong reason. The very tractors that the farmers drove to Washington (with air-conditioned cabs) showed what their proper concern should have been. These mechanical monsters are $20,000 to $50,000 items, and there is a lot more expensive hardware back home on the range. The capital requirements of efficient farming and the value of land are getting to be too much for a single family. Unless the situation is relieved, business—big business—will take over the nation's farmland. This is what the farmers *should* have been beefing about. Any operation that gets too capital intensive, in the United States or in Moola-Moola, is in danger of falling into the lap of business or government.

Other things happen on our island as the business community grows. The people who remain independent are not happy with the distribution of profits, which is in the hands of the business community. In fact, a lot of regimented workers are unhappy too: they think the business leaders are taking too much for themselves. Without staging a civil war (Moola-Moola is not yet sophisticated enough for this diversion), workers turn to the government, to the old tribal chief. He is a bit surprised by all this just when things seemed to be going so well, and he doesn't want to lose his job: he now has a palace, a limousine, and a cute secretary. He sets up a staff to investigate and regulate. The staff members have to be paid, and since business controls most of the wealth of the island, he has to set up a system for skimming off part of it before it is distributed. Corporate taxes. Moola-Moola has a bureaucracy and a new alternate life style. Bright, ambitious young people can now choose to go into government instead of into industry. The business leaders are outraged and hurt. "Look what this island was before we took over; we are being persecuted for our success." Their disappointment is justified. The job they are doing—managing production to create a modern, efficient society—is a difficult and important task, what Chandler calls the working of the "visible hand."[2] The business leaders feel betrayed but there isn't anything they can do about it.

As the island prospers under business leadership new types of people rise and shine: CPAs, auditors, consultants, lawyers, teachers, and doctors. This is the professional class and it provides yet another competing life style for bright people. These professionals are not self-sufficient. They are dependent on, and live on, the business community, which after all controls the wealth of the island

[2]Alfred D. Chandler, Jr., *The Visible Hand*, Cambridge, Mass.: Harvard University Press, 1978.

until someone else takes it away. Doctors are included among the professionals, not because many of them work directly for business but because modern medicine is an offspring of industrial society. When the late Margaret Mead first did her busybodying in Samoa, she found very few doctors. Those in residence were not qualified members of the American Medical Association. There were no lawyers on Samoa—any society without lawyers can't be all bad. Life on Moola-Moola is getting complicated and business is losing its power: power to determine the distribution of wealth.

Business fights back. It fights a running battle with government and with the hangers-on; its most effective strategy is growth. By growing it can pull more and more good people into its orbit and improve its relative position and wealth. Unfortunately, the natives of Moola-Moola tend to be a complacent lot. Once they have houses and cars, they like to sit on their verandas, put their collective feet on the railing, and drink Mai-Tais. Something has to be done: every person must be turned into a consuming machine. Advertising (and advertising agencies) are born. If people don't have needs, create them! Life is a hollow mockery without a swimming pool (a tough sell on Moola-Moola), a power boat, and a motorcycle. "If we can make 'em, we can sell 'em."

Early in the transformation of the island economy money had to be introduced. Since it didn't already exist, it had to be invented as a way of allocating and rationing goods and (later) services. The old cowrie shells or the huge immovable stone discs used on the island of Yap, featured in old *National Geographic* articles, just wouldn't do the job. Something convenient and transferable was needed— paper money.

From the business point of view, only paper money is money, whether it be Treasury bills or promissory notes. Gold is gold: it has intrinsic value like any other item on the commodities exchange. Paper money is the creation of business—historically, one of its proudest inventions. Governments *print* money (which actually represents only a small fraction of the total credit), but only business gives it value. The actual bills or notes may carry pious statements declaring them to be legal tender, and may have handsome pictures of kings or queens or presidents, but this is window dressing. The only value of a bill is what it will buy; and what it will buy is determined, in a capitalist country at least, by the number of bills the government grinds out and by the business community, which has a monopoly on the turning of the riches of the earth into consumer goods. The value of dollars or pounds or yen is determined by the price sticker on the window of a new car—and by OPEC policy.

Without goods to buy and respect for it as currency, paper money is worthless. This was demonstrated to me on the little island of Biak, off New Guinea, just after World War II. Biak had been an important American base with PX, officers' club, and WACs—all the paraphernalia of total war. When I arrived, there wasn't much left except the beach, old barracks, and beer. We took a jeep into the bush to see if we could buy artifacts from the natives. Bingo! Here were some lovely Melanesian maidens, their hair dyed an attractive yellow by atabrine tablets, waving some products at us. What they wanted to sell were handfuls of dollar bills! Another example from World War II: The Russian soldiers had money but they didn't have PXs. They would gladly buy an old Mickey Mouse watch from an American soldier for a hundred dollars.

The business leaders of Moola-Moola invented money—they had to in order to allocate goods—but a funny thing happened on the way to the bank. Those little pieces of paper with good chief Um Gua's picture on them became something more than ration coupons. They took on a value, a desirability, in themselves. They became symbols of status and prestige. Business had invented something much more significant than it had bargained for. Control of money implies the almost divine power to create important people. By handing out enough money to the right people, business could create a financial aristocracy.

Obviously, on Moola-Moola the most deserving recipients

were the business leaders themselves, plus a few judiciously chosen outsiders like chief Um Gua who could help the cause. It was not even necessary to pass the stuff out with a shovel to entice the right sort of people to enter business. A modest starting salary with the promise of riches later as a reward for long and faithful service would do the job.

Another advantage of money worship is that it creates order in the ranks. He who has more money is more important than, and is respected by, he who has less. He who is in a position to hand out money has got to be revered. For the purpose of keeping a business organization in decent subordination, money is the best invention since flogging.

Of course, the other social groups on Moola-Moola aren't going to stand idly by and let the business community have a monopoly on money power. They want theirs too. The professionals can get theirs by restricting their numbers and by legislating the need for services to them in a comfortable blackmailing position. ("You *must* have an annual outside audit.") Government can get the stuff from business—the only real source—by raising taxes, or it can muddy the waters by printing more bills. In fact, the Moola-Moola government did both: it began to act like a modern, enlightened parliament. The fight for money power between social groups goes on in all Western nations. It may still be going on in Moola-Moola if the island has not yet been destroyed by one of those convenient volcanic eruptions that used to climax South Sea island movies.

Our World

Let us leave the beautiful island of Moola-Moola and look at modern business in the Western world. Things are not too different. Business is the great destroyer, converter, and creator of all that defines a modern society. The strength of the business community is based on its control of wealth: money is its power and its god. Its leaders may pay lip service to, and genuinely strive for, more noble doctrines, but the virility of business still comes down to the bottom line.

That business is in charge of production in most nations is the result of historical accident. It is allowed to stay in charge only because it produces. As in Moola-Moola, there are alternate life styles in modern nations: different social groups competing for money and power and hearts and minds. The most direct threat is the increasing powers of central government. Whenever a central government loses its usually justified diffidence and decides to run things rather than keep its normal role of critic, gadfly, and dependent, the business dynasty is over.[3] When bright people fail to heed the siren call of business—as the road to personal wealth— or when they lose faith in business integrity, business is through. Business is still on trial in most Western nations.

If this account portrays the business community as an embattled minority (business *is* a minority in most countries), it is a true picture. The average employee doesn't know this—he is carefully insulated from harsh realities by corporate policies—but business leaders know it well. Today the most financially powerful people are running scared. Management spends millions of dollars on public relations and institutional advertising to support its case; it pays its taxes and accepts repressive regulation with (usually) only token protest. The best security blanket for management is to surround itself with happy, prosperous, loyal supporters—the courtiers of our age. How can business invoke this kind of support from its people?

[3]When there is a change in administration, the U.S. government publishes a directory of high-level appointed and career civil servants. The latest edition, November 18, 1980, has 161 pages! The listees can point to it with pride as a sort of Debrett's Peerage. For the taxpayer and the businessman it is a chamber of horrors. Here in anatomical detail are listed those people of varying competence who tell us how much profit is decent, what is and what is not pollution, how to design our cars, and where we can send our children to school. These are our unelected masters.

INCENTIVES

The components of remuneration to employees—the price paid for their competence and loyalty—may be classified as security, prosperity, and wealth. The mix varies from country to country and from pay level to pay level. All employees get security; this is the Big Brother role of management. The aim is to shield the worker from all chances and perils of this life. He is provided with life insurance, paid vacations, and a pension plan. Even his personal savings program is subsidized by the corporation through stock purchase and savings plans. The sting of the tax bite is spread over the year by calculated payroll deductions (insisted on by the government). He is protected against inflation by cost-of-living (not merit) salary increases. Any new employee of a big corporation enters a sheltered environment designed to protect him to the end. It takes a brave man to voluntarily leave Big Brother and strike out on his own. All this costs a lot of money. For its investment, management gets (or hopes to get) loyal, competent people. It makes sure that the employee knows what a good thing he has going for him. There are usually "orientation" courses to convince the new employee and continuing propaganda in house organs and newsletters to convince the already convinced.

TENURE

The ultimate security is job security. The assurance that an employee will not be fired except for flagrant misbehavior or criminal activity is what the academic community calls "tenure." Job tenure is traditional in Japanese companies and in the civil service; it is becoming more prevalent in business in all Western countries. (Some automobile workers in the United States get 95 percent of their regular wages when the production line is shut down; high-seniority workers get first crack at this "paid vacation." Tenure is bad business. It erodes control and discipline in normal times and is disastrous in recessions.

Security, or Big Brother, benefits go to most workers. In the past a lot of these benefits were won by union action, but in most Western countries today workers would get a similar package without a strike threat. Management wants its people to be secure and content—walking advertisements for the company. In the United States, at least, most union members pay for a support hierarchy that would otherwise be provided in the form of a company personnel (or employee relations) department. Union power can be abused, as it is in England, with leaders making unreasonable demands that ultimately hurt both management and labor. The threat of union excess is another reason companies try to be generous even to nonunion employees.

Does all this security buy loyal employees? Probably not. There is a perversity in people that resents benefactors; gratitude is possibly the rarest and least enduring human trait. Management can be cruelly hurt by evidence of disloyalty. "How sharper than a serpent's tooth to have a thankless child." An executive friend of mine was really shocked when strikers against AT&T (one of the most generous of employers) carried signs saying "Ma Bell Is a Mean Mother." To him this was heresy. It was nothing of the sort. It proved only that some striker had a perverse sense of humor.

MIDDLE MANAGEMENT

While all regular employees of a big corporation are covered by its security blanket, the distribution of salary and other remuneration is more selective. Management tries to pay its production people and clerical types—the working stiffs—only the going rate, which is hammered out in hard bargaining and mediation or by the precedent set by other employers. Above the worker level there are middle management people and professionals, such as chemists and accountants. To these people management is more generous: it *wants* them to be prosperous. This may seem to be a paradoxical position. Why should business jeopardize its earnings by paying fat salaries to a whole class of employees who probably don't deserve it and who certainly won't be grateful?

The position is not only logical; it is necessary for survival—for business to retain its privileged position in society as the main exploiter of natural resources and the main converter of resources into consumer goods and services. Top management may only dimly understand this need. ("We have to pay good money to get decent lawyers.") The beneficiaries take it for granted—this is the reason they went to school. The goal of the manager of the personnel department is simple: to get as much as he can for others in order to get more for himself. The real reason for top management to support a prosperous middle management is that these people present the image of the business world to the public. They are the living symbols of the success of the business (capitalist) system.

The Covenant

When a new employee whose background and training imply his (eventual) inclusion on the middle management or professional team, there is an unwritten covenant agreed upon between him and the company. The employer's side of the bargain goes something like this: "We will provide for your security, both job security and protection against financial emergencies. We will pay you enough so that you can move smoothly into the middle class, and if you keep your side of the bargain we will continue to raise your social standing (at least to a point) as the years go by." The employee's commitment goes something like this: "I will do my job adequately. I will obey the tribal mores and respect the taboos of the business community[4] in behavior, philosophy, and dress, both on and off the corporate turf. I will be an involved member of society and will promote the business position." This may seem like a reasonable loyalty oath, or it may seem like selling one's soul to the devil. It all depends on one's point of view.

[4]See *HIM*, Chapter 14.

Actually, employee compliance is not *always* required: it may be waived, for example, for certain gifted scientists, for exceptionally brilliant business types, or to fill a racial quota. For the average Joe, the typical business school graduate, it is binding. To break the faith means at best a no-growth career and, more likely, termination at the first convenient opportunity. For most employees, compliance is natural and satisfying: from the employer's point of view, it is a must. Let us consider both sides of the bargain in more detail.

For the average businessman the unwritten covenant is the best invention since canned beer. He has to do his job adequately, which is no strain. Most business jobs are not very demanding; after 20 or so years in school, the average Joe may well be overqualified for his assigned tasks.[5] He is expendable; job security is a good deal. As far as observing the behavioral conventions, he has been eager to do just that since he started career training. (Most business school students anticipate the command by dressing more or less like young executives while still in school.) His wife is proud of him in his three-piece suit with dispatch case carried at the ready. Social involvement—church, service clubs, and so forth—is a bit more demanding but relatively painless, since the pertinent organizations are already run by business people in a comfortable businesslike way. No distressing radical ideas, please.

After tenure, the most important perquisite is regular advancement both in salary and in position. As long as the businessman keeps his nose clean he will progress, possibly even to the Olympian heights of becoming a hyphenated vice president. I have been frustrated watching cooperative team players move smoothly up the corporate ladder,[6] people who either never had an original idea or carefully refrained from expressing any. I was uncharitable.

[5] True in the Western world. In Third World or emerging countries it may be difficult to recruit competent help. See job offers in *The Wall Street Journal* and in various trade journals.

[6] The same sort of thing must happen in the civil and military services, maybe even in education; but this book is about business.

The thing that makes a nation a good place in which to live is the possibility for the *average* citizen to achieve the good life. The exceptional person can be assumed to be able to take care of himself; the rest of us need help. This is what the early immigrants meant when they said that the streets of America were paved with gold: not that there were nuggets lying in the road (what was lying in the road was something else), but that by hard work and dedication even an ordinary man, or at least his children, could join the ranks of the middle class—what Marx called the bourgeoisie (and Mencken, the boobeoisie).

This is the American dream. As long as it persists, private enterprise, capitalism, business—whatever you choose to call it—is safe. Big business can sustain the dream (or myth if you prefer) by giving status to its middle people and professionals without obsessive regard for their abilities. Business needs these success stories to support its image: to show that the nation is in good hands, that the system works.

Management wants its protégés to go forth into the world as evangelists for the business system, to be very models of the modern corporation man: trustworthy, loyal, helpful, friendly, courteous, kind, obedient, cheerful, thrifty, brave, clean, and reverent. The armed services have this same craving for respectability. In their case officers are decreed to be gentlemen (or ladies).

Most companies, after a probationary period, provide their people with a tasteful lapel pin to be worn as a mark of faith like ecclesiastical jewelry. Some go further. In its most successful years, IBM insisted that its representatives not only sing company songs but observe a strict dress code: dark suit, white shirt, conservative tie.[7]

The good company man will voluntarily and eagerly get

[7]This image thing may be the one reason American business was slow to move minority people into middle management positions. No more prejudiced than other parts of society, business wanted to preserve its conservative image, which was WASP/male. Now things are changing.

involved in community projects. I know of no company that is so intrusive as to *require* such participation. It is part of the unwritten compact between employee and employer. By the time the young businessman does get involved, he is an honest, committed supporter of the corporate position.

The emergence of the businessman as the exemplar of the modern way of life, as a leader in the community, is a recent development. It represents a successful marketing of the image of business by business.

TOP MANAGEMENT

With the workers secure and middle management prosperous, we can turn our attention to the remuneration of top management. The goal here is different: more than prosperity, it is wealth. Business leaders want to be part of a financial aristocracy such as arose on Moola-Moola—they want to belong to a special class. Since the intellectual and cultural contributions of most leaders are not obvious (most people don't know what the hell they do), the easiest way to set leaders apart from the rest of us is to make them richer. There is a cheaper option—official public recognition. The only nation that seems to have adopted this approach effectively is England, which grants knighthoods and life peerages. The great advantage is that such honors don't cost either the country or the corporation much money. To be addressed as "Sir" or "Lord" for the rest of one's life may be worth more than mere gold. It is a pity that republican governments can't have such a system. It would be nice if we could borrow Her Majesty for installation ceremonies.

Only large corporations can afford the luxury of creating members of the financial aristocracy. And only a few people in these organizations qualify for such favored treatment—the members of the management team. The titles and qualifications of such team members vary from company to company: chairmen of the board, presidents, group and senior vice presidents, perhaps the corporate council. Not all people with such titles are team members: the controlling group in any company is small (it has to be for efficiency) and its members are individually selected for their compatibility, competence, and creativity. These are the few real leaders in any corporation who make policy and strategic decisions rather than doing defined jobs. No mediocrity allowed. One of the decisions they make is to set their own remuneration:[8] to set it high enough to awe the workers and to impress their peers in other companies—not one of their more unpleasant jobs. Nominal salaries may be very high indeed—six and even seven figures in the United States, depending on corporation size and industry type. Salary alone is not the route to wealth; it is only part of what is called the executive compensation package.

Perquisites and status symbols are the most important rewards of a top manager, the things that set him apart from the herd and allow the accumulation of real wealth. Salary has a nasty tendency to go for living expenses and taxes. Monetary perquisites include things like stock options, bonuses, low-interest loans, and deferred payments—a mix that is limited only by the imagination of the tax accountant. The nature of the package varies from time to time and from country to country. As the purpose is to leave a residue, an estate, for one's beneficiaries, the details depend on the nation's income tax and estate tax laws. In countries like England, where income tax is high, status perks include the use of company planes and limousines, lavish expense accounts, and club memberships. The isolation of top managers (social distance) in a plush executive suite complete with dining room and gymnasium is a perk that sets them apart from other employees.[9]

Does this self-generosity work? Does it create a respected business aristocracy? The answers to these questions are yes and no. In a money-oriented society—which is the position in which

[8]Close enough to a true statement to be useful. The board of directors has an executive compensation committee to oversee the process, but usually what top management wants, top management gets.

[9]See *HIM*, Chapter 13.

business feels most comfortable—the captains of industry must be distinguished by having more of the stuff than other people. If they didn't, the whole system would seem rather pointless: like having an important golf tournament in which the winner is rewarded by a firm handshake. Since money is power in the capitalist system, business leaders should have some of their own. A lot of people would consider them damn fools if they didn't take care of themselves. For years, Walter Reuther took only a nominal salary as president of the Automobile Workers Union. This didn't seem to help his image, except to be remarked on as an idiosyncracy by columnists.

Wealth and Privilege

While most people accept the propriety of a highly paid and privileged business aristocracy, there is a vocal minority that considers such privilege obscene, if not criminal. Socialists automatically object to the idea of anyone having too much money (five times the average seems to be their upper limit). When this is an honest ideological position, it has to be respected. When it is used as an argument against free enterprise itself by characterizing the system as a rip-off, it is unfair. The number of people who properly qualify as top management is so small that the effect of their own remuneration on general prosperity or on earnings per share is trivial—after all, they have to pay themselves something. Management's generosity to middle management is a much more important money drain.

A lot of people without any particular socialist or leftist leanings resent anyone making much more money than they do. Part of this is envy and part of it is the feeling that rich people must despise the rest of us. These are not very noble or rational sentiments, but they are a force. Basketball players are reviled for making too much money (which the owners must pay to keep them). Barbara Walters was a flop as an anchorwoman on TV news largely because viewers could switch channels to protest her making a million dollars a year. In defense of the tradition of high executive remuneration, concentration of money in few hands has given the rest of us a lot of good things, such as museums, libraries, college endowments, and educational foundations.

Are business leaders *worth* these fabulous salaries? This is a question that is inevitably asked but that should not arise, since it has almost no meaning. As we have seen, both in Moola-Moola and in modern society there is no way to put an absolute value on anybody's work. Money is used to recruit a workforce, to allocate resources, to create a business (or bureaucratic, or educational) hierarchy, to enforce discipline, and to set social distinctions. A value approach is self-contradictory: an American doctor is not worth five times as much as an English doctor.

The question of the justice of high executive remuneration is meaningless. And yet, on a purely comparative basis, some leaders do seem to deserve more than others. The definitive element is *risk*. Some brave souls take their destiny in their own hands and create new companies, most of which fail. Some take their chances by pulling together existing ho-hum companies and building a new dynamic organization—people like the Leidtkes, who built the new Pennzoil, and Forest Shumway, who breathed new life into the Signal Company. These leaders are driven; they are Gamesmen[10] who enjoy taking chances: Why else would Seymour Cray leave a top job with Control Data to set up his own computer company?

Such upheavals occur only rarely in most corporate histories. In the interim, the organizations are run by professional managers—competent people but people who reap the benefits made possible by their more daring predecessors. Most top management people get their jobs by a combination of intelligence, competence, opportunism, vitality, good team play, and a little bit of luck.[11] Less

[10]Michael Maccoby, *The Gamesman*, New York, Simon & Schuster, 1976.

[11]Schumpeter would not agree *(CSD)*. He claims that business is an almost perfect selective filter for finding the best people. Anyone who has been in business knows, however, that it is fortuitous to be in the right place or even the right company at the right time.

endearing routes such as nepotism, office politics, backstabbing, and credit grabbing are more common in fiction than in well-run companies. The movement of a professional manager from the middle ranks into a top spot has all the suspense and excitement of a military promotion from major general to lieutenant general. Somehow, such people don't seem as deserving as the founder whose picture hangs on the board room wall.

7

SANTA CLAUS
AND SOCIETY

IT IS A characteristic of Western society that business passes out a
lot of money to its own people at all levels. Is this a good thing?
Does it promote general prosperity or is it a burden borne by the
working people as the Marxists would have us believe? There are
obviously some good effects and some bad ones. On the credit side,
business helps support an affluent middle class, which is the
backbone of Western societies. Balance-sheet items don't make a
prosperous society; money in the hands of consumers does. The
obvious way for business to be generous with its discretionary
money (tax money is not discretionary) is to pay its people well.
Businesses do make outside contributions which have lesser effects
on society for better and for worse. We will get to these later. On
the debit side, the Big Brother and Santa Claus posture of business

hurts the social system by dividing society and by promoting inflation.

INNIES AND OUTIES

Modern Western societies are divided by the policies of the business community (and by those of the civil service) into two groups: the "innies" and the "outies"—those who work for business or government and those who do not. The "innies" are secure; they have tenure. They are protected by company or civil service policies from medical expenses, from insurance costs, from their own improvidence, even from inflation. The "outies" are on their own in a harsh world. If *they* get sick they don't get sick leave; unless there is socialized medicine they pay their own expenses (if a hospital will have them); they must provide for their own insurance and retirement in a cruelly inflationary economy. An American dentist on his own making $35,000 a year is no better off than a run-of-the-mill corporate accountant making $20,000. At that, professionals are better off than artists—the very symbols of civilization. To cite a familiar example, consider the organist of your church. He probably has a master's degree in music and has to do the equivalent of three jobs—directing, performing, and teaching—to make ends meet.

The present value of a job offer by the business establishment is high: in the United States it is closer to a million than to half a million dollars.[1] With this sort of built-in security and success, why would anyone be an "outie"? Bad planning perhaps—majoring in history instead of something useful like data processing. Some "outies" are reluctant to enter the business world or the civil service until it is too late (age is a bar to entry). Others suffer from poor schooling, or stupidity. Still others are driven to follow their own

---

[1]It is surprising that job offers in Western countries are usually honest. In Third World countries government and business jobs are often awarded by patronage or to the highest bidder. The payroll of Pemex, the Mexican oil company, includes people who never report for work.

muses: to dance, to sing, to write, to make music, to paint. Business may feel a little guilty about such people, who work much harder than do most businessmen, but it has little room for them. With deep envy or resentment at somehow being cheated, these "outies" form a natural antibusiness constituency. Fortunately for the business world, they rarely organize; they tend to be individualistic. They do pose a long-range threat, as we shall see when we discuss competing life styles.

It takes a brave man to go it alone. Not only must he compete against big business in the marketplace; he must bid against business and government to hire people. The latter may be far more difficult.

SOCIETY'S STEPCHILDREN

There are a number of institutions in Western nations that we didn't observe on Moola-Moola: cultural organizations such as churches, private colleges, and symphony orchestras; and service organizations such as the YMCA and the Boy Scouts, which we might as well lump together as "United Fund organizations." Churches and private colleges are survivors of preindustrial society: United Fund organizations appeared late in the Industrial Revolution.

All these institutions are concerned with improving the quality of life. Most of them rely heavily on volunteer help, but all of them have to have some paid career employees, and this is where business competition hurts. Private colleges must compete not only with state-supported schools but with business itself to hire good professors. If they can't pay competitive salaries they must, and do, fold. The Boy Scouts must pay going wages to its key professional people; even churches have to compete with business for secretarial help. Maybe this is a good thing. Business and government policies ensure that anyone who works makes a "decent" wage, but competition places an almost intolerable burden on service and cultural institutions—a burden over which they have no control.

INFLATION

Inflation seems to be a modern fact of life. We all have our own stories of two-cent newspapers and seven-cent streetcar rides, but the great self-taught economist S. J. Perelman said it best:

> As recently as 1918 it was possible for a housewife . . . to march into a store with a five-cent piece, purchase a firkin of cocoa butter, a good second-hand copy of Bowditch, a hundred weight of quahogs, a shagreen spectacle case, and sufficient nainsook for a corset cover, and emerge with enough left over. . . .[2]

Business hates inflation. Business spokesmen will fulminate against it whether a hat is dropped or not. The villain of these diatribes is always the government and its unbusinesslike ways. There is a lot of truth in what they say; there is also a lot of cant. The fact is that business itself is a major contributor to inflation.

Mulling the Moola-Moola model, we might wonder why business should object to inflation. Since paper money was invented to allocate goods and to structure society, the denominations written on the bills would seem immaterial. Business might even welcome inflation. Most companies have large inventories in the form of real estate, natural resources, raw materials, or finished goods, and inflation gives them a "windfall" inventory profit that looks good on the balance sheet.

Business honestly doesn't like inflation. For one thing it doesn't like windfall profits, which stir up labor leaders and demagogues. For most companies inflation means a loss of real revenue. Costs go up in dollar terms; and depreciation, based on original cost,

[2] S. J. Perelman, *Listen to the Mocking Bird,* New York: Simon & Schuster, 1949, p. 86.

becomes inadequate to cover replacement. Sure, companies try to recover by raising prices, but usually only *after* their expenses go up: they are playing catch-up and this costs money. Another reason business opposes inflation is that it erodes the value of personal fortunes, unless the assets are in some inflation-proof form. The preferred inflation hedge of American business, the New York Stock Exchange, has been a sorry failure (foreign markets have done better). From 1969 to 1979 the Dow Jones average of stock price performance remained constant. Investors are not "bullish on America." The competitive position of our industry has not improved.

Cost Efficiency

The salaries and wages of business employees in the Western world are almost guaranteed to rise from year to year for sociological reasons: so that the employee feels that he is getting on and his family is proud. The cost efficiency (productivity) of business would thus seem to have to get progressively worse. That this has not happened in most nations (England is an exception) is due to fantastic improvement in the efficiency of operations—on the shop floor and in the mine. Capital investment in production tools increases the effectiveness of the worker or eliminates the need for him entirely.[3]

A good place to observe this is in the canning plant of a large American brewery. The striking thing to a casual observer is the lack of workers. Cans come in on a conveyor belt from the can factory next door, and from here on machines take over: filling, sealing, labeling, and packing a lot of indifferent beer for shipment. There *is* a man down there filling can top dispensers, but he looks like a candidate for redundancy as soon as a new machine arrives. That business productivity is not even higher than it is is due to the

[3]So much for Marx's surplus value. The surplus value in modern factories comes from machines, not people.

overhead of corporate staff—the white-collar contingent—whose ranks keep growing for a variety of reasons, as we shall see.

WHITE-COLLAR PRODUCTIVITY

We have already seen that top management wants its staff people to be prosperous. Middle managers are an ungrateful lot: only mildly interested in the welfare of the company, their goal is to build empires of people, space, and hardware. Management's traditional response to this pent-up demand is to allow the proliferation of departments by splitting old ones into several new ones. Each new department head then follows a Parkinsonian[4] course of building up his staff and influence: he knows that his own remuneration is a direct function of the number of people he supervises and of his department budget. It is a rare company that doesn't have ten different accounting departments, possibly feuding with one another. This was the old pattern but now things are worse.

Government regulation and the increasing litigiousness of the public and private sectors have forced corporations to defend themselves by adding new staffs of specialists and lawyers. Lawyers beget lawyers. Even worse, a whole new batch of specialists are competing to get on the corporate gravy train: computer scientists, operational researchers, word processing personnel, market researchers, communications technicians, economists, safety specialists, econometricians, even psychologists and outright quacks.

Management is out of its depth; it knows about law, accounting, and finance but it sure as hell doesn't know anything about nonlinear programming. It is hard to oppose the installation of a new technical department when the proposal is backed by multicolored slides, is given in an unknown tongue, and is supported by a prestigious hardware manufacturer and probably by an outside

[4]C. N. Parkinson, *Parkinson's Law*, Boston: Houghton Mifflin, 1969.

consultant. The technical revolution in business is causing top management to lose some of its control. Management's logical response, hiring technical advisers, is often self-defeating: such people may be more dedicated to their own discipline and to acquiring hardware than to corporate health. All this must cause some presidents sleepless nights. Let us look at the most visible, and expensive, example of the technical revolution: data processing.

COMPUTERS

There *are* good computer applications in business. These are usually operational uses, such as on-line process control and passenger reservation systems. They are hideously expensive to install, but they do pay off. What we are interested in is data processing, paper shuffling, which is the largest computer cost to business. In 1978, IBM's domestic leasing income was $8.6 billion. This is a fairly good estimate of the cost of data processing hardware to United States business.[5] Add twice this amount for associated personnel costs[6] and we have a reasonable estimate of the data processing overhead in this country.

What does American business get for all this money? Not too much. Before computers (BC), companies paid their employees, billed their customers, reported to the government and to the SEC, and generally made a higher rate of return on equity than they do now. We used to justify computer installation by the number of clerks we were going to replace. We didn't eliminate any clerks, at least no more than the number of keypunchers we had to hire. The new pitch for more hardware (on which the professional status of the computer manager depends) is data availability—a terminal on

[5]Not all IBM computers are used for data processing, but not all data processing computers are made by IBM. Since I omit direct sales, the estimate is conservative.

[6]We used to try to keep the people cost to no more than hardware cost. Computers have become so difficult to program and now require so many specialists that the two-to-one ratio is appropriate.

every executive's desk. The added value of instant data is moot. Is it really more useful than compiled information from a reasonable operating period? The same manager who is supposed to make brilliant decisions using a corporate data base and his own terminal routinely ignores daily fluctuations in the stock market. The Industry Scoreboard in the *Oil and Gas Journal* presents four-week moving averages.

I know the arguments for data processing: the old clerical staff couldn't possibly handle the new complicated procedures (true); computing is cheaper (true). These are misleading arguments. One of the reasons for the new complexity is the computer itself: procedures that would once have been rejected out of hand as ridiculous are now routinely accepted and programmed. Computer processing, the cost per operation, is at least an order of magnitude cheaper than it used to be. But this is irrelevant. Computer usage rises to meet computer capacity! It would be a brave manager (or a damn fool) who allowed any other situation in his shop. He would forfeit his chances to get new hardware and status, and he could be criticized for not using what he had.

One last shot at computers. They are security risks. Not that they draw bomb throwers (they often do) but that companies are vulnerable to computer failure or to a technicians' strike. Computer procedures are almost impossible to audit, and there is an increasing danger of undetected irregularities and computer fraud.[7]

GROWTH

The increase in corporate overhead goes on almost independently of operational activity. It is based on the cumulation of individual ambitions, not on corporate profits. The result is to sabotage efficiency, raise prices, and promote inflation. An excessively staff-ridden company is a candidate for extinction, or for

[7]See "Annals of Crime—Computers," *The New Yorker*, August–September, 1977.

government subsidy. Uncontrolled staff costs are a threat to free enterprise. Remember that the capitalist system is still on trial! Only as long as business shows that it can do a more efficient job on its own will it be allowed to remain in the private sector. Inefficient industries will be, and are, nationalized (or socialized if you prefer). Penn Central went this way. As corporations become more staff-oriented and less profit-oriented (more bureaucratic), they look more like government departments, and the temptation to socialize them becomes irresistible. To remain profitable, to remain alive, a company has to fight staff encroachment.

Draconian methods usually fail. To make across-the-board cuts or to perform major surgery demoralizes the troops. Management may get away with eliminating an unnecesssary research department, but it can't shake up the paper handlers too violently. Efficiently produced or not, reports are essential to a company. (Henry Ford tried to control accounting costs—staff in his simpler time—by restricting the accountants' working space. He wound up with chaotic books.) A novel approach, one that might even work, would be to reward managers for doing a job cheaply rather than according to the size of their empires. Still, the only really effective control method is *growth*. The logic is simple. Staff is going to grow more or less at its own rate in any case. If the corporation can grow at least as fast, the overhead burden, as a ratio, will not increase.

Growth is the magic word—remember Moola-Moola. If a company doesn't grow, it will founder or get taken over by a more aggressive company that is growing. Without growth, industries revert, by a sort of Second Law of Thermodynamics, into a state where paper shuffling and personnel problems swamp operations and production.

Not many people, in or out of business, want a no-growth society. It may be forced on us by the decline of natural resources, by overpopulation, and by inadequate technical or political response. No-growth would destroy the free enterprise system by converting businesses into bureaucratic rationing organizations. A more immediate threat is the desire of a lot of people to achieve the same result by changing our economic system. It is time we looked at the enemy.

PART TWO

The Enemy

8

THE ENEMY CAMP

PEOPLE SEEM to have an innate craving for the doctrines of socialism. Although the participants in undergraduate rap sessions don't realize it, their proposals for a brave new world usually zero in on concepts familiar to socialists—at least until someone opens the windows to let in some fresh air and daylight. Telling points are usually introduced with the opening phrase "Wouldn't it be nice if" or "Why couldn't we," as in such statements as "Wouldn't it be nice if there were no poor and no very rich people?" and "Why couldn't we organize society so that everybody shared the common wealth?" Years ago, I participated in such discussions walking over Ohio farmland at night. The bit about sharing the wealth appealed strangely, particularly since my typewriter was then in hock with the local, friendly, usurious banker. If anybody had told me that what I was spouting was almost pure socialist (or even communist!) doctrine, I would have been shocked.

Actually, the natural leaning to socialism shows up even earlier than in college days. It is manifested in the familiar cry of the small child who realizes that his big brother gets to stay up later than he does: "Things aren't fair."

Being so intuitive, the doctrines of socialism would be expected to have, and do have, a long history—from the ancient philosophers through ages of utopian dreamers. For our purposes we need only go back to Marx. He didn't invent socialism but he gathered existing threads together and gave the movement its holy writ. Marx was concerned more with the coming revolution and class struggle than with what a mature socialist society would be like. But no matter. He and Engels provided the dogma and the dialectic; later thinkers have filled in the messy details.

Before describing the (more properly, "a") blueprint of a socialist society[1] I had better say something about the difference between socialism and communism. Many people consider socialism a "nice" or "respectable" form of communism, one that does not involve hanging the fat, bloated capitalists from lamp posts. This was certainly my mother's point of view, which she expressed before going to the polls to vote for Norman Thomas. ("Such a nice man." He was.) As far as Marx was concerned, the two terms were synonymous. *The Communist Manifesto* is about socialist revolution. Today we think of communism as hard-line socialism with political overtones. The "dictatorship of the proletariat" is a communist phrase which, in practice, seems to translate into "dictatorship" period. Socialism as preached today is more of an economic than a political philosophy.

Socialists come in all shades of pink, from the very pale whose goal is only the nationalization of basic industries (not doctrinaire socialism) to red-flag-waving communists. The following discussion

[1]Schumpeter's term. See *CSD*, Chapter 16, for a definitive discussion.

of socialism for beginners covers what seem to me to be the generally accepted concepts of today's Marxist scholars. Trained economists can read it for kicks or for laughs.

The Criteria of Socialism

The definitive features of a socialist society are (1) public ownership of the production and distributive apparatus of society, and (2) the absence of significant savings by individuals. The first feature means that factories, mines, land, communications, and the distribution systems—railroads, airlines, ships—are owned and run by the government for the benefit of all the comrades rather than for capitalist masters. The second feature, absence of personal savings, implies that almost all goods at or above the "big ticket" level—automobiles and housing, for example—would also be owned by the state and somehow leased to the users. Money or its equivalent would exist only as an allocation device to permit the citizen some discretion. He may prefer steak to pork chops, for example. Such money would not have lasting value but would become worthless, like an automobile safety sticker, after a certain time period. The money might have designated uses like food stamps. The citizen would have neither the desire nor the capability to save. Important savings in the economic sense—to build new factories and roads, for example—would be made by the government from the "profits" of socialized industries.

Such a socialist system is generally conceded by both Marxist and other economists to be feasible. It would "work." There must be a warning here for the general reader. When a modern economist says that a system will work, he means that it can be reduced to a mathematical model of society and fed into a computer. If the model does not "blow up," the system is feasible. A serious objection to the socialist blueprint was made in 1920 by von Mises,[2] who claimed

[2]I have to bring him in because I studied under Richard von Mises—not economics but aerodynamics! He was one of the last great universalists.

that without a free market there would be no way to set reasonable prices or relative values or whatever they would be called. The answer to this dilemma is that socialism is workable only when it takes over a mature capitalist state and can adopt the existing price structure.

It seems to me that the absence of individual savings poses a problem. Nobody could save up for the "nice" things of life, such as travel, art objects, and pianos. I guess these things would be stashed in "Halls of Culture" or given as rewards for exceptional service. In any event, I will bow to superior intellect and admit that the model is theoretically possible.[3] Incidentally, very few Marxists will claim that the Russian system is a fair example of socialism. Even they will admit that it shows what *can* happen when a socialist experiment is tried.

If we accept these two criteria—public ownership and absence of personal savings—we can see things we often *call* socialism are not the real McCoy. They may be steps that soften up our society for an eventual takeover, but they are not the genuine article. Nationalization of industries by itself is not socialism. Increasing government regulation is not socialism. For one thing, such actions can be reversed in a democratic society. We have the English example and Maggie Thatcher (whom the *Manchester Guardian* refers to both in sorrow and in anger as "ax-happy"): the return of public housing to private ownership, the denationalization of BOAC, the "shape up or ship out" approach to British shipbuilding. In the United States we had deregulation of the airlines. Even Sweden, the Marxist's shining example, is not truly socialist when Björn Borg can get rich without renouncing his citizenship. (That he lives in another country is a detail.) As long as a country allows its citizens to save and to keep, it is not truly socialist.

---

[3]It does work in special situations. Even in the United States there are people who, for all practical purposes, live a socialist life. Consider an Army man whose family lives on a military base in a furnished house and who drives a "motorpool" car. He gets paid regularly but all his money goes for food and necessities in the commissary and the PX.

Conversion to a socialist society in a Western nation must be a deliberate, conscious act. In the case of the United States it would involve rewriting the Constitution. Whether the transition were bloody or peaceful (voted in as a last democratic act under the old regime), it would be recognized as a change: as the start of a new way of life. The proposed form of the new system could vary. It could be egalitarian socialism where everybody gets the same-size slice of the pie or it could allow "wage" differentials and perks. The new commissars might find it convenient to leave small businesses and, particularly, farmlands in private hands for at least a generation to ease the transition. They might allow the rich to stay rich and appropriate their property through death duties. The one sure thing is that all the comrades would know that their country was now a socialist republic (or democracy!): if they didn't also know they would soon find out that the change was irreversible.

ADVANTAGES OF SOCIALISM

Socialism has been a dream of mankind for centuries; many people have died fighting under the red flag. It must have merit and it does: both economic and sociological. The most obvious theoretical advantage—which can be verified on a computer—is its efficiency or, better said, its elimination of the inefficiencies of the commercial or capitalist society. (Schumpeter says that the socialist blueprint is drawn at a higher level of rationality.)

In most Western countries an inordinate share of the national wealth goes into supporting the running battle between business and government. There are exceptions. The Japanese government works hand in hand with business. The Italian government has traditionally been too weak to fight back.[4] Both these nations have an advantage over their trading rivals. In other Western countries the battle is joined. Armies of government lawyers, regulators, and bureaucrats compete with armies of industry lawyers and specialists

[4]See Jonathan Spivac, "Italy Booms Despite Crisis," *The Wall Street Journal*, July 18, 1980.

to the benefit of the participants. In the tax area, IRS auditors compete with corporate tax accountants to get money that corporations are increasingly reluctant to divvy up. It is the consumer and the taxpayer who support the troops in this civil war. In a true socialist society, of course, this sort of thing cannot happen, since government and management are the same. That a transition to socialism would put most lawyers out of work (criminal lawyers excepted, although even here we can expect certain new efficiencies) is almost enough to convert me. Schumpeter says the state would have to do something with them—something kind, I hope.

There are other inefficiencies in commercial society that would disappear under socialism. Advertising would be reduced to an information service to keep the bureaucratic managers abreast of recent developments and to inform citizens of the remaining discretionary items.[5] I can visualize something like a *Consumer Reports* stressing utility: "What the young comrade is wearing this season." Another wasteful cost of business is money spent for industrial warfare and overcapacity—too many corporations fighting for a market or trying to invade each other's territory. A familiar example from the days before the gas crunch was the sight of four large filling stations at a single busy intersection.

A more fundamental objection to the capitalist system, and a corresponding plus for socialism, is that the working of the profit motive does not always lead to sound economic conclusions. This is a field for the theorist and I won't compromise myself by getting too far into it. There is one anomaly of the capitalist system which even I can understand: the balance-of-trade paradox. Our traditional folk wisdom states that a nation should have a "favorable" balance of trade, that it should export more than it imports. But this is nonsense: it is equivalent to saying that a household gets richer

[5]The Russians *do* advertise—for Aeroflot in the English-language *Sputnik,* for example. Russia is not a pure socialist country. It has to compete with the capitalists on the international scene.

when it holds a garage sale of goods at distress prices and gets poorer when it buys and installs a grand piano. Exports should be considered a forfeit that a nation must pay to get the imports it must have. This is true of crude oil. The best way to conserve a nation's own reserves is to import foreign oil, with the payment made in printed dollars. How much better to export renewable resources like food, technology, and financial skills and to import nonrenewable resources from others. The Japanese and the Swiss do very well without oil of their own. (We will talk more about energy later.)

It is in the sociological field that socialists wax eloquent and that the movement takes on evangelical overtones: the end of class distinction; the demise of poverty and privileges; all men brothers, or comrades, striving for the common good. If the source weren't tainted, Paul's epistles might offer some rich quotations for socialists, but Marx and Engels gave them plenty of ammunition. How much this line represents a longing for a better society ("Things aren't fair") and how much it is a reaction against the inequalities of the present system depends on the speaker. Even the most ardent supporters of the capitalist system, even Rotary Club speakers, have to admit that as long as social worth is based on net worth, things aren't fair.

"Windfall" profits and "lucky" money make socialists see red.[6] So does an inheritance system that allows one child to be born with a silver spoon in its mouth while another has nothing. A society in which social standing largely depends on personal wealth[7] *is* warped. It encourages crime and selfishness, it downgrades personal contribution and merit: the Coca-Cola franchise holder is

[6]An interesting example involves the United States Dag Hammarskjöld commemorative stamp issued in 1962. One sheet of stamps was improperly printed. A collector bought it, but like a fool he let this be known. Rather than let him keep his "windfall" profit, our bureaucrats (who appear to have socialist leanings) printed a whole issue of error stamps so that everybody could have some and nobody would get rich.

[7]See. R. P. Coleman, *Social Standing in America*, New York: Basic Books, 1978, particularly Chapter 8.

more respected in a community than the dedicated teacher or social worker. A man like Somoza, who was so crooked and greedy that the Nicaraguans were willing to sacrifice thousands of their own people to get rid of him, could live in affluence and respectability in the United States because he could afford to do so.

At the other end of the existing social scale, the typical worker (a breed that Marxists refuse to admit is becoming an endangered species) would be emancipated under socialism. He would be a full partner in a classless society. His morale would be high, he would work eagerly for the common good, and his productivity—the key to prosperity—would increase. Much of the apparatus of labor relations, union management, and arbitrators could be thrown out along with the lawyers and tax accountants.

DISADVANTAGES OF SOCIALISM

I am not going to climb on to a soap box. I continue to accept that socialism is workable and I assume that the transition to a "worker's paradise" is made in a humane an intelligent way.

A favorite objection to socialism is that people just aren't good enough, smart enough, or unselfish enough to administer such a system and that the central planning board and the management apparatus would be too large, inefficient, and expensive. These are not necessarily valid objections. Government bureaucracy is not always stupid, inefficient, and greedy. There are excellent counter-examples, such as the German bureaucracy before World War I and the old British civil service in India. The latter can serve as a model for any management effort.[8]

Even in the reviled American civil service establishment there are pockets of efficiency, such as the county agent system and the administration of the national parks. If the transition to socialism were made intelligently, the best managers in business and

[8]See P. Woodruff, *The Men Who Ruled India*, London: Cape, 1971.

government would move smoothly into corresponding socialist management positions. There is no reason to believe that the new management and planning apparatus would be any larger under socialism than the old regulatory and fiscal bureaucracy. When you add to the existing government establishment the bureaucratic employees and the lobbyists employed by business itself, the new socialist control organization might even be leaner than that of "fettered capitalism."[9]

The usual demagogic objections to socialism appeal to its presumed erosion of freedom and democracy. Such arguments are important—they may even be critical—but they don't belong in this discussion, which is supposed to be objective. The terms "freedom" and "democracy" are usually defined on the basis of convenience. One man's freedom is another man's tyranny. "A" may object to the installation of a traffic light which increases his commuting time as an excess of a power-mad establishment, "B" may be happy to see that the government is finally getting traffic under control. "Democracy" is one of those few words like "cat" that remain almost orthographically invariant under linguistic transformations (wow!). "Democracy" may *look* the same in most modern languages but it sure doesn't mean the same thing. Until it has an accepted consensus meaning there isn't much point in dragging the word into this discussion, which is supposed to be an objective analysis.

To my way of thinking, the greatest threat to the working of a socialist economy will come from the workers, from the little folk for whom the whole noble experiment is supposed to be made. Remember, we are talking about a civilized, bloodless revolution; the proletariat has not had the uplifting catharsis of seeing the fat, bloated capitalists swing from lamp posts. In fact, at lower levels, most of the old bosses are still in charge. I don't think that the working comrade will like the self-styled intellectuals, at high levels, who are running the new order. If he doesn't have the

[9]Schumpeter's term for a highly regulated commercial system.

feeling that the new system offers him and his children better prospects, if he doesn't have confidence in the new leaders and commissars, he is going to respond with the classic negative vote of the working stiff and the enlisted man: "This is a crock!" The new social engineers are going to have to put a lot more teeth in the new order than the benign Big Brother operation they had in mind or they are going to see socialism go the way of the two-dollar bill and the Susan B. Anthony dollar coin in the United States.

There are at least two reasons why the working comrade may not be content in a classless society. All citizens may be equal but not all jobs are equal—somebody has to pick up the garbage. Some of our clear-thinking Marxists argue that comrades should be paid a premium for doing dirty work. I wonder how the other comrades are going to like *this* arrangement. A lot of workers, good workers, just don't want a classless society. They will even accept a low-prestige position as long as there is the possibility for themselves or for their children to move up. As we have already seen, personal satisfaction (prosperity, if you like) involves odious comparison with others who haven't done as well—at least not yet. This is not a pretty side of human nature, but it is one that socialists ignore at their peril. There isn't much point working your way up if you have no place to go, or if the only route to power is through party membership. The advocates of socialism have some indoctrination to do before their system will be accepted by the working stiffs.

THE SOCIALISTS

Who are the socialists in Western society? I have divided them into four classes which pretty well cover the lot: (1) the honest socialists, (2) the chic socialists, (3) the opportunists, and (4) the haters.

Honest Socialists

Honest socialists are those people who have taken a long look at commercial society, with its strengths and weaknesses, and at the socialist blueprint, with its good and bad features, and have come to the conclusion that socialism is the better system. If they feel strongly enough, they will work for the cause. I have respect for such people; they may even be right. Some honest socialists like Norman Thomas and G. B. Shaw were even lovable. (The late Mr. Shaw might have objected to this description, but I certainly enjoy his writing.) Such people are honorable opponents in the most important confrontation in Western society. I can't say as much for the others.

Chic Socialists

My prototype of the chic socialist is a professor of economics at a small college. He is an economist and he has a Ph.D. to prove it. He isn't very bright (not an incompatible situation). He never worked outside the academic establishment and has no business experience. He is a socialist and an "intellectual." As an intellectual he is a member of a large class of people who have advanced degrees (scholastic rather than professional); who write and who talk; and who are in academia, in government, in the media industries, or even in the business community. Many are frustrated at having to work at jobs that they consider to be below their capabilities. Many are overeducated—a situation that will continue as long as our schools turn out more graduates than nature turns out candidates with the necessary abilities.[10] Most of these people have a beef against society; some turn to, or at least toy with, socialist doctrine. But let us get back to our hero.

Of course he is a socialist—Marxist is the term he prefers. He has spent many years of his life working for the day when he could stand in front of a class rather than sitting in one. He wants to impress his students with his learning and his intellectual courage. What better way than to take a socialist position against the running dogs of capitalism. To be an iconoclast is an advantage on the academic cocktail circuit. (Who's afraid of Virginia Woolf?) Each

[10]See Schumpeter, "The Sociology of the Intellectual," *CSD*, Chapter 13.

morning when he sees himself in his shaving mirror (to trim his beard) he can murmur, "Oo, oo daring fing oo." Not the guy I want beside me manning the barricades.

I may have parodied my prototype, but I do not despise him. Being a teacher, he is in a position to influence a generation of students—to help create more intellectuals with leftist leanings. When these new "liberals" and chic socialists leave school they will infiltrate the most influential areas of society: journalism, the visual arts, foundations, government bureaucracy, and academia itself. They will have, or will think they have, a vested interest in social unrest. The result will be a subtle slant in the media that suggests not necessarily that socialism is the way to go but that business is somehow bad and needs to be "exposed" and ridiculed whenever possible.

The Opportunists

The opportunist is a revolutionary. He is closest to what the average person thinks a communist is like. His is a power play. He looks to the revolution for personal gain, as an opportunity for him and his fellows to take over. He recognizes the basic fact that most liberals will not quite face up to: *socialism is the only viable alternative to capitalism in the Western world*.[11] If capitalism, commercial society, falls, socialism will take its place. There is no alternative—it is that simple. This makes the opportunist's job easy. Anything he can do to stir unrest, to humiliate the business community *or* the elected government, works in his favor. There are no scruples in revolution. He will use any route and any group to these ends—the chic socialists, the workers, the labor unions, the liberals, the haters (whom we consider next), even organized religion.

---

[11]To capitalism only. It does not sprout from undeveloped economies. Guerrilla leaders may be Marxist and wear colored berets and carry submachine guns, but they are going to get military dictatorship rather than socialism. Without the preparation of capitalism, socialism just won't wash.

Honest socialists should oppose the opportunists; they should fight the impulse to embrace anyone who professes the Marxist doctrine. Honest socialists want the revolution to benefit the proletariat and not the new leaders. They want a smooth transition from one system to the next. The revolutionary may not be vicious, he may not *want* a bloody transition and the hunting down of the capitalist swine; but if that is the way it goes, if that is the route to power, so be it.

The Haters

The "haters" is a large group that includes a lot of the chic socialists and intellectuals. The group also includes a lot of people who have no intellectual pretensions but who just hate the existing system for any number of reasons. They may not consider themselves socialists—just antibusiness or antiestablishment—but we have to include them in the enemy ranks because of the natural succession of economic systems. Most hate is based on greed or envy, or on a sense of social injustice. It may even be a love/hate thing. A terrorist may fight a Western nation until the day when he is granted asylum and when he becomes a super patriot.

A lot of people become haters when they contemplate the high salaries and privileges of business and government leaders and even of special groups like sports figures. Some workers have a grudge against their employers and will sabotage production if they can get away with it. There are many cases of disgruntled former employees returning with bombs.

The most obvious candidates for the haters ranks are from the minority groups that feel robbed. All Western nations have such groups—if they didn't they would probably import refugees to create them. In its mildest form, this discontent becomes civil rights activism; in its most virulent form, it turns into terrorism and the demand for a separate state. The Basque minority in Spain is just one example. Haters can be a real threat to the establishment, either when they are pursuing their own goals or when they are being used as cat's-paws by the revolutionaries. Prejudice is rooted in people and not in economic systems. The Russians have minority problems just as serious as those in the West.

CONVERSION TO SOCIALISM

A violent uprising of the proletariat and the overthrow of the bourgeoisie in the tradition of Marx at his most militant is not the goal of most honest socialists. For one thing, revolutions are messy and destructive. The new leaders want the productive capacity of the nation to remain functional[12] and they want to avoid monetary chaos so that a pricing structure can be preserved. (Runaway inflation may be useful later to erase private property, but not yet.) The preferred method of conversion involves a softening up of the capitalist system to prepare for painless change. This system is often called "creeping socialism."

Creeping socialism operates both from the outside and the inside of business establishments. From the outside: by imposing more and more controls and regulation so that business decisions are increasingly made to satisfy government requirements rather than to serve the profit motive. From the inside: by a loss of spirit and true grit in the business community. As corporations grow and the swinging founders become only memories and pictures on board room walls, they are taken over and manned by salaried professionals who were trained in business schools and in law schools. Some of these new managers are wheeler-dealers, Gamesmen, but most are not; they are Craftsmen or Company Men[13] whose working philosophy puts them closer to a GS-12 in the civil service than to a free enterprise bravo. When these inside and outside trends intersect,

---

[12]Somoza left things in good order for a takeover. Since he owned 80 percent of the industry of Nicaragua, it was necessary only to expropriate his holdings.

[13]For a discussion of Gamesmen and other "types," see M. Maccoby, *The Gamesman*, New York: Simon & Schuster, 1976. See also *HIM*, Chapter 12.

when all corporate decisions are made for regulatory reasons and all business managers are essentially civil servants on corporate payrolls, nationalization is an easy step. The shareholders may have to be appeased, but as far as corporate operations are concerned the thing can be handled by a company newsletter.

Nationalization of industry is a giant step toward socialism. It is the first criterion of a socialist society and one that can largely be satisfied before conversion. In fact, some people define complete nationalization of industries and services—with everybody working for the government—as socialism itself. This is not the classical model, not if there still are personal savings and wealth lying around.

It is almost impossible to confiscate private property and savings before the act of conversion; it is only a little less tough to do so after the act. Even hard-line Marxists admit that farmers and small shopkeepers are going to be hard sells. Socialists *should* encourage the growth of corporations and the emergence of oligopolies, particularly of agribusiness and of giant retailers, to move property from fractious citizens to more amenable corporations. An associatd benefit is the reduction of the ranks of small businessmen, who can be effective soldiers for free enterprise. That most socialists actually fight business growth is a consequence of their own prejudice—a weakness they usually reserve for their reactionary foes. They just don't like to see any business prosper or any businessman make too much money.

A lot of softening up of property owners can be done while a society is still capitalistic; this is another aspect of creeping socialism. The strategy is to get a more equitable distribution of wealth. If this can be done, the objections to a new, classless order are blunted. After all, people wouldn't have much to lose. Western nations haven't quite got to the point of robbing the rich to give to the poor (although a "wealth tax" is a euphemism for this), but they regularly use taxation and transfer payments to do the job. (See

Chapter 4.) The introduction of "directed" money like food stamps is particularly effective. The most useful, or notorious, mechanisms are the graduated income tax and inheritance taxes or death duties.

In a way, industry itself unwillingly contributes to this leveling process. As labor unions use strikes and threats to get higher pay and benefits for the workers, management is forced to reduce the pay differential up to and through middle management ranks in order to stay competitive. In American industry today a large slice of all employees, with job titles ranging from maintenance man to accounting department section head, get a salary of plus or minus $20,000 (1979 figures). Such employees are unlikely to think they have much to fear from a socialist takeover: "someone" has always taken care of them, "someone" always will. In fact, if they are "haters" they may even look forward to seeing their bosses come down a peg or two. (They should be apprehensive, however. Most employees don't realize what a good deal they have as "innies" compared with the "outies" out there.)

These are the two principal mechanisms of creeping socialism: nationalization and equalization. The working socialist will push them along whenever he can, using any rhetoric that is currently acceptable or stylish. He doesn't fight alone. There are lots of people, groups, and movements that will help even though they fight under other banners. By the very nature of the two systems, anything that hurts commercial enterprise promotes socialism. This is a big enough subject to deserve a new chapter.

9

AID AND COMFORT

IN THIS CHAPTER we consider the carryings-on of a lot of people who are not declared socialists but who, in one way or another, undermine the existing commercial system and so give aid and comfort to the enemy. Most of the characters in these scenarios are referred to as liberals or as intellectuals—both terms being used improperly. The word "liberal" is an old friend of freedom lovers: it used to have something to do with liberty. It still retains its original glorious meaning in some parts of the Western world[1] (as used by the Liberal party in England, for example), but in the United States it has been bastardized to cover a multitude of things from leftward

---

[1] In the communist world and in the Third World, terms like "liberal" and "freedom" are used not as words but as political ammunition.

leanings to declared socialism. I use the word in its new, improper sense: a political philosophy which at its finest implies concern for the unfortunate and at its worst is a euphemism for "screw the establishment."

"Intellectual" is another fine old word which has been badly jobbed. Properly, it describes a person who puts study and reflection, integrity of mind, above the prosaic. If I ever have to use the term in its proper sense, I will refer to such a person as a "true intellectual." True intellectuals naturally have little use for such trivia as money, power, and possessions and this makes them almost the antithesis of the intellectuals of our story. *Our* intellectuals are people who spend a large portion of their lives chasing advanced degrees, usually in what are called the social sciences (sic). They use their degrees as clubs to beat the rest of us about the head and shoulders: to demand power, remuneration, and respect. The best place to get these good things is in government service or in academia, where one doesn't have to put up with back talk from inferiors or the give-and-take of the marketplace. Most of our intellectuals honestly think that they have a mission to control the rest of us and that it is a waste of time to suffer objections. The intellectuals stick together—Irving Kristol calls them the "new class."[2] If they can arrange it, they prefer to communicate only with their own kind. Only a few, the "super intellectuals" (see later), realize this goal.

If there weren't so many of them, the intellectuals would provide amusing case studies for anthropologists, but there *are* too many of them and they aren't funny. Our universities continue to grind out so many that there isn't room for them all in the happy hunting grounds of bureaucracy, even with the help of their fellows (read: the growth of government institutions). Some intellectuals

[2]I. Kristol, *Two Cheers for Capitalism*, New York: Basic Books, 1978. It seems to me that these people are too diverse to be lumped into a single class. A more friendly discussion of the new class is Alvin W. Gouldner, *The Future of the Intellectuals and the New Class*, New York: Seabury Press, 1979.

have to wind up in menial jobs like carrying mail or working for the enemy—for business. This does emasculate some of the breed— they may change their orientation or, more likely, just become "haters"—but there are plenty left in positions to harass the business community.

The terms "liberal" and "intellectual" are almost synonymous but not quite. Most intellectuals are liberals but not all liberals are intellectuals. President Johnson, for example, did not have enough "learning" to qualify. I shall try to reserve "liberal" for politicians and "intellectual" for bureaucrats and members of pressure groups.

ELECTED LIBERALS

I really don't have much objection to elected liberals. They can, and do, hurt the business community, but at least they get their jobs from the people and not just by passing one more written test. In democratic Western governments both the left and the right *should* be represented, as this mix reflects the leanings of the people. I find it hard to like Senator Kennedy, the liberal standard-bearer in Congress, but I have to admit that he is a hardworking, well-informed senator, popular with his colleagues and with his constituents. I couldn't vote for the man, but then I don't have to.

Elected liberals hurt the business community directly and indirectly. Directly, by passing laws to take money from corporations and to further fetter free enterprise. Indirectly, by fostering the growth of government bureaucracy and by supporting the "in" crackpot or hater groups. The indirect attack, like a body blow in boxing, is probably more effective in the long run.

NONELECTED LIBERALS

Elected liberals have to put their jobs on the line every few years, but high-ranking bureaucrats remain with us through changes in administrations *and* through changes in the political leanings of the electorate until they finally retire on handsome, indexed pensions (paid for by business, the productive element in society). To varying degrees in Western nations, these people *are* the government. (A recent article in the *Manchester Guardian* suggested that MPs' salaries be tied to the "appropriate" civil service level!) In some countries, these leaders are carefully raised like hot-house plants for their responsibilities. In France only graduates of the *École Polytechnique*, the *École National d'Administration*, or the *Institut des Études Politiques* need apply.[3]

While much of the work of our huge government departments is counterproductive, the intellectuals who run them believe that what they are doing is right and good. How can this be in the face of one disaster after another? The United States government agencies have fouled up (to name a few examples) our educational system, welfare programs, urban renewal, and the lumbering industry of Alaska. Our liberal bureaucrats have a record that makes that of General Aloysius P. Cornpone look good. Like Douglas Haig in Flanders, all they want is lots more troops, one more try, and no new ideas. The answer is found in the training of our intellectuals— the same training that made them intellectuals in the first place.

Most disastrous liberal programs are based on a few dubious principles learned in school from professors who may or may not be Marxists but who are often just repeating what *they* learned. These are fundamental misconceptions about things like education, poverty, motivation, and environmental influences that are accepted as doctrine. As any mathematician knows, calculations based on false principles create garbage. Let us take an example that is not too close to home, one that we can look at more or less unemotionally: our relations with the developing countries.

According to Bauer[4] the relations between the Western

---

[3]See William Pfaff, "Aristocracies," *The New Yorker*, January 14, 1980.

[4]P. T. Bauer, *Dissent on Development*, Cambridge, Mass.: Harvard University Press, 1972.

countries and the developing countries (development economics) are based on four simple propositions:

1. The vicious circle—that poverty begets poverty.
2. The necessity of central planning in the poor countries and of support from outside.
3. The historical exploitation of colonies by the industrialized nations (pure Leninism).
4. The "obligation" of industrial nations to assist the developing nations in order to expiate past sins.

These are the articles of faith that are taught in our schools and that form the basis of our national policies. The only problem is, as Bauer carefully documents with counterexamples,[5] none of them are true. They do form a fine platform on which bureaucratic empires can be built and from which a lot of other people's money can be passed out. Axiom four, by promoting guilt feelings, is particularly effective in extracting money.

The four listed axioms are pure Bauer, but I can add a fifth "political" axiom from this side of the Atlantic. Our liberal leaders, like Andrew Young, would have us believe that American blacks are intimately concerned with the welfare of their brothers in Africa. Hogwash. Very, very few American blacks (or whites) can even locate Benin, Mali, Burundi, Kalimantan, or Ruanda (trivia question: which one of the former is not in Africa?), let alone capital cities like Niamey, Kigali, Bajunsbura, and Gaborone. Black Americans have the same concerns as WASPs: Johnnie's arithmetic, Suzy's teeth, mortgage and car payments, and why the Dodger relief pitching has come apart at the seams. These are important concerns but they don't build bureaucratic empires.

[5]Our social planners don't like counterexamples. One of the axioms of educational theory is that black children can't get a decent education without white children to hold their hands. A glaring counterexample was Central High School in Washington, D.C.—practically on the steps of the temple. It was a black school and one of the best in the nation. They closed it.

THE NANNIES

A real weakness of the free enterprise system is that it can allow a *short-term* advantage to the producer of shoddy goods. The manufacturer who sticks to better engineering, materials, and workmanship can be at a competitive disadvantage. The technological revolution has sharpened the problem. A hundred years ago a farmer knew a good wagon when he saw one. Today the purchase of a new car or a television set is largely an act of faith. Any product that moves or that uses electricity or chemicals is a potential health hazard. There is a real quality and safety problem in our society.

Manufacturers know the problem. They know that in the *long run* quality is rewarded: "A" will buy a Dodge pickup because "B" has been satisfied with his for five years. Companies work to protect their reputations, but they also know that in the short run they could go bankrupt. The answer is outside, noncapitalist regulation to maintain minimum quality, safety, and consistency. Control organizations, maintained by government or by industry (or by both), have a long and generally beneficial history—outfits like the National Bureau of Standards, Underwriters' Laboratories, the Bureau of Mines, and the API.

"Nannies" is my term for the intellectuals who exploit this weakness in the capitalist system. They use their pious concern for the consumer to build comfortable bureaucratic empires to harass business. They add two axioms of their own to the regulatory doctrine:

1. The consumer is a babe-in-the-woods who can't tell a good investment from a bad one. He must be protected from himself.
2. Big business is a con game that pushes unsafe junk at unfair prices.

Using these dubious propositions, the "all heart" nannies have attracted followers who are looking for a cause or who just hate big business. They have built huge empires like OSHA that are supposed to protect the consumer but that usually cost the consumer money and further fetter business.

The top nanny is Ralph Nader. He is a hater. His hit list is headed by General Motors, runs through all big business, and comes down to the poor consumer. Apart from shooting down a good automobile (which is now a collector's item), he glanced off General Motors and hit Chrysler instead. I doubt he sheds many tears over the mistake. An interesting man; a powerful man. He has cost you and me and American business a lot of money.

The rancour of our nannies does not extend to foreigners. We have been forced to install unused and ineffective safety devices on our own cars (any safety engineer knows the best way to protect motorists is to enforce speed laws and crack down on drunk drivers), but no objections are made to imported motorcycles, which really are "Unsafe at Any Speed." To keep the competition fair, I have to hope that other countries grow their own nannies.

NATURE BOYS

Another weakness of pure capitalism is that it doesn't place a value on preserving the environment. In fact, cutthroat competition encourages poor housekeeping. Most business leaders prefer not to leave gaping holes in the landscape or to foul the air and water. They welcome regulations that lay down civilized operating rules. Since the consumer pays for this tidiness in higher prices, he should decide what he is willing to pay for. The "nature boys" know better; they tell the rest of us what is proper.

I am a little uncomfortable objecting to the nature boys. I am for conservation and environmental protection. My wife and I were members of the Sierra Club and were saving the redwoods before this became the thing to do. Good ideas can be carried to excess by people who don't know what they are talking about: good ideas can be used as the basis for empire building and as a club to wallop business. I object to the nature boys because they are perverting my own cherished ideals to serve their ends. I am for the serious student of ecology.

The end of the Vietnam war and the winding down of the civil rights movement, as American blacks got about all the nondiscrimination they could handle for a while, left a lot of our intellectual leaders without a cause to lead and a lot of young people without a cause to follow.[6] Most of these people took the coward's way out and prepared to make an honest living. Ecology to the rescue! The old leaders polished up their speaking style—demagoguery mixed with cant—broke out the old blue jeans, put a dab of Grecian Formula on their beards, looked up the word "ecology" in the dictionary, and went to war: against business.

The axioms of the nature boys are not too well defined: that business *wants* to foul the landscape;[7] that there is something noble about beards, blue jeans, and backpacks; that the government is the only responsible custodian of the land. The new no-no is nuclear power. Never mind that it is the cleanest practical energy source available. It has to go—think what could happen! Since Three Mile Island we don't have to think anymore; we know what can happen: it was a mess, but as far as we know nobody got hurt.

What starts in the streets ends in new legislation, in new bureaucracies, and in the law courts. The resulting legislation and regulation make it too expensive and too time-consuming for business to act effectively to help solve the nation's problems. It took eight costly years to satisfy different regulatory bodies and finally built the Alaska Pipeline. Prudhoe Bay oil will forever be more expensive than it should be. Ninety percent of Alaskan land is in a sort of deep freeze, waiting for the experts in Washington to

[6]One of the problems in Western societies is that we are running out of causes. There are no colonies to be administered, no west to be won. The consequences of even a "noble" war look bleak.

[7]Oil companies are no more eager for oil spills and tanker collisions than bankers are eager to burn money in the yard.

decide how it should be used. We haven't built a major refinery in the United States in 20 years. Eastern manufacturers can't economically burn cleaner Western coal because of illogical air pollution standards. It can take up to 14 years to get permission to build a nuclear plant in the United States. The time lag not only deprives us of needed energy but also puts us at a disadvantage compared with the Europeans and Russians, who are building nuclear plants at an increased rate. We are throwing away our technological leadership.

The list could go on, but the point is made. Under the banner of ecology-gone-ape, our nature boys have succeeded in putting the brakes on our national dynamism. People who should be building or creating are writing environmental impact statements.

SUPER INTELLECTUALS

Within the classification of intellectuals there is an elite group, some of whom belong in this chapter and some of whom really don't: some are enemies of capitalism, some aren't. A distinctive characteristic of these people, apart from their impressive learning, is their staying power. They are always with us. I call them the super intellectuals.

Super intellectuals have safe home bases in university chairs, on foundation boards, in editorial offices, in high government jobs, and in law offices. From these sally points they bombard us with the written word. They move easily in government circles. A random list of names will set the pattern: Acheson, Brzezinski, Bundy, Galbraith, Harriman, Kristol, Moynihan, Podhoretz, Vance, Young—and the ultimate example, Henry Kissinger.

Few of these people ever run for elected office—they don't have to. Their power is exercised through influence on elected officials; in international agencies (of which the United Nations is only the most visible); by management of prestigious funds; and through writing. How they do write! And much of it is good. Most of them are immune to shifting political winds. The same names keep coming up in different administrations. This is only proper. Their ideas are bigger, their goals higher, than mere party politics.

Inasmuch as it is possible to divide a bunch of rugged individualists into two groups, the super intellectuals can be classified as liberals and as—well—liberals: old (liberty) liberals and new (leftish) liberals. In order to resolve the semantic problem, Peter Steinfels calls the liberty boys neoconservatives, a term which he says they accept.[8]

When leftish super intellectuals gain the ears of national leaders or move into power positions, business can usually expect the worst. On the other hand, when neoconservatives take over, business leaders can be excused a warm glow. This may be overly optimistic.

Our neoconservatives, typified by Bell, Kristol, Moynihan, and Podhoretz, are not super Rotarians. Most of them are reformed Marxists who rejected socialism for pragmatic reasons and accepted capitalism as the only game in town. Business leaders may clip Kristol's articles out of *The Wall Street Journal* with a chuckle (or scissors) and murmur, "That's telling 'em, Irving," but Irving is not one of the boys. He supports business because he fights socialism. In common with their leftish opposite numbers, most neoconservatives would like to do a little economic tinkering—benign, of course. They are for business but they have a little list of improvements in the back of their minds.

On balance, it might seem that the two types of super intellectuals would cancel each other out. To some extent they do; certainly they cut each other down. There is still something disturbing about a group of nonelected people having such power in a democracy. (The neoconservative doctrine of *pluralism*[9] even

[8]P. Steinfels, *The Neoconservatives*, New York: Simon & Schuster, 1979.

[9]The liberal concept that a person is best represented as a member of a like-thinking group. The corollary is that group leaders should be responsible people who respect other group positions. See Steinfels, *The Neoconservatives*, p. 33.

seems a little undemocratic.) The voter who thought he was electing his leaders may be disturbed to see the same old faces back in Washington.

Why do these people keep coming back? For one thing, they are experts—within their own persuasions. They have impressive academic credentials; and Americans, even senators and presidents, have an exalted respect for such people. (See Chapter 15 for a possible explanation.) This respect may not always be deserved. Certainly the super intellectuals do not always respect each other's work or that of previous generations. The only names that seem to stand the test of time are the old standbys: Locke, Smith, Mill, de Tocqueville, Marx.

Another reason the voter may feel uncomfortable is that the super people don't *know* him: they don't have to kiss babies and shake hands. In fact, they speak mostly to each other and to the powers-that-be. It would be nice if the super intellectuals had to make a trip "out there" at least once a year, out to the boondocks where people are scrambling to make a living, to raise their children, to pay their taxes. I suggest a *bus* trip through the piney woods of East Texas, from Shreveport to Houston, with stops at Kickapoo, Carthage, Henderson, Nacogdoches, Lufkin, Corrigan, New Willard (on demand), Livingston, Cleveland (furs bought), New Caney, and Humble. Don't cheat—and don't bring your own lunch.

THE MEDIA

A lot of our intellectuals wind up in the media—in journalism and in the visual arts. This gives them a rare opportunity to get the rest of us up to snuff. In order to do their thing effectively, they have had to veto the old first principle of journalism.

When I studied journalism, the cardinal rule was that editorials belonged on the editorial page. To inject personal opinion into news stories was a sure route to a failing grade and an indication that you

130 / THE MOVING FORCE

might be happier in creative writing. The assumption was that the reader is as smart as the writer and has a right to form his own opinion from neutral reporting. This old rule was not even given a decent burial. It was superseded by something called investigative journalism, an approach based on the axiom that the reader not only wants facts but also wants (and needs) a lesson at the same time. That the new approach in the United States comes from the Eastern seaboard (particularly from Columbia University) is not surprising. The East has always taken seriously its responsibility to upgrade the rest of the country.

The vectors of new journalism are papers like the Washington *Post* and magazines like *The New Yorker*. I used to be able to curl up and have a good cry reading articles about how our American troops were savaging the Vietnamese—most of whom became so bitter that they now want to become Americans. The real triumph of investigative journalism was Watergate.

As an American I am supposed to be proud of my country for cracking down on the principals of the Watergate case. I guess I am. We did show the world that no Republican, of whatever rank, is above the law. I just wish we hadn't come off looking like such damn fools to foreigners, who never could understand how a powerful nation could suspend normal operations to track down the actors in what was never more than a victimless piece of unmitigated stupidity. Overkill.

American journalists do not have a monopoly on this sort of thing. French newspapers have always worn their hearts on their sleeves, but the British press just might win the green weenie. The recent media trial of Jeremy Thorpe, the leader of the Liberal party—who was vindicated in a real trial—is one of its better efforts. To ruin a good man's reputation is a small price to pay for the advantages of investigative reporting.

Politicans of the right (or wrong) persuasion are still fair game for our new journalists, but these targets have been shot over and are getting wary. The secondary target is big business.

The fourth estate can speak for itself better than I can. The following three specimens were collected in a single week in the summer of 1979. This was after the disastrous crash of a DC-10 airliner and at the time of a gasoline crunch. The nannies wanted to shut down DC-10 flights forever and, if possible, execute the top managers of Douglas. Intellectuals wanted to pin the blame for the gas shortage on the big oil companies.

A UPI release on July 28, 1979, carried the following headline in 20-point type in our local paper: "Tenneco Draws Fine for Hiding Gas Data." The lead paragraph allowed that Tenneco had pleaded guilty to illegally shipping natural gas and had agreed to pay a million-dollar fine. Not much point reading further in the face of this damning evidence, but read on. Tenneco admitted that it *might have* illegally transported natural gas, without the required approval of the Federal Power Commission, in *1973* and *1974*. The company itself brought the matter to the attention of the government and agreed to pay a fine rather than go through litigation. This is "hiding" data? The crime was the equivalent of a private taxpayer reviewing a five-year-old tax return, deciding he might have made a mistake, and telling the government that he might owe some money.

During the same week on the evening TV news, the commentator detailed the number of times since being reinstatd that DC-10s had been forced to change flight plans because of engine trouble. It was enough to send us listeners running to the phone to cancel bookings. As an afterthought, before turning to something else, the anchorman remarked that this was the *best* reliability record of any plane type during the period.

While visiting a friend, I got trapped into watching a TV sitcom. The hero of the series was a rugged, educated slob—one of the new class—a public servant who chopped up corpses to protect the people. His sidekick was a smart and sassy Oriental—which provided good image and racial balance. These two *apparatchiks* spent as much time hugging each other as baseball players do patting each other on the fanny. The heavies on my night were three businessmen who ran a chemicals company seemingly from a communal office about the size of the old Forbes Field. They made money by concocting chemicals which first killed their research workers and then destroyed the public. Our hero went out of his way to be as rude as possible to these managers, whom he immediately recognized as the overpaid fiends they were.

Who finally came to the rescue? Why OSHA, of course—with banners flying and ballpoint pens at the ready, trailed by a legal squad to initiate a class action suit.

We used to laugh at Russian propaganda about noble tractor drivers. Get yourself an "antacid" and watch our bureaucrats in action. On commercial television yet! Paid for by American business. Who needs enemies when he has an advertising department?

LAWYERS

Most lawyers are not intellectuals. For one thing, their education was interrupted by attending law school. Few lawyers have strong ideological leanings; they just want to use the law to make money. Their pursuit of this end usually hurts the business world, and so we have to include them among the aid-and-comfort people.

The legal profession sends a lot of its people into government. According to Matthew T. Valencic, former Rhodes scholar and director of HALT (Help Abolish Legal Tyranny),[10] one out of every nine white people on the streets of Washington, D.C., is a lawyer. A majority of our congressmen are lawyers. This gives the profession an advantage: congressmen write laws that only other lawyers

[10]A young man fighting a losing battle. See his essay in the *Kenyon College Alumni Bulletin*, Summer, 1979.

can understand. A similar situation would obtain if the medical profession had its own group of doctors inventing diseases. If lawyers can spend time in Washington without impairing their careers, businessmen should learn to do the same.

It is hard to estimate the legal burden on industry by reading corporate annual reports or 10Ks, since the costs are hidden in other categories, such as cost of sales and outside consulting. In any event, the imposed cost of government legal activity would not be shown. A better approach is to consider the total legal expense in our country and to assume that industry, as the main productive element in society, will pay for most of it.

Both Valencic and Robert Hudec[11] agree that by the year 2000 we will have a million practicing lawyers in the United States (we have half that number now). Assuming that the rest of us continue to support lawyers in the style to which they have become accustomed—upwards of $50,000 a year—a quick multiplication gives us an expected annual cost of $50 *billion*. This is a lot of money.

What does business get for all this money? I am tempted to say "nothing" but that is not true. Business does not spend this kind of scratch for nothing. What business gets is protection—protection from other lawyers. *Only a lawyer can safely confront a lawyer.* Dickens understood this dictum a hundred years ago: "Perhaps you would like to assault one of us. Pray do it sir. . . ."[12] Legal battles are the only ones in which both contestants are winners.

The picture is still not complete. An increasing number of lawyers are no longer satisfied with salaries and fees. They go directly to where the money is: class action suits[13] against corporations and malpractice and damage suits against individuals. Unreal

[11] A law professor who rebutted Valencic's essay in the same issue of the *Kenyon Bulletin*.

[12] Fogg speaking, of the dynamic duo of Dodson and Fogg. The case: Pickwick v. Bardell. See *Pickwick Papers*, Chapter 20.

[13] See *HIM*, Chapter 9.

settlements in such cases are paid for by the rest of us in the form of higher prices and increased insurance premiums. There is also an adverse psychological impact on business. Multimillion-dollar awards cheapen the value of earned dollars—they dilute the lifeblood of industry.

Surely this is unfair criticism in the face of our continuing reverence of common law as the protector of justice and decency and the respect we accord lawyers in our society. (Such respect has been documented by Coleman and Rainwater,[14] who seem to be masters of the obvious.) Even though our criminal system has glaring weaknesses—minorities tend to have the book thrown at them and Texas millionaires beat the rap—I wouldn't want to live under any other code of law. *But* the actors in the justice game are only a fraction of the American bar. Justice is hardly a factor in corporate law. ("Young man, if you are concerned about justice, I suggest you enroll in divinity school.") The corporate legal game is the interpretation of contracts and regulations—a modern-day equivalent of the question "How many angels can dance on the head of a pin?" This is the law that corporations pay for.

Unfortunately, all lawyers are accorded the status and perquisites earned by the justice-seeking minority. Perhaps we should resurrect the old term "barrister" to identify the truly deserving.

This legal burden cuts the productivity of American business, raises costs to consumers, promotes inflation, gives aid and comfort to the enemy, and makes it difficult for our products to compete against those from less lawyer-ridden countries like Japan, Germany, Switzerland, and Italy. Only a capitalistic society will tolerate such a debilitating legal structure. Only a country as rich as the United States can afford the legal community it maintains. When the burden gets intolerable we may throw out the baby (common law) with the bath water.

[14]Richard Coleman and Lee Rainwater, *Social Standing in America*, New York: Basic Books, 1978.

THE OTHERS

There are other, less regimented aid-and-comfort people in our society. I have described a few of them: educators who would rather be trendy than responsible; religious leaders who try to save souls through sociology. I haven't mentioned labor organizations and unions, which are natural homes of aid-and-comfort people.

In countries like England, the labor hierarchy includes a lot of real socialists. With a few exceptions, like the old Longshoremen's Union, American union leadership is not Marxist. For one thing, the workers tend to be conservative "good old boys." That the leaders are more liberal than their followers is not surprising or even alarming—they have to adopt this posture in order to oppose management and serve their members. A trained management should be able to hold its own in a collective bargaining situation, *unless* liberal lawmakers have stacked the deck in favor of labor.[15]

The threat by labor to industrial stability in America is more apt to come from the greed of labor leaders themselves than from their concern for the prosperity of their members. The result is the plundering of pension funds and the negotiation of sweetheart contracts with industry. This is part of the crime threat to business which we consider in the next chapter.

SINCERITY

Do all these people, the socialists and their helpers, really want to overthrow the capitalist system? The honest socialists, of course, really do. But I doubt this is true of the others—the opportunists, the haters, the aid-and-comfort people. They attack the system because they feel confident that they will lose. They are like the Icelanders who criticized the "decadent" American troops stationed in their country and subsequently panicked when we agreed to pull them out.

[15]As they did in Australia. See *HIM*, Chapter 5.

It is fun and intellectually stimulating to twist the lion's tail or to pluck the eagle's feathers when we know that the beast will survive, is infinitely rich, and will not strike back. If the hazing is also profitable, and it often is, the temptation is irresistible. Our intellectual teachers and journalists don't really want to work in a socialist society. If our lawyers thought about it, they would realize that their excesses are tolerated only by a benign society. Labor leaders look in vain for their Russian counterparts. As Southern evangelists remind us, "There are no graveyards in hell."

I think these gadflies are too complacent, too confident of the eagle's strength. As we shall see, there are powerful intrinsic forces working against the commercial system—the bird may not be all that healthy in the first place. We may not always be able to afford the luxury and the expense of subsidizing the "new class"—the parasites and critics who are the pampered children of the system they claim to despise.

10

NATURAL ENEMIES

A thirsty old wino from Lynn
Confessed as he wiped off his chin,
"It wasn't the sin.
Or the broads or the gin.
'Twas 1099s did me in."

IN THE LAST two chapters we have examined the breathing enemies of capitalism. Now we look at its natural enemies—at the home court advantages enjoyed by socialism.

As it was in Moola-Moola, so it is in our world: business is *tolerated*. When the majority of the people in a democracy lose faith in free enterprise, the system will pass. Business must somehow maintain the image of being responsible, fair, and efficient, of being the best way to provide the good things for the most people. In the old days—in the 1920s, say—this was easier: it was necessary only to brag about living standards to justify capitalism. Today the public is harder to sell, if only because it has lost some of its pathological fear of socialism or at least of government ownership, which seems to work well in other countries.

It is not really necessary for our eager journalists to advertise corruption, favoritism, greed, and inefficiency in business: the workers and consumers are smart enough to see these things for themselves. Business must maintain a decency and morality well above legal requirements. Outside forces and competition can make this difficult.

Another requirement for the health of the commercial system is a sort of "business attitude" on the part of the citizens: a gut feeling that the business life is a good life, that the salaries paid are worth working for, that corporations are somehow worthwhile. To a large extent, this attitude depends on the integrity of a nation's money—on its real value and on the share of it controlled by business. The business life is *not* a good life if employees are paid in "funny" money; it is not very attractive if there are other, easier roads to riches.

There are devastating forces over which business has little direct control: inflation, depression (business will be blamed), crime, the appeal of alternate life styles, the decline of the status of business.

CRITICAL RATIOS

This section is dedicated to graduate students. I know that there are certain critical ratios that must be preserved for free enterprise to prosper, but I don't know the threshold levels or the qualifiers. Dissertation writers take note.

Government Workers/Industry Workers

If the ratio of the number of government workers to industry workers gets too high in an ostensibly capitalist nation, the economy is going to collapse or change. (In a socialist system, the ratio is meaningless.) There cannot be a cleancut threshold. All government workers are not useless. In the United States, for example, mail carriers and TVA and AMTRAK workers perform useful service, while some government agencies are counterproductive. The critical threshold will be highly qualified, but I suspect that it is about 25 percent, which is the point where Greek democracy came apart after World War II (and which is the ratio in Israel today).

Service/Nonservice

At a recent meeting of the League of Women Voters in Shreveport, Louisiana, a woman rose to her feet to comment that Shreveport did need new industry but that "we should look for nice, clean service industries—we don't want to get like New Jersey." (Sorry, N.J. I like the Garden State.) Somebody has to pick up the shovel. We can't live by taking in each other's wash.

In all Western nations the ratio of service to nonservice people is increasing. In the United States over half the workers are in service rather than in industry or farming. How high can this ratio safely go?

Supporters/Supported

The ratio of supporters to supported can be expressed in terms of people, regions, or countries. The best-known people-to-people example is provided by the American Social Security system. When recipients take out more than workers put in, our leaders get panicky and try to figure out how to put more bite on business. Another example is the ratio of workers to welfare dependents. How many other people can a working family support without straining the capitalist system?

As Garreau poind out,[1] North America can be logically divided into nine economic regions, or "nations": Quebec, New England,

[1]J. R. Garreau, *The Nine Nations of North America*, reprinted in the *Manchester Guardian Weekly*, March 25, 1979.

the Foundry (capital: Detroit), the Breadbasket, Mexamerica, Dixie, the Islands (capital: Miami), the Empty Quarter, and Ecotopia (the Northwest and Alaska).

The cultures of these "nations" are quite different. The most sinister is that of the Islands, headquartered in Miami. It is armed and dangerous and a large part of its income comes from dope smuggling.

Most of these "nations" are not self-supporting. Even potentially rich Ecotopia has been restrained by our nature boys. A large part of the deficits of other "nations" is picked up by one "nation"— the Breadbasket. This is the great Canadian and American Midwestern plain, the part of the continent most maligned by our Eastern intellectuals. To what extent and for how long can the decent, hardworking people of one region carry the others?

I have mentioned that the United States has accepted Puerto Rico and several Pacific islands as dependent countries. The ratio I am concerned with here is the number of foreigners that our country sponsors compared with the native population. We have already received a portion of the Cuban population, which has taken over Miami. We prop up the Israeli economy. We scour the China Sea for refugees and are now flirting with Mexicans and Iranians. There must be an upper limit to the number of exotic people a country can absorb without losing its identity and prosperity.

Business Money/Other Money

In order for a nation to be considered capitalistic, business must play a dominant role in the economy. The most measurable index of relative importance is the ratio of money under business control to that in other hands—government, nationalized industry, organized crime, real estate holdings, and nonbusiness worlds like education and medicine.

Business has one advantage: the stock market stands ready to take in money from any source and move it into industry. This used to be about the only game in town for people with an embarrassing amount of money to invest, but the stock market is losing its monopoly. More investors are turning to real estate (still dominated by small-time operators), to gold and coins, and to commodities.

There are other important ratios and rates kicking around, such as the balance of trade, the national debt, and tax rates. These tend to measure economic health rather than the status of business in society. If I introduce too many ratios, this section will look like a Dun & Bradstreet course on stock analysis. The ones I have defined will suffice. They are changed—unfavorably for free enterprise—by the natural enemies of business.

Depression

American business survived the Great Depression; German democracy did not. How did we get so lucky? I think it was because of our stoical and submissive attitude. We blamed the "times" for our troubles as much as our government. Thurman Arnold, who wrote during the Great Depression, said that "persons on relief who had seen better days and were imbued with middle class culture felt it only proper that they should be pauperized before aid was extended to them."[2] My father's job was in jeopardy for years, and he dreamed up various heroic survival schemes to use if the blow fell. The thing he never considered was turning to the government for help.

I don't see this fortitude today. Our people, all people, would turn to the government as naturally as a child with a skinned knee runs to his mother. The liberal response (the conservative approach having been discredited) would be first to ruin business—by violating the critical ratios—and then, as a last resort, to take it over.

The scenario is something like this. As the number of unemployed becomes intolerable, government requires that busi-

[2]T. Arnold, *The Folklore of Capitalism*, New Haven: Yale Univerity Press, 1937.

ness hire more people and give priority to the least effective workers. As productivity goes down, business has to raise prices. The standard liberal response is wage and price controls. At the same time, increased welfare spending and reduced tax revenues force the creation of more (cheap) paper money. Hit by the double whammy of inflation and losses, corporations must fold or be nationalized. Government cannot allow wholesale closures and more unemployment—it has to take over the whole mess.

This is a simplified scenario. Some corporations may be strong enough to survive, but we would emerge from the depression (if we did) with a changed, more socialistic economy. After all, we did, to a lesser extent, after the depression of the 1930s.

Our economists assure us that we will never have another depression. Recession, yes, depression, no. (A recession is when someone else loses his job; a depression is when you lose yours.) Unfortunately, from a business point of view, the preventive medicine of the liberals is almost as traumatic as the disease: government spending, increasing national debt, inflation, and cheap money—all of which dilute the lifeblood of business.

CHEAP MONEY

Some of my friends still have the first dollar they ever earned. They tend to drag it out after a few snorts. The old bill even *looks* better than the ones in my pocket; it may be bigger; it certainly would have bought a lot more in its day. The point is that in *those* days dollars were something worth working for, something to clutch in your hot little hand and carry home in triumph. Today's salary is printed by a computer on a check along with a string of deductions that threaten to swallow the total.

The smart worker has to wonder if working for business is such a good deal. (This has nothing to do with the "decline of the work ethic" that columnists view with alarm. See Chapter 14.) If a Swedish worker gets a raise, the government share can be 85 percent. If an American businessman's wife sells real estate on the side, the government buys *her* a car through depreciation and investment tax credits. The cute waiters and waitresses, tipped so generously with expense account money, just may not report all their earnings. The corporation worker doesn't have a chance of a tax break—the government gets its money before he gets his. Potential business leaders leave business (or the country, in the case of England and Sweden) to see what they can do elsewhere.

Lower down on the corporate scale, some American and Canadian workers opt out: they work six months and draw unemployment compensation for the other six. Some smart people avoid business as a career. They go into the professions or into civil service of military service.

For a person of average ability, working for the United States government is probably a better deal than working for business. Our leaders are so generous with taxpayers' money that civil service pay rates are at least comparable with what business can afford and the fringe benefits (except at high levels) are better. Government departments don't care too much if employees are there or not and they are generous with holiday time and sick leave (take it whether you are sick or not!).

The best thing about government jobs is retirement benefits. Pensions are generous and they are *indexed*—tied to the inflation rate. Few companies can afford such a system. The practice of indexing bureaucrats' pensions is common in Western countries; it has been particularly valuable in England, where the inflation rate has been high.[3] Things aren't fair! The people who are largely responsible for inflation are protected from its effects.

The American military establishment may have the best retirement deal of all. A colonel with 30 years of service (this is no longer a high grade; it is the rank the average officer can expect to reach if he keeps his nose clean) will retire in 1982 at $30,000 a

[3]A Permanent Secretary who retired in 1977 on a pension of 7,000 pounds received 19,000 in 1980.

year—indexed.[4] If the retiree then wants to take a shot at civil service he is given preference.

EASY MONEY

Business used to be about the only legal route to wealth, and businessmen basked in the prestige of their position. Times have changed and the social standing of businessmen is declining.

In 1950 the estimated market value of the land in Harris County, Texas (the county that includes Houston), was $4.6 billion; in 1979 it was $44.2 billion.[5] This is a hell of a difference. Even in Houston the "big rich" more likely made their money in real estate than in the oil patch.

"Pig farm" millionaires are not the only people who are competing with business leaders for the top of the money tree. Certain professionals have been able to maneuver themselves into a blackmailing position against the rest of society by performing required services under favorable conditions. We have already talked about lawyers but there are others, such as auditors, actuaries, and CPAs, who have very good things going. The most successful group in the United States is the medical profession.

Back in the 1930s, about the time that physicians were first able to help patients more than hurt them,[6] our doctors made the discovery that people would pay almost anything to prolong life or to keep from hurting. The medical profession has parlayed this simple fact into a multimillion-dollar operation, creating the most privileged faction since the medieval clergy. Medical schools and

[4]Tax-free if an understanding medical board rules that the retiree has incurred a physical disability in the last 30 years. The route in the Air Force is from flight pay to disability retirement.

[5]Based on assessed values provided by the Tax Research Association in Houston—20 percent ratio assumed in 1950 and 32 percent in 1979.

[6]The advances were made by biochemists and other researchers rather than by physicians.

training are subsidized: hospitals, not doctors, pay for the expensive equipment and working facilities. The practitioners (and the hospitals) are free to charge what the traffic will bear and still go to the government for more. Our exclusive suburbs are as likely to be populated by doctors as by businessmen.

The easiest money around is that handed out in our courts in class action and damage and malpractice suits, such as that of the lady who discovered she had a misplaced navel after plastic surgery. Multimillion-dollar settlements are so common they are no longer front-page news. Why such large awards are made I don't know. Perhaps judges and juries like to stick businesses and insurance companies; perhaps they do not think of money as something to be worked for.

I do know that ultimately, in one way or another, the productive elements of society—industry and agriculture—will pick up the tab not only for unreal court settlements but for all easy money. It will be paid in the form of taxes, increased costs, and inflation.

UN-MONEY

As far as business and the tax collector are concerned, real money is that which appears on financial statements: money on which profits can be made and taxes collected. Money or transactions that escape the accountant's Pentel pencil can be considered "un-money." It is of two types: transactions between people that are unreported and perquisites and privileges that are not given monetary value. The more un-money there is in an economy, the worse it is for business, which makes no profit on unrecorded transactions and which has to make up in real money for uncollected taxes. Let us consider a few familiar examples.

My neighborhood has a free local newspaper, *The South Town Courier*. There *are* news items in this paper, but its reason for being is its want-ads, which offer for sale or trade everything from bantam hens to "antique" furniture to zithers. There are thousands of such papers in the land, and together they constitute the world's largest flea market, garage sale, or suq. All this marketing is outside the business system and largely outside the taxing system. Cars (a big item) *are* taxed, but only at the price admitted by the buyer and seller.

An orthodontist might make a mutually profitable deal with a plumber (two high-tax-bracket professions). The dentist will straighten Suzy's teeth and the plumber will build a new bathroom for the dentist's mother-in-law. No messy accounting entries need be made. An English telly repairman or a retired American handyman may prefer to be paid in cash. The service industries—people doing things for people—do very well with un-money.

Un-money in the form of perquisites and privileges is common in countries like England and the United States, which have steeply graduated income tax rates. The manifestations are well known: club memberships, "business" vacations, company cars, rides on corporate jets.[7] In a social democracy like Sweden where incomes are supposed to be equalized, un-money perquisites are used to retain status or pecking order. Key goods and privileges such as choice apartments and medical service, transportation, loans, and business expenses are effectively "demonitized" and used to reward the privileged class in a classless society.[8]

Un-money, or the underground or black economy, is promoted by punitive tax laws and other government edicts like income control and the strange American law that limits the amount a retired person can earn and still receive his Social Security payments (which were once supposed to be his own money coming back). It is business, and its shareholders, that pays for this underground economy—which is estimated to be as much as 20 percent of our total economy.

[7]See *HIM*, Chapter 13.
[8]See the lead editorial by Melvyn B. Krauss, "The Social Democracies: Equality Under Strain," in *The Wall Street Journal*, February 1, 1980.

MORTAGING THE FUTURE

To debase currency is to hurt business. The decline of the dollar is usually blamed on profligate and wasteful government, which is fairly accurate finger pointing,[9] but in a democracy the voters cannot evade all responsibility—their elected representatives are supposed to be doing their will.

The members of my generation have been pigs. We have mortgaged the future and left our children to pay for our excesses. After World War II we returned home with the delusion that our nation was infinitely rich and that we were all entitled to our share. We hadn't fought for "Mom's apple pie" after all, but rather for a free education and a ranch-style house with a "wet bar, cathedral ceiling, and wood-burning fireplace." A surprising number of us got these things. The only catch is that we didn't pay for them—not for all of them, anyway.

The government made up the difference by printing money, increasing the national debt, and debasing the dollar. The most incurable spendthrift of all was Lyndon Johnson, who didn't see why we had to make sacrifices even to fight a war.

We have left a sad legacy for our children: houses they can't afford to buy, raging inflation, and a whopping national debt. The unkindest cut of all is that we won't even quit and turn the mess over to the next generation. With the help of geriatric congressmen, we have abolished civilized retirement ages so that we can keep on spending and grabbing—and continue to run the economy we have ravished.

CRIME

Crime, organized and unorganized, is an enemy of business. Free enterprise can succeed only when a society has a legal tradi'ion and at least a rough-and-ready working morality. It is no coinci-

[9]Documented, for example, by William E. Simon, *A Time for Truth*, New York: McGraw-Hill, 1978.

dence that most prosperous nations are honorable. The degree of honor varies from country to country. Germany, for example, allows business bribes to foreign politicians to be written off as expenses; but all Western nations do maintain at least a minimum standard under which (most) contracts are honored and (enough) taxes are collected. This section is not about morality (we get to that later, when we consider religion) but about crime. Crime does undermine national morality: it also has other, more immediate effects on business.

The leaders of organized crime are living enemies of capitalism, but I did not include them among the aid-and-comfort people in the preceding chapter because they are honestly *for* free enterprise— the freer the better. Organized crime flourishes in a liberal society where there are legal safeguards for all people, where the acquisition of wealth is not looked on with suspicion, and where the tax system is designed to take its cut from reported profits. (Crime works with un-money.) Crime leaders in the United States know that if the worst happens, smart lawyers will probably get them off: they can expect no such favors under socialism or a dictatorship. The easygoing business world even provides a comfortable retreat into which they can invest their profits and retire respectably.

According to Kwitney,[10] organized crime is the biggest "business" in the United States. So many billions of dollars, for example, flow from northern cities to Florida banks (the center of drug traffic) that the Treasury Department wants these transactions reported.[11] Such huge amounts of illegal money decrease the ratio of business money to other money. Insofar as illegal profits are not taxed, business profits will be taxed the more.

What is the structure of organized crime in the United States and what sort of activities does it infect? The reader who really wants to study this problem (and the ineffectiveness of government

[10]Jonathan Kwitney, *Vicious Circles*, New York: Norton, 1979.
[11]*The Wall Street Journal*, September 6, 1979.

in suppressing it) should examine Kwitney's book. All I can give here is a summary.

Contrary to what some of our fuzzy-thinking intellectuals write, there is a Mafia in the United States. Its roots go back to Italy and its members are Italians and Italian-Americans. They are only a part of organized crime: WASPs, Jews, blacks, and Latinos are also in the rackets. However, Mafia members (Mafiosi) are both the stormtroopers and the elite of organized crime.[12] They control the areas they want to control and allow others to operate where it is mutually agreeable. The Mafia maintains this position through fear—the Mafia can and will kill.

What types of operations does the Mafia prefer? It has all but abandoned the traditional areas of the numbers racket and prostitution, leaving these untidy operations mostly to the blacks; it has even surrendered much of the dope traffic to the Latinos (which may be due to a strange sort of decency on the part of the Mafiosi). Apart from fencing (disposing of stolen goods), today's favored operations are on the edge of legality: gambling, resorts, food and restaurants, and the financial citadels of banking, stock market manipulation (including counterfeiting certificates), and commodities trading. The Mafia also makes power plays by controlling labor unions.

Apart from business itself, the victims of these shenanigans are nice people: shareholders whose bank or corporation is being swindled, shoppers who buy bad food and meat, union members who see their pension funds plundered, even gamblers who play against more than the usual odds.

Mafia influence in labor unions is particularly bad for business. Crooked unions do not necessarily put a deeper bite on business (they may even arrange "sweetheart" contracts), but they do foul up the labor–management equation. Management may not like unions,

---

[12]There are other "Mafias," at least in the press; the very real Japanese "Mafia" (the Yamaguchigumi), the Chinese "Mafia," the Jewish "Mafia," and others.

but if it has to deal with them, it needs to deal with responsible people who understand industry problems. Union leaders should not only take care of the needs of their members; they should also know enough of economics, finance, and management to make reasonable deals.

Corrupt union leaders, like the convicted teamsters, use union control for personal gain. They do not take care of their people— they screw them by misappropriating funds. The possibility of corrupt union control of whole vital parts of our economy is scary.

If internal, *un*organized crime were a terminal disease, Western business would have died long ago. My favorite image is of Jim Fisk, Daniel Drew, and Jay Gould holed up in "Fort Taylor" against the forces of Commodore Vanderbilt, with Fisk and his mistress entertaining the press while Gould reorganized the plundered Erie Railroad in the back room. This has more of a red-blooded American touch than the Stavisky affair or the South Sea bubble.

Today business suffers more from poor management and the crimes of lesser employees than from corrupt leadership. For some reason business takes a lenient position on "white-collar crime." It is apt to quietly dismiss the criminal, set up a contingency accounting fund, and try to forget the affair. This makes it hard to document the internal crime load that business carries, but it is not trivial.

Computers have added a new dimension to white-collar crime. It is just much easier for a smart programmer to set up an electronic swindle than it is for an auditor to detect it.[13] Detected stealing by people and by computers is only a fraction of the total. In some industries, like retailing, theft is a significant cost of doing business.

ALTERNATE LIFE STYLES

A friend of mine, knowing my contention that the United States needs knightly orders as a cheap way of recognizing

---

[13]See "Annals of Crime—Computers," *The New Yorker*, August–September, 1977.

outstanding people, suggested an American order—the Order of the Jackass. Now this does not sound like a high honor, but as he described its conditions it makes a certain amount of sense. His idea is that the candidate must be well known and *well liked*. The qualifier is that members of the order would not be taken seriously. For example, if a Knight of the Jackass were to give a stirring speech, the audience would be free to cheer loudly and to stamp its collective feet—but it wouldn't have to believe a word. My friend had certain politicians in mind but my nomination goes to Charles A. Reich, author of *The Greening of America*,[14] which is the bible of the alternate life style people. I like his writing, I envy him his royalties, but I don't believe him.

Reich divides us all into three types: Consciousness I, Consciousness II, and Consciousness III. (It is always a good idea to invent new terms.) Consciousness I is so far beyond the pale that I won't waste much time on it. Imagine a flat-headed brute wearing a vest decorated with dollar signs and carrying a club and you get the idea. Consciousness II is what most of us are: a condition forced on us by the "corporate state," an unlikely union of government *and* business that turns us into little consuming and producing machines. (I figure that I am about Consciousness I.8.) We CII types are in a hell of a shape. Our only goals are material things and status; our brains are wasting. We are so far gone we don't even know when we are having a good time! We only "think" we enjoy ourselves. (I wish Reich had published a toll-free number so I could call and find out.)

Now there *are* Consciousness II people in business and in government: workaholics who justify themselves by their organizational slot, people who are afraid to face life on their own resources. This posture is not forced on them by business; it is not required or even rewarded. I have known so many varied characters in the business world that the idea of a single prototype is absurd. Consciousness II as described is the refuge of the mediocre mind.

[14]New York: Random House, 1970.

Consciousness III is going to save us! According to the objective library file card, it is a way of "making American society livable." As I understand it, CIII involves living in the "self" and in the "now" (existentialism?) with a large dose of rejection—rejection of CI and CII and of the order, hierarchy, and status symbols of corporate society. Outward, visible signs are important: long hair, worn-out jeans, and bare feet. The mind of the CIII is "blown" by electronic rock, by the contemplation of nature, by psychedelic drugs, and by casual sex. To take a structured job or even to tolerate a structured education is apostasy.

I don't believe in CIII or at least I am not ready for it. I believe in decorum, order, and consideration. I believe that before one can play Chopin one must learn technique. I believe that one competent civil engineer can do more to preserve the environment than a horde of untidy marchers. I don't believe it makes sense that "a group might elect a chairman without conceding him authority."

Some young people still buy this line. They drop out of traditional society and into their own thing. Business and government lose potentially talented people and eventually have to support them. I am just enough of a CI not to worry too much about the *boys;* it is the *girls* who concern me. They are the ones who hide their blooming youth in rags, who are stuck with babies and venereal disease, and who sometimes escape by committing suicide. There has to be a better alternate life style.

Postindustrial Society

The "better way" usually proposed is called the postindustrial society—a more rational, relaxed, and civilized life than the CII rat race we are presumed to be in. Two arguments for the new way are well presented in *Future Shock* by Alvin Toffler[15] and *The Decline of Pleasure* by Walter Kerr.[16] Toffler proposes that things change too fast in our present world for most of us to cope; we must slow down

[15]New York: Random House, 1970.
[16]New York: Simon & Schuster, 1968.

or we will all become neurotic. Kerr argues that we must change our value system from one based on utility to one that is more intuitive and instinctive—more civilized.

Under the values of postindustrial society, it is better to sing bawdy songs in a tavern than to discuss business (and write the binge off as an expense); it is better to reread *Huckleberry Finn* or do a jigsaw puzzle with one's spouse than to bring work home. Postindustrial man does not reject the workplace but he observes more rational priorities between work and pleasure—between the material and the spiritual. It may be more important to go skiing than to work overtime.

I like the concept of postindustrial society. (It is not goofing off! It may be harder to pursue human and cultural goals than status and profit.) I even think that business can learn to live in a postindustrial world. The problem is to keep from getting too far "ahead" of other nations. England may have made this mistake: it is supposed to be well on its way to a better life. (Judging by the lack of zeal of salespeople in British stores, one might say England has arrived.) England has trouble competing in world markets.

As long as there are competitive countries with compulsive work ethics, the trend to postindustrial society—advocated by labor unions and also by just thinking people—is a threat to business efficiency and prosperity. We could become amateurs, possibly lovable amateurs, playing against professionals.

BUSINESS ITSELF

The last natural enemy of capitalism is business itself. Marx predicted that business would be its own worst enemy, that as corporations grew and became staff-ridden they would lose their entrepreneurial zip, become preoccupied with continuity and security, and pave the way for the revolution. Governments long ago elbowed autocannibalism aside as the first enemy of business, but corporations still do hurt their own cause.

Companies, big companies, can get so senile that they founder.

Railway Express is a memory; 20 years ago Western Union looked like a dying company. Business can rally to its own cause: the services these organizations provided are still available. Aggressive outsiders like United Parcel Service and Federal Express took over the delivery functions; enlightened management of Western Union turned the company around. Business will usually take care of its own backsliders. Unfortunately, a few big ones like the Pennsylvania Railroad do get away.

Business can project a "public be damned" image if management becomes preoccupied with its own perquisites, balance sheets, and income statements. There is now a new internal threat that management has to deal with—the technological revolution.

The problem facing the top management of an even mildly technical company is the same one that faces a modern congressman (or president): there is just too much knowledge around to be absorbed and understood. It is not enough for a senator to be a good politician. He must understand foreign policy, economics, the pros and cons of nuclear energy, and the SALT treaty. It is not enough for a business leader to know accounting, administration, and finance. He must know something of computing, communications, regulatory law, statistics, and the disciplines of his own industry, which may include organic chemistry, physics, or nuclear engineering. I felt sorry for the managers of the Three Mile Island power plant when they appeared on television. Obviously, they were trying to reassure us on the basis of incompletely understood technical information.

The marriage, in a single person, of business sense and technological ability is rare. Good researchers move up to be lousy administrators. High-technology corporations have been founded by brilliant scientists who didn't know they were underfinanced.

The solution for both the business leader and the senator is the same—team management: put together a staff or team that has the necessary skills. The danger is that the team, unless forcefully led, can develop internal strains and rivalries. In the best of cases, it is difficult for a committee to provide the clear leadership of a single individual. Management by teams can follow a Marxian road to a business bureaucracy and decline.

THE YARDSTICK

How serious a threat do these "natural enemies" pose to Western business? The measure is their effect on the efficiency, creativity, and response capability of corporations. "Productivity" would be a better word than "efficiency," except that it has been misused by me and by other writers.

As generally used, "productivity" confines itself to exhorting the working stiffs to get cracking. This is the "John Henry" approach to productivity. ("John Henry was a steel drivin' man.") The ideal productive employee is someone who works 60 hours a week with skill and dedication, tugs at his forelock as he approaches the pay table at the end of the week, and mumbles, "Is all this for me? It seems like more than I deserve." American, German, English, Japanese, Italian—workers will work hard. They would rather work than goof off, but only in the right environment and for what they consider fair reward. They will not, like John Henry, work themselves to death (he must go down as the biggest ass in history, competing in a strong field). Worker efficiency is more a function of good industrial engineering, personnel policy, and management than of eliminating trips to the water cooler.

Corporate efficiency, or productivity, depends on many things: the natural enemies we have been talking about, tax policy, the regulatory and environmental burden, and the efficiency of management itself. Padded expense accounts and "three-martini lunches" cost a company just as much as lazy workers. Ham-handed management and overstaffing cost a lot more.

The latest threat to business efficiency is the high cost of energy. As far as this chapter is concerned, we can take the energy problem as an unfortunate "given." Energy cost is too important today to dismiss so quickly. The following (optional) chapter gives my views of the current mess.

11

ENERGY

There was a young Ms. from Quebec
Who said to her Hs. from Great Neck,
"Now oleo's fine,
And butter's divine,
But I much prefer Oil of OPEC."

THIS WILL BE a short chapter. There has been so much written about the energy crisis that there isn't much point in my getting into the act. The book *Energy Future*,[1] for example, by the people at the Harvard Business School, is a fair statement of the current problem. My interest is in the impact of the crisis on business in general, on the oil companies in particular, and on the future.

---

[1] Edited by R. Stobaugh and D. Yergin, New York: Random House, 1979.

As far as *non*energy corporations are concerned the crisis hurts them in several ways: their manufacturing and overhead costs go up; they suffer from the general inflation caused by increased energy cost; and they are hurt by the reallocation of the customer's money—more for energy, less for other goods and services. Good management will have to cope.

The electric utilities are in a particularly bad spot. They don't know whether to convert to coal, to natural gas, or to nuclear fuel. And they get precious little help (and lots of static) from governments, which are just as confused as they are. The confusion stems from the scientific community, which is violently split into warring factions—for and against coal, for and against nuclear fuel—and so is incapable of giving useful consensus advice. This confusion has scared the American government out of the spent-fuel treatment business, which makes the disposal of nuclear waste an almost impossible problem for existing nuclear power plants and discourages the building of new ones. Lack of leadership plays into the hands of the nature boys and the nannies, who presumably want us to go back to burning buffalo chips. It looks as if the scientific community is no better prepared to provide leadership than the lawyers who run our country.

THE PIECES OF THE PROBLEM

To be fair to readers, I state my own position on energy problems. The neatest way to do this is to list my own conclusions and then to briefly support them.

- There are two different energy problems: short term and long term.
- Short-term problems are due to policies rather than to shortages.
- The oil companies have succeeded too well. We and they are now paying the price of their success.
- Economic laws, ancient and modern, have been overridden by OPEC policies.

- There is a feasible solution to the long-term problem.
- Oil and natural gas are not appropriate long-term energy sources.

Now to support these possibly controversial positions.

The Short-Term Problem

If we divide the energy problem into two different periods, short term (about the next 40 years) and long term (beyond that), we have two different problems and two different solutions.

For the short term, we have enough fossil fuel (oil, gas, and coal) to maintain our present level of industrialization and to allow growth. The reserves in the Near East and the declining developed reserves in the West are sufficient by themselves.[2] Add to these the new reserves that have been confirmed since oil prices went through the roof—North Sea oil, the Bombay High, Alaskan oil, Mexican oil—and the new reserves that are just now being developed—the Beaufort Sea, the Overthrust Belt in the American West, East Coast and Maritime Province offshore, the Artic Islands reserves, new Alaskan reserves—and it is obvious that there is no fundamental oil and gas shortage for the short term.

Oil and natural gas are nonrenewable resources and we must run out of them (and of coal, and copper, and iron ore, and mercury, and so on) if we continue historic patterns of usage. The short-term crisis, however, is the fault not of niggardly nature but of the deeds of man—deeds done partly through greed and partly through the legitimate concern for the long-term future.

Energy Future deals with the short-term problem. Its analysis and conclusions are a remarkable commendation of the decency and forbearance of the Western nations. There is no suggestion that we fail to respect the policies of the OPEC nations, which do not want to produce at higher rates for good reasons: to conserve their national resources and to keep the inflow of Western money at a

[2]*International Petroleum Encyclopedia: 1979 Edition*, Tulsa, Okla.: Petroleum Publishing Company, 1980.

manageable level. We will live with the shortage they impose, making do with substitution and conservation—with conservation being the best-available "quick fix." I agree. I prefer austerity to a return to gunboat, or nuclear, diplomacy.

The danger is that we confuse the short-term with the long-term problem. There is not much point spending the next generation building cumbersome solar energy facilities[3] and "syn-fuel" plants which could come on stream when the short-term crisis was over and be as useless as our synthetic rubber plants were after World War II. It is the big oil companies that must be the main actors in the short-term scenario.

The Oil Companies

The multinational oil companies have had a bad press. I cannot redress the balance in a single section of this book. I can make the case that if the big companies did throw their weight around in other countries, they really had little option, given the political, strategic, and military facts of life. In many cases the multinational oil companies acted as willing (or unwilling) extensions of a foreign office or ministry.

During the time period that writers and demagogues review to show the perfidy of the oil companies, a lot of things happened. Oil was discovered in Persia; the British navy decided to convert from coal to oil; the Germans lost World War I and their Middle East holdings became spoils of war; the Americans, who had provided the oil to run the war, became worried about an oil shortage (really) and tried desperately to break into the Anglo-French-Dutch Near Eastern monopoly; Venezuelan oil was developed by American companies; East Texas oil was discovered; a global depression hit and oil sold for as little as five cents a barrel. World War II shattered world economics: it was fueled by American oil. The nuclear age dawned. OPEC came into being. This is only a partial list, but it is

---

[3]They *have* to be cumbersome because sunlight is a low-level energy source. See the Second Law of Thermodynamics.

enough.[4] It is a lot to have happened to any industry within the lifetime of living men.

The important point of this review is that these happenings were not just industry problems. They involved foreign policy dealings at the highest levels. In many cases the oil companies were sent in after international diplomatic maneuvering in much the same spirit that a mother might send her child out for an evening with a very eligible date: "Have a good time, dear, do whatever you have to do, and *please* don't tell me about it tomorrow." It hardly seems fair for later administrations to criticize the oil industry for loyally implementing the policies of earlier ones.

The rise of the multinational oil companies is more interesting than most fiction: there are enough plots, counterplots, politics, wars, revolutions, unlikely characters, and (yes) even chicanery for a dozen novels. A recent, readable account is Anthony Sampson's *The Seven Sisters.*[5] Unfortunately, this book, like most current reporting, is biased against the oil companies. Writers may be unable to resist bringing in villains; more likely they have the typical intellectual's mistrust, or even hatred, of big business. The chapter headings in Sampson's book are not the sort to create a warm glow in oil company board rooms: "The Carve Up," "The Intruders," "The Reckoning," "The Seduction."

The overriding fact that no prejudice can obscure is that the Western oil companies were fantastically successful in finding and developing almost unlimited reserves of foreign oil. We, and they, have been paying for it ever since.

Economics

After the initial development of the huge Near Eastern fields, the economy of the West was transformed by a flood of cheap energy (in the nineteenth century kerosene cost \$42 a barrel). From

[4]For the complete story, see Neil H. Jacoby, *Multinational Oil,* New York: Macmillan, 1974.

[5]New York: Viking Press, 1975.

being a luxury, energy became almost a throwaway item. Oil could be profitably produced and loaded in the Persian Gulf at 15 cents a barrel. The Europeans cushioned the impact of this bonanza to some extent by high taxes on oil, but in America it was "all systems go."

Cheap oil changed our life style, our architecture, our transportation, our demography. Cheap foreign oil put the domestic oil industry on "hold." Cheap gasoline and new highways gave us big cars and suburban living; it shot down the passenger train and turned central cities into distressed areas. Not that this was all evil or irrational; it was the natural response to an economic stimulus. It was great while it lasted. The problems came when cheap energy became a memory and we were left with an infrastructure unsuited for an energy-scarce world.

But I have said that we are *not* short of oil. How did it happen? It happened because OPEC repealed economic laws. (How did the OPEC people get so smart? They sent their sons to American universities and hired Harvard MBAs.)

Classical economics says that you produce abundant resources first and move to lower-grade sources later when new technology comes on stream to ease the transition. It also says that competition will set a market price that has some relation to costs. These are the laws that have been revoked. We are now producing high-cost Alaskan and North Sea oil that cannot be sold at a profit at less than some $12 a barrel. People snatch at Mexican oil, which *is* abundant but which is produced so inefficiently that it could not compete in a free market. Economics is turned upside down. The economic scene is so warped that it would be just as devastating for the West if OPEC were suddenly to return to a more reasonable price level of, say, $5 a barrel.

Let us leave the short-term energy problem, leave it in the hands of congressmen with the uneasy feeling that they will reject the only real source of expertise—the oil companies. Let us look at the long-term problem.

Long Term

The *Energy Future* writers tell us not to look for a technological "fix" for our energy problems; but this is exactly what I think we should look for, long term. After all, it was coal technology that got our ancestors out of the "wood crunch" and new oil technology that saved them from choking to death on coal smoke. The elements of the next technology may already be apparent.

The new energy age will be a fusion-hydrogen age. Most people have heard that nuclear fusion is the ultimate energy source: nonpolluting, inexhaustible. Not as many know how close it is to being a reality. Not long ago an excellent report came out of Princeton on the current state of the art in technology and on the continuing international efforts by Americans, Russians, Europeans, and Japanese.[6] Things look good. The Princeton scientists feel that enough breakthroughs have been made that engineering rather than theoretical problems are what stand between us and the building of the first fusion reactor to create more power than it uses. Not easy problems, but solvable ones. Two such installations are planned for the early 1980s: the TFTR reactor at Princeton and the JET reactor at Culham in England.

It would probably be a mistake to try to move ahead quickly with a "crash program" (remember the breeder reactor). Competing commerical designs must be evaluated. We are going to have to learn to live with the short-term energy problem and fossil fuels before making a gradual transition to something better.

The energy *transmission* problem in a brave new energy world is as critical as supply. Even if we had a new unlimited source of electrical power, we would still have to get it to the user. To move the energy now transported by oil and gas pipelines would require lacing our country with an entanglement of high-tension power lines. Unless a storage battery an order of magnitude better than existing models is invented, highway vehicles will still require liquid or gaseous fuel.

[6]H. P. Furth, "Progress Towards a Tokamak Fusion Reactor," *Scientific American*, August, 1979.

The best answer seems to be to use hydrogen (the most abundant element) as portable energy. Reactor heat can be used to directly dissociate water into hydrogen and oxygen. Hydrogen, which is as good a fuel as natural gas, burns back to nonpolluting water vapor. Hydrogen can be transmitted in our existing pipelines system; it can be used to fuel cars and buses—experimental converted vehicles are already in use.[7] Trains should probably be electrified and airplanes should continue to use liquid fuel.

There remain many long-term problems that I have ignored or glossed over, but the conversion to a fusion-hydrogen system does seem feasible with intelligent national planning and an economic commitment no greater than that required to fight a medium-size war.

Hydrocarbon Energy

Some years ago at a technical meeting I heard a speaker argue that natural gas and oil were just too valuable to burn up for heat. At the time, when we were pushing outdoor gaslights as a way to sell gas, this sounded silly but now I am not so sure. Oil and natural gas are the most important chemical feedstocks in the world. They supply the makings of products from plastics to cosmetics to food. It is hard to imagine alternate sources. Perhaps we owe it to future generations to conserve this resource, this bounty, for their use rather than burning it up in boilers and automobiles.

A PHILOSOPHICAL NOTE

The elements of the ancients were earth, water, air, and fire. If we equate earth with arable land, air with breathing room, fire with energy, and water with fresh water, these are still the very elements of life—of prosperity. They are far more important for most of us than the elements listed on the periodic table.

The Arab nations must feel frustrated. Although they have

[7] J. J. Reilly and G. D. Sandrock, "Hydrogen Storage in Metal Hydrides," *Scientific American*, February, 1980, p. 118.

plenty of fire and air (and money, but that is not an element), they are short of earth and water: two elements that are almost impossible to buy. (Arabs can, and do, buy land in the West but this is hardly a permanent solution.) The Western world may be temporarily short on fire and long on frustration, but it is otherwise better balanced. The United States and Canada are particularly favored. If we don't jeopardize our "air" position with unwise immigration policies and if we can survive the short-term and solve the long-term "fire" problem without sacrificing our freedom, we should be able to face the future with goodwill and confidence.

PART THREE

Battlegrounds

12

THE SOLDIERS
OF CAPITALISM

WE HAVE IDENTIFIED the people who fight for socialism, either
from conviction or out of hatred of Western business. It is time to
look at the other side, at the people who stand up and fight for free
enterprise. The most obvious candidates are businessmen. To say
that all businessmen are, by definition, soldiers of capitalism is too
easy. For one thing "businessman" is a poorly defined term, one
that becomes as enigmatic as the blind men's elephant when we
consider different manifestations: the moguls and robber barons of
folklore, the mysterious money men who work in financial centers,
the "executives" who populate our suburbs. Somehow all these
people are businessmen with something in common, but they seem
like different species. Some are soldiers and some are not.

In this chapter I concentrate on the American scene rather than on all Western countries. This is not entirely laziness: it is almost impossible for a child of one culture to describe fairly the workings of another.[1] Fortunately, in the Western world at least, the American model seems to be pervasive. It is hard to get beyond the range of a three-iron shot from a Kentucky Fried Chicken or a McDonald's eatery in any Western city. Actually, what the United States is to Europe, California is (or has been) to the rest of our country. The smart businessman keeps an eye on California. He may not like what he sees, but there is a good chance that what is "in" there—from gay bars to new sports clothes—will soon spread to the rest of the nation. The West Coast even has a tourist pattern analogous to American travel in Europe. To be on Route 66 (a main east–west artery) in Arizona or Texas after schools let out in California is to live dangerously (at least when gasoline is available).

THE LEGENDS OF BUSINESS

The folk heroes of American business—men like Gould, Fisk, Huntington, and Guggenheim—were a colorful lot.[2] By modern standards they were probably crooks (even in their day they often had to "fix" legislatures), but still we tend to admire them. "They made our nation what it is." As a matter of fact, we do owe a debt to the robber barons if only because they directed the energies of the country to exploitation and development when other nations (in South America, for example) were quite content to preserve class privilege and the status quo. (Religious background may be important here—Catholicism versus Calvinism. See Chapter 14.)

The moguls themselves were a mixed lot, ranging from highly intelligent to vulgar. Some were idealistic: Carnegie called his

---

[1]It can be done but it takes time. Ezra Vogel spent two years in Japan before writing *Japan's New Middle Class,* Berkeley: University of California Press, 1963.

[2]See S. H. Holbrook, *The Age of the Moguls,* Garden City, N.Y.: Doubleday, 1954; or T. B. Brewer, ed., *The Robber Baron: Saints or Sinners,* New York: Holt, Rinehart & Winston, 1970.

THE SOLDIERS OF CAPITALISM / 169

wealth "God's money" and John D. Rockefeller felt he had a divine calling to bring order to the oil industry. What they had in common was energy, pragmatism, and a love of competition and of winning. They succeeded but they could hardly fail. With a rich nation to plunder and cheap labor they succeeded like fat dung beetles on a particularly rich manure pile. Americans love winners and a lot of us long for strong leadership. We regret the passing of the moguls: most of us would get a vicarious kick out of the excesses of a Diamond Jim Brady or of a Jim Fisk or from the parties that the Astors threw.

The myth lives on in the image of Daddy Warbucks—the father figure who singlehandedly takes on the dirty commies and our own government. The highly successful musical *Annie* is a celebration of this deity. Are there moguls today? A few, a very few. The manure piles are drying up, tax rates are higher, and the government is more obstructive.

People like J. Paul Getty had to look overseas for resources. Ross Perot found his own manure pile *within* American business. Corporations were running their computer departments so poorly that he could move his own people in to do the job (facility management), do it cheaper and better, and make a handsome profit. (He lost more dollars in one day than J. P. Morgan made in total.) In the Daddy Warbucks tradition, Perot even sent a private army to Iran to get his people out. There are still a few real swingers left, but most business leaders today look like any other American Express cardholders.

INSIDE SUPPORT

The executive who lives next door is not a tycoon. Tycoons live in a different world, a private world of executive suites, exclusive clubs, and housing enclaves like Grosse Point and River Oaks. Your neighbor works for big business all right, but he does what he is told. He may or may not support the system. In order to classify the business employees who mingle in middle class society, we have to take a closer look at the worker hierarchy in big business.

Employees can be separated into six categories, some of which we have already encountered: (1) production line workers and unskilled laborers, (2) skilled technicians, (3) staff workers (business bureaucrats), (4) professionals, (5) middle managers, and (6) top managers. Some of these people support the system; some do not.

The easiest way to dichotomize these people is to define a businessman as one who has a perceived[3] vested interest in his own company and in the free enterprise system. This eliminates the unskilled workers, who look to their union and to their fellow workers for security and prosperity. Skilled technicians—welders, machinists, mechanics—rely on their own skills: they could, or think they could, just as well work for the armed forces or for a socialist government. Professionals include both businessmen and nonbusinessmen. Engineers, researchers, even lawyers whose work is discipline-oriented rather than company-oriented would be just as happy in academe or in a government think tank. The true businessmen (and executives) are members of top management and a subset of the professionals—particularly those who are bucking for management positions. These are the people who have a strong vested interest in their own company and in the free enterprise system.

Most staff workers and middle managers know that they are expendable, that they can be replaced with only minor inconvenience to the company (at a saving, if the incumbent is a long-term employee). Their security and progress are protected by the unwritten covenant as long as they play the business game—they will play the business game; they will support the system. A top management person, on the other hand, has a personal vested interest in free enterprise and in his own company: not only is it the road to his own wealth; it is also an extension of his own ego.

[3] A necessary modifier. While it may be argued that we all have a stake in preserving the capitalist system, only those who recognize this are properly called businessmen.

OFF-DUTY SUPPORT

Businessmen rarely defend capitalism during working hours, any more than soldiers defend their country when in barracks. Unlike the soldier, the businessman sees action during *off-duty* hours. As noted in Chapter 6, corporations need to infiltrate their people into society to speak up for the business position and, more important, to be living examples of the business, or executive, image.

What is the executive image? It is nothing more or less than the attainable American dream. The exemplar comes from the media—from television, from bad novels, and from advertising. An ideal executive is well educated, interesting, and above all rational. He is reasonably good-looking, with a background, perhaps, of high school football; he is honest and public spirited and lives in a neat suburban home. He is financially secure and a good neighbor who can be relied on in a pinch. His pretty, but not flashy, wife is a wonderful homemaker: she may not have been a cheerleader in high school, but she is a cheerleader now—for her husband and for his career advancement. The happy couple have two children, Dick and Jane. (Jane has trouble with arithmetic and Dick hates Latin, but otherwise they are doing fine.) The delightful family is often seen together at church dos and at the country club.

Joe Dalton

Now let us spit on our hands and look at reality. How well does it compare with the ideal? Icon smashing (the columnist's disease) is fun, but it is not always in good taste. In this case the true life style of the average businessman is too important a shaper of our society to be accepted as read. Suppose the ideal *were* the actuality: that business did send into our society millions of these young and middle-aged executives whose good sense, intelligence, and rationality would ensure stable, well-run, and prosperous communities. Even the next generation would be taken care of—Dick and Jane would see to that. With this army of leaders and evangelists, with this sort of performance, no one could convincingly argue against the free enterprise system: business would quite properly be respected and businessmen would be heroes.

Business is not generally respected in our country and businessmen are not heroes.[4] No businessman has ever been drafted to serve as President, as we have drafted generals after winning wars. Something is wrong.

Joe Dalton, your neighbor, is a businessman, a minor middle manager in a big company. He *looks* like an executive,[5] at least when he leaves for work in the morning. He even played some football in high school. Joe tries to play his proper part. He does live in the suburbs, has a reasonably attractive wife and two children (Eloise and Hector), is an elder in his church, and is a member of the Lions Club. He is an excellent neighbor and a fast man with a drink. But—there are some cracks in the picture window.

Joe is no brain: he runs more to *corpore sano* than *mens sana*. He is technically qualified for his job and has an advanced degree to prove it. But in other fields—esthetics, anthropology, biology, ecology, history, languages, literature, philosophy, philology, political science, semantics, syntax, and theology—he is a mental adolescent. Job-oriented higher education didn't allow much time for such frills. The offered television menu of sit-coms suits his entertainment needs quite well, at least between football seasons. Once a year Joe springs for tickets to a major football game, complete with a chrysanthemum for his wife so they can relive college glories.[6] The only significant reading material in the house is *Reader's Digest* condensed books.

---

[4]For a study of this social animosity, see Ernest van den Haag, ed., *Capitalism: Sources of Hostility*, Washington, D.C: Heritage Foundation, 1980.

[5]The dress code is well defined and much copied. (See *HIM*, Chapter 14.) The impractical business uniform is adopted by researchers and engineers who are going to spend their day over a hot test tube or a drawing board. Even baseball players are respectable; off duty they wear gray flannels and blue blazers.

[6]Football is the game for young "upwardly mobile" people. Baseball appeals to another constituency—the old, the poor, and the black—people who spend their money just because they enjoy the game. I prefer the baseball crowd.

Mrs. Dalton doesn't do a lot of homemaking—she works. She has to, to make ends meet. The house, the stationwagon, and the wall-to-wall carpeting still have to be paid for, along with the kids' education. Since the unpleasantness about integration, Eloise and Hector go to private schools. The children are manifestations of the optimism of early married life—offerings not about to be repeated. Hector's only interest is his motorcycle, with which he terrorizes the neighborhood; Eloise wants to be a stewardess or cocktail waitress if she outgrows a tendency to be flat-chested. They would both like to exchange their parents for something better. For their part, Joe and his wife wonder if the children are into drugs yet and live for the day when the kids finally leave home so they can do something.

Joe is a loyal, hardworking company man. He carries his plastic dispatch case home most nights, more to ease his conscience than to satisfy the demands of his job. He votes for the most conservative candidates in the running—at least for those who make the most effective noises about opposing gun control, cutting taxes, and increasing defense spending. He is quite willing to speak for the "American way," although his arguments could be shredded by any reasonably educated socialist (read "dirty commie"). He supports his own company—"a great place to work." Still, after a few drinks he has been heard to insinuate that his immediate supervisor "couldn't pour swamp water out of a boot with the directions written on the heel" and to beef about unfair personnel policies that give all the good jobs to women and blacks.

Joe may not be quite the effective evangelist his company would like, but he is not all that bad. The important point is that Joe is a nice guy; people like him. He is a "good old boy." Other people may distrust his company for other, possibly valid reasons, but not because of the Joes of this world; in fact, he and his peers provide a living rebuttal to the common notion that big business is powerful and inscrutable. His main shortcoming, as far as his company is concerned, is that people don't take him very seriously—as seriously as they might (just might) take the college professor and the minister who live on the same block. Fortunately, business has other, more effective propagandists working for its cause.

SMALL BUSINESSMEN

The most effective propagandists for big business just might be small businessmen. These are the entrepreneurs—the owners and managers of shops, small factories, automobile agencies, service firms, and neighborhood department stores. Not farmers. These small operators may not like big business very much, since it gives them tough and possibly unfair competition, but they support the free enterprise system and if big business is part of that system, so be it. The small operator lives dangerously—he is one economic cycle or one generation removed from disaster. If he wants to stay competitive he cannot afford to put something away for hard times; nor does he enjoy the security of the businessman working for a big corporation. He has to "meet a payroll"; he is "street tough." Many small businessmen are recent-generation Americans who do not take economic freedoms for granted, as most of us do. To them, they are worth fighting for. In fact, they often identify free enterprise with democracy (a connection many of our academicians would find amusing). Such people can stand up to socialist dialectic and support their own position with names and dates and possibly even with scars.[7]

The small businessman may go beyond rhetoric in his support of the capitalist system: he may stand for a minor political office such as alderman or school board member or even for mayor of his town. If elected, he considers it an honor to serve, even at a personal financial sacrifice. The average big businessman would hardly be foolish enough to interrupt his career in this way—you don't get promotions when you're on leave. The competitive world of the

[7]This is not to argue for unrestricted immigration into an overcrowded country, but rather to propose the entry of a selected group of the right sort of people.

small businessman is better training for the harsh world of politics than the usually less demanding jobs in big business and civil service. Harry Truman went all the way.

OTHER SOLDIERS

Other supporters of the business system include outsiders who are either supported by business or sympathetic to the business position. Bribery is not implied; it is not common in the American business establishment. If two people are running for the same public office and one supports the business position and the other does not, it is perfectly logical, legal, and in the democratic tradition for businessmen to support the one who favors the business position. It is also logical and legal for corporations to send spokesmen (lobbyists) to state capitals or to Washington to present their points of view to incumbents who are considering legislation that concerns the business community. The influence of business on government deserves fuller treatment: we shall consider it in some detail in Chapter 17.

The free enterprise system does have unsolicited outside supporters.[8] There are, for example, columnists like William Buckley who follow the capitalist line and who know what they are talking about. But for every friend in the fourth estate there are foes. Many journalists consider themselves to be liberals or intellectuals or both (for some reason capitalism is regarded as anti-intellectual) and assume a leftist or socialist stance, which gives them lots of room for righteous indignation.

There *is* a loyal business press which publishes periodicals like *Forbes, Barron's, Fortune,* and *Dun's Review*. The best, and best known, is *The Wall Street Journal*. There are also scholarly reviews

[8] I suppose I have to mention the all-American flag-waving groups that are for desperately free enterprise. All Western nations have these embarrassments: the National Front, Neo-Fascists, the Birch Society. With their bigotry and hatred, these are the sorts of friends business can do without.

like *Commentary* and *The Public Interest* which support the capitalist ethic. The trouble with all these publications, from a propaganda standpoint, is that they are mostly read by, and speak to, the already committed and their impact on the outside world is limited.

Business should expect support from the academic community if only because our great universities are monuments of the capitalist system. No such luck. There is not much help from academia—with a few glorious exceptions, like the economics department at the University of Chicago and its doyen, Milton Friedman. Many economics professors in other schools preach a pedantic, leftish doctrine and give the impression that they look forward to the demise of big business.

Business schools would seem to have to be loyal supporters. They are for business, all right, but they are of little help in the ideological war. Their curriculum is preoccupied with the nuts and bolts of business and finance. Try to find a course on the capitalist dialectic—or the socialist dialectic for that matter (know your enemies). Business schools measure their success by the earnings of their graduates. Harvard, for example, is proud to show the updated curves of its alumni salaries—perfect ammunition for socialists.

THE MIX

These are the soldiers, or better, the noncoms and officers of the free enterprise system in its battle for survival: businessmen (like Joe) who are willing but uninformed; small businessmen who may be more strongly motivated but who (usually) have less status in the community; top management that uses shareholders' money to pay for institutional advertising, which often does speak out on its own behalf (usually to the shareholders) and which buys support when it legally can; finally, a few outside friends of the court— columnists, writers, and a handful of professors. This is a motley cadre to lead the fight against an organized and informed enemy.

The foot soldiers who fill the ranks must come from the sociological mix—the infinitely varied citizenry of a modern democracy. Somehow enough unity, spirit, and conviction have to be mustered in this heterogeneous crew not only to support the nation but also to at least tolerate the capitalist apparatus that makes it work. This is the subject of the next chapter.

13

MOTIVATION, MORALE, AND PROPRIETY

WHEN I WAS young, I was blessed with a useful number of English aunts—the real thing, not American imports, maiden aunts living in England whose natural partners had died on the Somme, at Passchendaele, or at Ypres ("normal wastage": 1,000 men a month). As far as my brother and I were concerned, these aunts qualified as fairy godmothers. They were far enough away not to be a nuisance and they were reliable in sending us good British goods: pound notes, ten-shilling notes, plum puddings, toffee, and wooden jigsaw puzzles. Every Christmas we got a huge book, *Chums Annual*. This was a collection of all the stories and articles that had appeared in the boys' periodical *Chums* in the last year. The serials were predictable: a school story, a pirate story (on the Spanish Main), and a series on the outposts of the Empire. We loved it. I now realize that the writing was good[1] and the pen-and-ink illustrations of a quality unheard of today. It was magnificient propaganda.

As we devoured *Chums* (my father told me there had been a competitor, *Boys' Own Paper*, but this was before my time), two little boys in Chicago who wore horn-rimmed spectacles ("four eyes") and who made up the tail end of the gym line became loyal soldiers of the King. We longed to attend an English "public" school even though the main indoor sport seemed to be beating the bejesus out of the "fags." We wanted to carry the Union Jack to the far corners of the earth. All things British were best and Englishmen were fine, upstanding, cleancut chaps or at least well on the way to this desideratum largely through reading Latin and playing cricket. (There wasn't much in *Chums* about Englishwomen except for an occasional reference to a golden-haired girl with clear blue eyes.) Other nationalities hardly existed. If Americans appeared they were brave, a bit crude, and ineffective—a description that disturbed us but one we took in stride.

This was the reading of the middle class English boy; this was what shaped his self-image and his concept of England and Empire. This was mindless propaganda for the privileged minority that was to provide first-class junior officers for the army and the navy. That the image was not representative did not matter. *Chums* is long gone, the British Empire is gone, and British capitalism is on the ropes. I think there is a connection.

GROWING UP IN AMERICA

Even professional educators, possibly the last group to recognize self-evident truths, are agreed that the critical time of learning is the early years. (The church has always known this.) Not that the ten-year-old is into integral calculus or theology but that he is

---

[1]Some of the material might be deleted by an alert modern editor: "Don't shoot any more Wogs, Geof! We will have to carry our own gear to the coast."

busy forming his attitudes, his manners, his priorities, and his prejudices.

If a child grows up convinced that his country is not only the best but is somehow an example to the rest of the world, it is an easy step to assume that its form of government and its economic system are proper. No matter that the child knows nothing of political science or economics; whatever the system is in his country (England, the United States, Germany, Russia), it is good enough for him. He may later fight for it. Dictators, who are practical men, know this. It was from the Hitler Youth that an (almost) invincible army was built. It is from the Pioneers that Russian party members come. This early indoctrination is the first step to motivation. Without a minimum of consensus motivation, a nation is vulnerable not only to the invasion of foreign armies but also to the invasion of alien ideas.

Sophistication and liberalism are enemies of the nationalistic indoctrination of youth. I am not arguing against these admirable concepts; I am just stating an uncomfortable fact. A country can become too cultured and rational to tolerate the simplistic propaganda that contributes to nationalism, unity, and strength. A similar situation exists in academic disciplines, particularly in those that are relatively exclusive. An American nuclear physicist feels more at home with an English or a German or even a Russian counterpart[2] than with his banker. Archaeologists, zoologists, and many other scientists split their loyalty between their own countrymen and an international fraternity of peers. To such people, the relative merits of capitalism and socialism don't seem too important.

In a simpler and earlier day—not much earlier—we did indoctrinate our young people in the United States. Every school morning started with the Pledge of Allegiance and a verse or two of "America." The stories in English class usually had a moral to them. Our songs in music class tended to be patriotic and inspiring:

[2]Read, for example, C. P. Snow, *The New Men*, New York: Scribner's, 1954. Also available in Penguin paperback.

We are the men of the coming generation,
We are the men who will build a mighty nation.

We loved patriotic liturgy: the Fourth of July, one of our few holidays, was a big day. As far as outside reading was concerned, we didn't have anything with the impact of *Chums*, but *The Open Road for Boys* and *Boys' Life* were safe. For heavier reading, books like the Hardy Boys series and the Tom Swift series (which explicitly supported the capitalist system, as in "Tom freely stated enterprisingly") praised the pluck and ingenuity of the American boy.[3]

The early radio offerings such as "Jack Armstrong, All-American Boy" and "Little Orphan Annie" would be laughed out of court today by our more sophisticated, but not necessarily smarter, young people. The visual arts were simpler. In early movies the establishment was boosted: in *The Dancing Fool*, for example, the hero was a salesman quite different from Willy Loman in *Death of a Salesman*.

I am not claiming that this was a better world—I will let my prejudices hang out later—but it was an easier world for children. We knew what was right. We saluted the flag. Our system was more than right; it was the only way to go. If our country needed us, we were available.

While the first aspect of motivation is the indoctrination of the young, the ultimate motivation comes from social pressure and from mature conviction based on study and reason. You can indoctrinate a child in Sunday school or in the synagogue, but meaningful Christian or Jewish faith, the faith on which the future of the church or temple depends, comes only after long and sometimes painful learning and reflection. Before getting on to this final critical path to personal economic and political conviction, let us consider the fruits of collective motivation: the morale of a people, their willingness to support their way of life.

[3]Even earlier, the Horatio Alger books were pure capitalist propaganda. How effective they were I don't know.

MORALE

Morale, as I use the term, refers to the morale of groups—of workers, of soldiers, of citizens—rather than to that of an individual. (Another French designation, esprit de corps, might be more accurate, but it sounds too military.) I suppose it is possible to talk of individual morale but it doesn't help much: if a person's convictions and goals are different from those of his fellows, he diminishes rather than increases group morale. The morale of any group, whether it be a football team or a communist cell, is the result of a sense of *unity* (togetherness), a feeling of *confidence*, and a common *purpose*.

The starkest demonstration of the need for all three of these attributes is seen in a nation at war. War, like hanging, tends to "concentrate the mind wonderfully."[4] In a stress or panic situation, such as a strategic bombing attack, soldiers or civilians *must* feel a closeness to each other; they *must* have confidence in their comrades and superiors and in ultimate victory; they *must* recognize a defined goal or purpose, whether it is to "save the world for democracy" or just to beat the enemy. Without all these factors, the war is probably lost. History provides many examples: the French army in World War II, the Americans in Vietnam, the Shah's army in Iran.

These three morale factors are less obvious in peacetime, but they are just as important to group success. Morale is critical in any group venture, up to and including the preservation of a way of life and a social and economic system.

The proliferation of organizations with many different goals may be a good measure of the level of a country's civilization. In a primitive or deprived society, people are too preoccupied with staying alive to be much concerned about saving the redwoods or the whooping crane or supporting a symphony orchestra. In England, a highly civilized country, there is even a Campaign for

[4]Hill Powell, ed., *Boswell's Life of Johnson*, Oxford: Clarendon Press, 1934, Vol. III, p. 167.

Real Ale. Such organizations are effective out of all proportion to their size as long as they have the necessary morale ingredients and a social climate that tolerates and respects them. In a truly democratic society, *any* group that feels deprived or that has a specific goal can make itself heard. The results of such efforts are usually good: the promotion of racial and sexual equality, the preservation of our natural and man-made heritage, better beer. The danger is that people can put parochial or special interests above national well-being—an Irish-American, for example, may support the IRA in opposition to national policy.

Socialists and communists are traditionally a high-morale, single-minded group. The capitalist system needs equally motivated and organized support. The very ideology of the free enterprise system and the diversity of creatures involved in it (consciously or unconsciously) make this almost impossible.

In a Western nation almost everyone has a stake in the capitalist system, whether employed by business or not. The independent artist needs a prosperous society; he depends on the working of the system to market his wares. The government bureaucracy needs prosperous business as a source of tax money. In other words, with the exception of the conscientious objectors (socialists), the same constituency that would fight a war should support the system. Let's see how this constituency stacks up in terms of its morale factors: unity, confidence, and purpose.

Unity

A feeling of unity in a people comes from a shared social and historical background. As long as we can define the typical American (or Englishman, or German, or Canadian) and as long as our youth can identify with this image, we feel a sense of unity—we are among friends. Easy identifications are usually false. The public school boy in *Chums* did not grow into the typical Englishman, as the English found out when they could no longer afford to confine their army to privileged regiments. The "other ranks" in World War

I turned out to be a head shorter than their officers; they didn't speak "received English."[5]

To leave a sheltered environment and enter the services or the workplace is a cultural shock. Fellow citizens come in all sizes, shapes, and colors; they may not even speak the same language. The hardest accommodation is spiritual rather than physical—to try to identify with people who have completely different priorities and tastes in sex, music, literature, learning, and religion, even in recreation and in the spending of money. Through World War II, the American armed services followed the tradition of keeping the races (and the sexes) separated. My first outfit was all white: a sprinkling of college boys, working stiffs, and some dedicated refugees earning American citizenship the hard way. We got along; we broke into natural groupings and we found unity in purpose. It must be harder for today's recruits.

Language disparity is an almost insurmountable barrier to national unity. Only the Swiss seem able to cope with this hurdle. Where there are well-defined linguistic groups in a country, there are almost always separatist movements based on real or imagined discrimination. Canada is an outstanding modern example, but there are and have been many others. I am alarmed by illegal immigration into the United States. I am more concerned that the Hispanics cling to the Spanish language. (They may have logic on their side; after all, Spanish was spoken before English in much of our country.) Earlier immigrants rejected their native languages as soon as they could. (I have friends who understand German because their parents spoke it but who never learned to speak the language themselves.) I would hate to see us become a two-language country. Other Western countries increasingly face the same problem as a result of the postwar migrations of peoples.

Even *within* English-language communities there are linguistic threats to unity. I have no problem identifying with any person who speaks what I consider reasonable English. I have difficulty even

[5]Fowler's term. See Henry Fowler, *Modern English Usage*, 2nd ed.; New York: Oxford University Press, 1965.

understanding one who speaks "jive talk" or "street jargon" or whatever it is called. I am turned off by people who use excessive obscenities. This is prejudice and it is indefensible. It is not group or racial prejudice: it is directed impartially against anyone who abuses the English language.

Confidence

Confidence is the innate feeling that group goals will be achieved or that a preferred status quo can be maintained. The most outstanding modern example of confidence was that of the English people after the fall of France. Hitler held all the cards; the only reasonable question was whether England would give up with or without a struggle. For their part, the English did not expect to fight a losing battle to the last man. They expected to fight and win. This is confidence. I had a friend in the Philippines who was interned by the Japanese. He made friends with one of the guards (there were decent Japanese even then) and asked his friend who would win the war. The guard answered carefully and very presciently, "It will be a long war. I think maybe the Americans will win." This is lack of confidence.

Confidence in the outcome of the ideological battle between socialism and capitalism involves a belief in the "wave of the future"—in unlived history. Only if a person is convinced that, in spite of its ups and downs, the capitalist system will prevail can he effectively work to maintain and strengthen it. Socialists or communists have no doubts. They may admire the free enterprise system, as Marx did, but only as a prelude to the inevitable new order. A soldier or a civilian who has faith in ultimate victory does not die in vain—at least not in his own eyes. He dies a martyr and furthers the cause. There is a martyrology of communism. Who are the heroes of capitalism?

Purpose

Fellowship and confidence don't have much value unless they are invoked for a goal, a purpose. The goal of socialists is well known: to instill a new political and economic system. It is laid out in *The Communist Manifesto*. Clear purpose gives any movement strength and efficiency. An organization dedicated to saving redwoods or to keeping beer natural knows its goals and its enemies and how to keep track of gains and losses. The goals of capitalism are diverse: they have never been packaged in a manifesto (remember the problems we had defining capitalism in Chapter 2), are not well understood, and keep changing.

Capitalism is like religion in that most people in Western society pay lip service to it but few understand it. (Socialism *is* a religion. See Chapter 14.) In the heyday of capitalism, there was missionary zeal to spread the doctrine to the corners of the earth. To convert a nation or a colony was to save it. In those days capitalism was identified with freedom and democracy (as it still should be). Smart foreign nations incorporated useful Western financial methods and technology into their own systems. Less sophisticated countries were left with the apparatus of industrial society after they had thrown out their benefactors, without the will or the wit to use it.

Our missionary zeal is gone. Today we are satisfied (or unsatisfied) to promote elections in which people who can't read or write are asked to choose between alternatives they don't understand—a Vernon Parish, Louisiana, election.

The purpose of the soldiers of capitalism today is defensive: to keep what they have, to resist change. Defense has always been the more difficult strategic position. The attacker has the advantage of looking for weakness, concentrating his forces, and obtaining local superiority. The capitalist system has so many fronts that even in prosperous times it leaves many openings to attack. In a recession it looks like a sitting duck:

What can be the stated purpose of an organization like the U.S. Chamber of Commerce, which is committed to the preservation of the capitalist system? To provide a better life for the people? This is the stated goal of *any* economic system. To create rich men? Guffaws from the Emirate countries. To conserve resources? None of these goals, based on outward, visible signs, is very convincing. Useful goals must be more subtle and more fundamental: to preserve free enterprise and free competition so that the capitalist system with all its faults and regulated by an understanding government can promote prosperity. (Unfortunately this can sound like special pleading for privilege.) I am convinced that the ultimate commitment to the capitalist system is to those old, abused concepts: freedom and democracy.

COMING OF AGE

The maintenance of the three elements that constitute morale—unity, confidence, and purpose—is part of cultural conditioning: of growing up; of learning and associating with the myths, traditions, and religions of a people. I have already talked about early exposure to traditions and myths. Up to a point I believe in this sort of thing. Children should be taught a decent respect for the symbols of a nation: for the flag or for the royal family. I believe in the preservation of myths: George Washington and the cherry tree, King Alfred and the cakes, Siegfried and the sword. Sharing a nation's myths is like sharing family secrets. Ultimately, children outgrow liturgy and folklore and graduate to the more solid food of cultural learning in school, in the home, in church, in the streets, in social groups, and from the media and the arts. These are the arenas in which the battles of ideas are ultimately fought and from which the survivors emerge as defenders of the system, as parasites on society, or as advocates of change.

History

The most manageable battleground of ideas is the classroom. The student gets a feeling of belonging, of being the inheritor of tradition, by studying his nation's history.

History, for goodness sake! The most despised subject of hardheaded businessmen is the key subject in our schools! There is a problem. Unless a student can identify with historical characters, he isn't reading *his* history; he is reading stories about some other people. In a country like Japan, which has a relatively homogeneous racial and social structure (and a bad case of xenophobia), this is not serious: the historical characters are the student's own ancestors. In racially and ethnically mixed countries like the United States, South Africa, and even to some extent England, it is hard for a black or an Indian or an Oriental child to identify—to feel a sense of belonging. The same problem exists in countries like Mexico that have sharp class distinctions. A child can consider himself a social outsider before he finishes the eighth grade. He sees black and white much earlier.

Even the sociologists and educators who write and prescribe school textbooks have grasped the problem. Not that these people are necessarily dedicated to the preservation of the capitalist system. They have other fish to fry: to improve the self-image of minorities and to correct real or imagined wrongs. Their answer, in America at least, is to rewrite history to give everybody a piece of the action. He who writes history makes history. (One of the terms of the Versailles Treaty was that the Allies would write the "official" history of the great war.)

Frances FitzGerald recently wrote a book on the changes in the versions of American history taught in our schools in the last century.[6] The writing of history texts is too important to be left to historians! The texts are created by teams hired by publishers: teams that represent the appropriate disciplines and that know the current requirements of school boards. It seems that our history changes not only in time but also by teaching location. There is a "Lone Star edition" for Texas (presumably to better document the Alamo). The "in" thing of course is to play up the role of blacks and Chicanos in American history. They are not, for example, to be pictured in "degrading" work clothes. It will be interesting to read

[6]F. FitzGerald, *America Revisited*, New York: Atlantic–Little, Brown, 1979.

the Vietnamese contribution to American history when we have assimilated the new wave of refugees.

This is bad history; it is even bad propaganda: propaganda should be believable. Western history has been made by kings and generals and popes and bishops and lawmakers, and these people have not necessarily been nice but they have been white. Of course minorities, which include all of us, have made contributions to American history—the Confederacy could hardly have fought the War Between the States without the loyalty and hard work of the blacks—but minority groups have mostly played supporting roles. (There I go rewriting history; the disease is catching.)

To rewrite history for nonhistorical reasons is a mark of desperation, almost of hysteria, and it is not effective. Even *Chums* and the Tom Swift books were better; at least they didn't have the stigma of being required reading.

PROPRIETY

Decent people are not going to invest their time and money to support a cause unless they believe it to be a "good" thing, to have an intrinsic rightness. The Shah's troops took a daily loyalty oath but deserted when things got rough. Not enough South Vietnamese thought their government was worth fighting for. If capitalism (business) is going to attract real support and not have to depend on mercenaries, it must come on as a worthwhile, honorable institution. If it doesn't, decent people will say "to hell with it" and turn their energies to saving the whales.

Western business is based on contracts and on verbal commitments. When a manager in one company tells a manager in another company that he will buy at a certain price, both parties know the deal will be honored. (Lawyers have to come in later to draw up formal contracts, which must meet regulations and which do muddy the water.) This level of morality is required for business to run smoothly. Western businessmen do not as a rule take bribes; to do so would completely foul up the pay structure and discipline of a company. They do not sell jobs. They keep honest books and pay their taxes. They try to maintain a decent correlation between ability and advancement. These things constitute a minimum moral code below which business will not be allowed, even by a permissive people, to continue to control the industrial wealth of a democratic nation.[7] Western business is not only willing to maintain these standards; it *has* to in order to operate efficiently, competitively, and cooperatively. There is probably less hugga-mugga in the business world than in government. This is being "business-like."

Relative rectitude may be admirable but it is not endearing. Government, the public, and business itself want to see more evidence of corporate heart and soul. The government wants business to do social work: to hire and train and promote more minorities and women and disabled people. (As we have seen, once employees are hired, business will guarantee their welfare.) Government wants business to locate in depressed areas. It wants promotions to be based on sociology as well as on ability. It wants industry to preserve the environment.

The public wants corporations to be good neighbors. It wants them to support cultural organizations, to provide community leadership, not to foul the air or waters, to look pretty, and not to make too much noise. Carried to the extreme, the public wants industry to go somewhere else so the natives can go back to picking breadfruit and digging clams.

Business recognizes these strictures, but top management at least doesn't have to like them. There are people and empires within corporations that like these things very much: the public relations department, the ecology department, and the open-handed executive who buys the champion hog at the state fair. Such

[7]At the time of this writing, many people are convinced that the oil companies are profiteering on gasoline prices. If this were to prove true, the pressure for nationalization of big oil would be irresistible.

charm packages are usually bad business. Besides, they extort money from the deserving shareholders, and aren't the deserving shareholders the first concern of management?

Ah, the shareholders—here is a noble cause: the welfare of the retirees, widows, and orphans who own American business! You see these shareholders on television commercials: the venerable octogenarian totters to the mailbox while his wife, in gingham and sneakers, leans on her hoe and watches fearfully to see what dear old Texaco has sent them to live on this quarter. Not an accurate picture. The important shareholders are steel-jawed, gimlet-eyed money managers for banks and pension funds whose loyalty to the company extends only until the next earnings report. The crying and concern for shareholders that emanates from executive suites is enough to bring tears to a man's eyes. Fortunately, business has other, more appealing gods to appease.

Nobility

Business leaders are convinced that *their* business is public benefaction—that the goods or services provided are really a favor to the nation. This can be a hard position to rationalize if the output is "Saturday night specials" or "tiger cages" or napalm, but it can be done. If all else fails, management can fall back on the old saw, "If we didn't do it someone else would." You can pick up the missionary zeal in addresses to shareholders and at employee gatherings. My wife and I found ourselves in a small restaurant in Arkansas seated near a party that must have been the total staff of a small manufacturer. The group had a company song:

> Dura, Dura, Dura,
> Dura, Dura Cloth,
> Dura, Dura, Dura,
> Wipes the spots right off.

A catchy song; I hope the outfit is still in business.

Profits

With a noble goal taken as read, the raison d'être of top management, and of most businessmen, is *profits*. This doesn't sound very lovable. Before closing this book and picking up your copy of Galbraith, consider what this reverence of profits does for all of us. Profits, lasting profits (not the kind that come from peddling shoddy goods), result from increased efficiency and productivity, from superior design, and from competitive pricing. These are the elements that create prosperity—a better life for all of us. Profits may be a heathen idol, but men have worshipped worse gods. A new employee, particularly in an operational or "line" position, in a well-run corporation soon picks up this persuasion. Everybody is trying to do things better and cheaper. The purchasing people shop for the best prices; production engineers, even production workers, try to improve throughput. Distribution, warehousing, inventory, and selling costs are constantly evaluated. For the most part the motive is not even selfish, which would desecrate a true faith. Profit increase or cost reduction (the same thing) is a game, a grand game that any number can play. Success is something to brag about in off-duty hours. The reasons for this commitment are both practical and psychological.

Look at the class pictures in your college yearbook. You can see in the faces of the young people an innate desire to do something worthwhile, to make this world a better place. Youth does have high ideals and dreams, even in our materialistic world. If a graduating class is lucky, as mine was, it will be called to fight a noble war. Some of today's graduates use their idealism and energy to fight for special causes, but most move quietly into business or government. On the face of it, there aren't many windmills that a trained computer programmer can tilt at; *but* if he can write a more efficient program that saves his company money and if he can make the mental adjustment to equate profit with virtue, he has justified his existence. He can live with himself, castigate the saboteur who wrote the old program, and be admired by his friends. This sort of performance will probably help his career, but that is a secondary consideration. He might describe his motivation as pride in workmanship or as professionalism, but the best term is self-esteem.

It is only in the business world that this worship of profits and efficiency reaches its full flower. For this reason, businessmen are more apt to be content than civil service workers or members of the armed services (in peacetime). The aim of government workers is not profit. Nor is it efficiency—or if it is, the target is so often missed that it must be more frustrating than comforting. The goal of most government agencies (and of many business staff departments) is simply to grow—to spend at least as much as last year so that their budget won't be cut. To me this is a strong argument against nationalized industry. By removing the profit motive you cut the heart, the cause, out of a corporation.

The pursuit of profit may seem to be a strange sort of cause. As long as it is largely selfless and parochial, I accept it as just. When companies are so large that the working of the profit motive can affect national or international policy—American automobile companies and international oil companies come to mind—then I am not so sure. Do corporations put national welfare ahead of profits? In war? In peace? I guess I would have to say "not always," and when they don't they may concede points to their enemies.

The other side of the coin is more sharply struck. A badly run company that doesn't strive for profits either goes out of business and puts its people out of work or becomes a parasite supported by government subsidy. If this is not sin, it is immoral. Business can and does look to a higher source than profit to justify its existence.

Gott mit Uns

Any group with a well-defined purpose whose aims are neither atheism nor the promotion of a rival religion (like communism) tries to invoke the support of organized religion. This seems to be more than a craving for a "Good Housekeeping seal of approval"; rather, it is an ancient need for the endorsement of higher authority.[8] The religious establishment, like the educational establishment, is older than industrial society. Recruiting priests or rabbis or ministers to support *any* cause is not difficult, since people with religious tenure, like those with academic tenure, modestly consider themselves to be experts on everything. We were treated to the spectacle of priests leading antiwar demonstrations to prevent the United States from establishing order in Indo-China and to leave the natives free to slaughter each other. Now the ecclesiastics, who turned out to be nuclear engineers[9] all the time, want to shut down nuclear power plants.

From the time of the Crusades the military and the religious have had a close and sometimes disastrous relationship. The German army wore *Gott mit uns* belt buckles, and my church gave all its sons little Crusader crosses to wear with their dog tags. (Tin-backed bibles were marketed for mothers to give to their sons for protection—a good example of semifaith.) Church music can come on pretty strong:

"Lord of our far-flung battle line . . ."
"He is trampling out the vintage . . ."
"Protect us by thy might . . ."
"Scatter her enemies . . ."
"God the all-terrible . . . lightning thy sword."

With all this spiritual support available, business wants its share.

In things spiritual, capitalism has a clear advantage over socialism. If communists consciously reject religion, business will consciously embrace it. (That the early Christian church was socialistic is best forgotten.) The fervor of the business community

---

[8]The Israelites carried the Ark of Yahweh into battle with mixed results. See, for example, I Samuel 4.

[9]Or land reformers. It was interesting when Pope John Paul II, possibily the single most effective fighter against oppression, told the South American clergy to stick to things spiritual.

varies from country to country and from place to place. It is best seen in the Bible Belt of the Southern United States. It is a rare meeting in these parts where someone doesn't call on Brother _____ to give the invocation. It always seemed a bit presumptuous to me to expect the Good Lord to take a special interest in a pipeline supervisors' meeting and almost an imposition to have to listen to a long-winded Baptist extol motherhood, fellowship, and God while I watched my food grow cold. I was wrong. Looking at the faces of my fellows I could see that for them this was time well spent. The Lord was with us in our deliberations or our devourings and all was right with the world. This is small beer: at the other end of the spectrum there were men like John D. Rockefeller, Andrew Carnegie, and LeTourneau who saw their empires as extensions of God's work. In any event, organized religion is another arena in which business competes for favor and support.

Unfinished Business

In this chapter we have examined the roots of the motivations that move people to fight for, or just to accept, a concept or an ideology. The roots are early conditioning and conscious or unconscious learning. We considered the elements of the morale of a motivated group: unity, confidence, and purpose. Finally, we considered the morality of purposes and goals, without which any movement is in trouble. We identified the arenas in which the battle of ideas is fought: schools, homes, churches, streets, the media, and social groups. This leaves unfinished business. We need to see how the business community throws its weight around in these arenas to support its position.

14

RELIGION

The vicar of St. Swithins-on-Poke
Instructed his curate named Hoke,
"'A reading from ____' is expected,
"'Here beginneth ____' is accepted,
But never 'The Lord saith and I quote ____.'"

RELIGION MAY SEEM like a strange topic to introduce in a book about business. For most of us religion is something that can safely be confined to Saturdays or Sundays, which doesn't have much to do with the give-and-take of the marketplace. It would be a brave (or a foolish) economist who dragged such an unscientific subject into a learned paper. I have no such inhibitions. My position is that Western capitalism as we know it is possible only in societies

196

tempered by their own religious convictions or those borrowed from others. Corporations do not usually support organized religion directly; the support comes from individual businessmen. Still, in my opinion, such contributions are well spent. Business owes more to the first estate than it can ever repay. It is going to take a bit of writing to support this position.

ORGANIZED RELIGION

Religious belief is an innate need of human beings. As far as I know, our busy anthropologists have never discovered a primitive tribe that did not believe in supernatural powers. The need for religion is part of the package deal of being human: of being able to contemplate ourselves and to ask questions that we are obviously incapable of answering. (The questions get more sophisticated as we get more "civilized," but they also get more numerous.) The goal of organized religion is to provide a set of beliefs that embrace the mysteries we cannot explain to ourselves.

All successful religions are based on mystic revelation; on visions of the ineffable. This is as it has to be. Since religion deals with the supernatural, our usual methods of investigation—the scientific method or a survey, for example—are useless. Any attempt to turn theology into a science is a waste of time. The unscientific foundations of religion can cause intellectual people to reject it as nothing more than a nice collection of myths. This is an inconsistent position. By the very nature of its origins, religion can neither be proved nor disproved (this side of the grave). Attempts to prove the existence of God, for example, are sophistry. No person can say that religion, any religion, is true or false; the most he can say is that "I, personally, believe or do not believe." Religion is an act of faith.

Mystic insight is a rare gift, as rare perhaps as the ability to bat .400. This leaves most of us who profess a faith in the uncomfortable position of having to accept the words of others: of prophets, saints, and incarnate gods. We need references, we need scripture, to preserve these insights. Every organized religion has such literature: the Torah, the New Testament, the Hindu Vedas and Sutras, the Koran, the Book of Mormon, the Little Red Book of Chairman Mao. The thing that distinguishes these bibles from other collections of books fundamental to other disciplines—*Bourbaki* to mathematics, the *Oxford English Dictionary* to English literature— is that, once written, they are never changed on the basis of new experiments or research. They are, as a good Baptist would say, "the word of God." (One of the reasons socialism is often considered to be a religion is that it has such holy writ—the writings of Marx and Engels.)

This immutability has to seem unsatisfactory to the scientific mind, but by itself it does not make such bibles demonstrably wrong. The remarkable thing in the prophetic writings of different faiths is not the diversity but the similarity of so many of the revelations. Mystics may be listening to a noisy channel, but if there is a message sent it seems to be consistent.

WESTERN RELIGION

The two primary concerns of all great religions are the relationship of man to God and the relationship of man to man. The first is a theological concern and the second is what we call moral. The most striking difference between Eastern and Western religions is their different emphasis on these two aspects: Eastern religions tend to be God-oriented and Western religions to be man-oriented. This may be a function of relative prosperity. Certainly, in the harsh Middle Ages, Christianity was more spiritual and mystical—even more superstitious—than it is today.

It is the moral tone of modern Western religions—the man-to-man thing—that I am interested in and this saves my discussion from being irresponsible. I have to leave the spiritual side of religion to theologians and to contemplatives. It is the moral climate, which ultimately stems from religious beliefs, in which Western business operates.

The great religions of the West are Christianity and Judaism. From the moral point of view (rather than the theological), I am going to lump them together as the single Western religion. This may be considered heresy by my Christian friends and shocking to my Jewish friends, but it is a useful simplification and at least has the virtue of eliminating the clumsy adjective "Judeo-Christian" from the text.

OUTWARD, VISIBLE SIGNS

The practices of organized religion show man at his best and at his worst, at his most respectable and most ridiculous. The Baptists dunk their people; the Mormons baptize people who have been dead for a hundred years; Catholics burn incense and dress in medieval robes; Jews blow on rams' horns. In some denominations people are "born again" and babble in unknown tongues and pound bibles and their chests. As any good Catholic would say, these are only the "outward signs of inward spiritual grace." Other outward signs have left us a heritage of beauty and terror.

There is beauty in religious artifacts: in the cathedrals of Cologne and Ely and Liverpool and Washington; in the codices and manuscripts of medieval scribes, and above all in sacred music. There is unworldly beauty in the triumph of Bach played on a great organ, in the voices of a boys' choir at evensong, in the chanting of a cantor. There is beauty also in the spoken word; in the liturgy of an Elizabethan service, in the thundering of a Southern black preacher, even in the wheezing of an English vicar over a somnambulant congregation in an old stone church at twilight. These are the good sounds, but there are terrible sounds too that intrude over the years like the shrilling of the oboe against the sweetness of violins: the screams of martyrs from the Circus Maximus, from the Crusades, from Oxford and Seville, from Auschwitz and Dachau, from Rhodesia.

What has all this goodness and badness, this agony and ecstasy, got to do with the Western business establishment? In my opinion, a great deal. From the still unresolved battle between the children of the light and the children of darkness, from hundreds of denominations and filtered through all sorts of mystical monkey business, there comes a simple message. This message is that people, individual people, are important—not because they are rich or powerful or talented but because they are *people,* and so they deserve respect and consideration.[1] This is the basis of Western morality; this is the shaper of the social climate in which business operates.

MORALITY

The moral climate of society is so pervasive, so much a part of us, that we are unconscious of its influence—we take it for granted. Consider a couple of examples.

Read objectively, the economic world proposed by Adam Smith was a prescription for a hell on earth (socialists take note)— the unbridled striving of man against man for personal gain. Smith was not an evil man, he was no Machiavelli, he had no intention to promote purgatory. He was writing as one "decent" man to another. He safely assumed that his readers were steeped in the concepts of honor and fair play and that competitive activity would be modified by respect for people. He was assuming the morality of Western religious tradition.

During World War II, the U.S. Air Force flew planes out of Kunming to help the Chinese in their battle against the Japanese

[1]There is another message: that things of *this* world are not really important: a message that might scuttle the free enterprise system if it were part of our culture. Fortunately, it is usually reserved for Sunday.

invaders. My brother was one of the flyers who took off from Kunming without adequate ground support or weather predictions. Planes were often lost or ran out of fuel and had to make forced landings in Chinese territory. This was a bonanza for the local entrepreneurs (warlords). It enabled them to pick up the survivors as valuable assets and ransom them off to the highest bidder: to the Americans, to the Japanese, or to another warlord who thought he could make a better deal. To us this seems shocking, but only because we are steeped in our own morality—in the idea that some things are "done" and others are "not done." To the locals it would have been the height of folly to let such a golden opportunity pass.

The failure of the United Nations as an effective international force may be due to the refusal of its Western authors to recognize the different moral codes of peoples. In adopting a "they're just like us" approach, they reached the same level of sophistication as the GI who is sure of the love of his foreign bride when she is looking only for a ticket to the States. The people of other countries are not necessarily bad or selfish, but their loyalties are to family, tribe, and possibly to nation. The idea of a brotherhood of man is as ludicrous to them as the doctrine of transmigration of souls is to us. The Western nations, the United States in particular, are considered fair game to be fleeced by public abuse, private flattery, or any other ruse. We should pay as much heed to moral tradition as to political and economic systems when dealing with other countries or when setting an immigration policy.

In theory at least, religion is not the only route to an accepted moral standard. Two other ways are through law and through the application of a philosophical system.

The use of law as the arbiter of morals has drawbacks—for one thing, laws change. To determine proper behavior a person would have to check to see what was acceptable today. Another problem is that laws are made by men and that evil or foolish men will make evil or foolish laws. (From what I have seen of lawyers, I have no desire to put my morality in their hands.)

A pillar of Western religion is that there is a "world order," that some things are forever right or wrong independent of legal statutes. Law, then, is the servant of eternal truth; its duty is to codify what is already accepted as proper.[2] The use of law as the implementor of eternal truth is neither defensible nor logical, but it is the tradition of Western nations. It is implied in the United States Constitution.

A more intellectual approach to the morality problem is to derive a philosophical model of human behavior based on a priority list to maximize the share of good things for most people. This is the socialist approach. Plato's *Republic* was an attempt in this direction. The arguments against the philosophical approach (from the religious point of view) are the same as those against the legalistic approach. Standards of behavior would be set by people and people are fallible and mutable. In the absence of a religious tradition, the philosophical (or ideological) approach is probably the only alternative. The law would then be written to support the latest morality model.

If business wants to operate in a religion-oriented moral climate, it had better support organized religion. Before we get down to the ways and means of support, we need to take a look at organized religion today.

The Denominations

The three great divisions of Western religion are Catholic,[3] Protestant, and Jewish. Jews and Protestants are further divided into denominations, while the Catholics manage to keep their differences within the family. While the deviations in Jewish

[2]On the other hand, to go back to ancient holy writ for laws and punishments—stoning, stripes, cutting off of hands—seems to me the worst form of regression.

[3]I use the term in its popular sense. Properly, there are three divisions of Catholicism: Roman, Greek Orthodox, and Anglican (Episcopalian), but for most people "Catholic" means Roman Catholic and this is the way I use the word.

practices are as great as those among Protestant denominations, this is not important to our story. Having been tempered by centuries of persecution, all Jews—to outsiders at least—present a united front in important policies such as their support of Israel. It is the great Protestant denominations, and the work ethic that has been blamed on them, which are interesting.

As Weber points out,[4] the attitudes and ethics of the Reformation did promote the capitalistic system. Our own more recent work ethnic in the United States was probably more a response to opportunity and a condition of survival than the result of religious teaching. Our early preachers did extol the virtues of work, but this may have been more a reflection of the · inclinations of the congregations than a deliberate policy. A lot of preaching is just that—telling people what they want to hear. Life on the frontier was hard and men and women had to work. Protestantism (particularly Methodism) was the religion of the frontier.

Back East, the financiers and the wheeler-dealers were also working hard—they had a whole new country to exploit. These men were mostly Protestants (the influx of Jews and Catholics came later) and their ministers had *better* tell them their efforts were sanctified.

Whatever its inspiration, we do have a work ethic in the Western world—the feeling that it is somehow improper to be idle. My wife has a fairly advanced case: she feels guilty when I am not working (then I feel guilty because she feels guilty). But the neurosis is not confined to Protestants. The Japanese, like Datsun, may be the most driven. Superannuated Japanese businessmen will carry their dispatch cases and sit in the park rather than lose face with their neighbors.

The work ethic today is a social and economic rather than a religious phenomenon. It will exist wherever workers can keep a portion of their earnings or wherever the alternative is ruin, as it

[4]Max Weber, *The Protestant Ethic and the Spirit of Capitalism,* trans. by Talcott Parsons, rev. ed.; New York: Scribner's, 1977. Translation of Weber's "Die Protestantische Ethik und der Geist des Kapitalismus" (1904, 1905).

was on the frontier. With the development of the country and the rise of the welfare society these motivations are losing their impact. To expect the famed Protestant work ethic to smooth labor relations today and to guarantee craftsmanship is a vain hope.

While the Protestant work ethic is pretty much of a myth,[5] the great denominations do affect our private and public establishments through individuals: through the religious affiliations of the leaders and followers. In the upper levels of most American organizations Protestant church membership is the norm; it is another bond that ties people together. While the particular denomination does matter, the main thing is to have a "P" on one's dog tag. If a few of the managers do turn out to be Jewish or Catholic, they are usually accepted once the majority decide they are good old boys and, really, "just like us."

In the Protestant pecking order in America, the Episcopal (Anglican) church is tops. That it outshines larger and richer denominations like the Methodist and the Presbyterian is due to its history and to its tolerant (some would say feeble) doctrines. For a rather small denomination, the Episcopal church has provided an extraordinary number of political, business, and social leaders in our country. (Episcopalians and Jews do make up an overwhelming part of the "super intellectuals" discussed in Chapter 9.) This preeminence exists not because of any particular virtues of Episcopalians but because the English were here first with the most—and because of the social traditions of the church. The permissive and liberal (in the true sense) stance of the Anglican church is unlikely to offend others. Episcopalians, like Jews, place a high value on learning and teaching, which helps them maintain their position.

The great faith that *should* be a businessman's or a politician's home is Presbyterianism. (America's closest answer to Westminster Abbey is the Washington Cathedral—Episcopal—but the so-called Church of the Presidents near the capitol is Presbyterian.) To an

---

[5]Or, as Weber said better, "The idea of duty in one's calling prowls about in our lives like the ghost of dead religious beliefs." *The Protestant Ethic*, op. cit.

outsider, the Presbyterian church seems grim—exemplified by St. Giles Cathedral, massive and gray, brooding over the Royal Mile in Edinburgh. Calvin doesn't come through as a good-time Charlie: he seems to have disliked the human race (possibly with good reasons) and supported the mind-numbing doctrine of predestination—that some got it and some ain't.[6] The good news is that success in this life is an indication of election in the next. To a Presbyterian, wealth and prestige are not things to be ashamed of.

Somewhere near the bottom of the pecking order come the Baptists. This is unfair. As the largest Protestant denomination in the United States, the Baptist church probably provides more spiritual solace than any other. Its members are very loyal. While it is gradually shaking off the reputation of being the home of the unlettered and the unwashed, the Baptist church *will* try to tell the rest of us what (not) to do. It blocks the building of breweries and closes sporting houses (*sic transit* Chicken Ranch), for which I guess the rest of us should be grateful. The fact is that many Episcopalians and Methodists feel more at home with Catholics and Jews than with Baptists.

To American Protestants, Catholicism seems a bit standoffish (the church, not the members). We vaguely sense that we are not welcome at Catholic services, that the communicants hold their priests in awe (we usually hire our ministers as preachers or just to do our believing for us), and that they regard other denominations as Johnnies-come-lately. From a practical point of view, the unity of the Catholic church, which is its strength, is also its weakness. It lacks the spirited competition of the Protestant denominations. I guess I am for free enterprise in religion as well as in the economy. A people who accept a single doctrine and religious hierarchy are apt to accept an existing social hierarchy as well. The Catholic states of Central and South America have yet to show the economic enterprise of their religiously unstructured Northern neighbors. I

[6]Characteristically, not rejected by the Episcopalians. See XVII in the Articles of Religion in the Book of Common Prayer.

hope we never have a single established church of any denomination in our country. Power, even religious power, corrupts.

THE POWER OF THE CHURCH

With millions of members, the great denominations might be expected to have great social and political power. Not anymore. The last flexing of religious muscle resulted in prohibition. The current controversy over abortion crosses all sorts of religious and social lines. One reason for this impotence is that religious commitment is now a minority position in the United States[7] (and in England and France and Germany, and even in Italy and Israel). When most people state their religious preference, they are naming the church they don't attend.

There is a notion that church leaders are trying to take over the country. The Pope is the most popular candidate. Rome threatened first through Al Smith and more recently through John Kennedy. A recent book, *The Power of Their Glory* by Kit Konolige,[8] implies that the Episcopal bishops are taking over. A similar book, *Our Crowd* by Stephen Birmingham,[9] showed the Jewish challenge. (Just who the Jewish panjandrums are I don't know; my neighborhood rabbi doesn't either.) Such threats are only fiction. Very few business or political leaders would consider consulting their ministers or priests or rabbis or bishops or the Pope on any other than spiritual matters. Churches today are the creatures of their congregations, not the other way around.

To be devout may be a disadvantage in business or in politics. (Based on the performance of our legislators, church membership does not even seem to lead to personal rectitude.) Too much

[7]Curiously, polls show that most Americans believe in an afterlife. They might be more concerned with their type of accommodations in the next world: something like first class on the QE2 or tourist on a jet—a modern definition of heaven and hell.

[8]New York: Simon & Schuster, 1978.

[9]New York: Harper & Row, 1967.

compassion for others can impede the climb up the business ladder. In government, it may result in a wishy-washy foreign policy. Religion can be used to rationalize indecision. On the other hand, it is nice to be in the position of dealing with someone who considers you to be a brother. "Nice guys finish last."

The real power of the church in Western society, of any church, of all churches, is what I have already stated: that it sets a moral standard; that it provides a sort of consensus conscience for all of us. This power does not come from Episcopal sees; it comes from the thousands of little churches scattered across the land. the minority who support these churches and practice their rites are preserving a heritage. The rest of us are what Gwen Raverat (a nonbeliever) called "Christian parasites."[10]

THE CHURCHES

It is in the running and supporting of individual churches that the soldiers of capitalism can help the cause. All churches and temples have three types of members: professionals (ministers, rabbis, and priests), activists, and churchgoers. Churchgoers are the foundation: without someone in the pews the professionals wouldn't have jobs and the activists wouldn't have a place in which to be active.

People go to church for different reasons: out of religious conviction, to be amused, because it is the thing to do, for political expediency, for the sake of the children, or just because it affords them an opportunity, at least once a week, to do something that nobody can say is not right. A lot of business employees go to church—it seems to go with the way of life they are striving for. For whatever reasons people do go to church and support the religious establishment, not without some personal anguish at the time of the annual canvass.

There are two types of lay activities: spiritual and temporal (not

[10]G. Raverat, *Period Piece,* New York: Norton, 1953, p. 189.

necessarily exclusive categories). In any church the spiritual activists are a minority. These people attend prayer and *chavurah* meetings and study biblical and other religious writings for their own spiritual development. In the long run, these are the people who, like the religious orders in Catholicism, keep the faith and preserve the church. In the short run, it is the temporal activists who solve the problems and keep the church doors open.

All churches have two types of management, clerical and lay, which are usually engaged in a gentlemanly power struggle. There are the secular governing bodies—vestry, elders, board of directors—on the one hand and the religious professionals on the other. In those denominations where the secular body selects the spiritual leader, it is in a strong position and the church is apt to have a more secular, businesslike tone. This is the case in most Protestant churches. (The great exception used to be the Methodist church, in which the bishop appointed the pastors. Today, in this and other respects, the Methodists are becoming more like "low church" Episcopalians.) Catholic laymen do not have such power and this helps preserve the status of the clergy.

For most churchgoers, the higher working of the church establishment—at the diocese or synod level, for example—seems far removed. In fact there is often an uneasy feeling that those "people in New York" don't know what is going on. It is the actions of the clergy and the decisions of the local secular governing bodies that keep people coming to church.

BUSINESS AND CHURCHES

Businessmen support churches; for the most part businesses do not. In a multidenominational society corporate support would be hard to explain to the shareholders. The idea of supporting all Western religion as a "good thing" (as business does education) would be even harder to explain.

In the past, rich industrialists have made munificent gifts to the religious establishment: the Rockefeller chapel, the Princeton chapel, the Riverside Church in New York, which was specified to be nondenominational and whose mission is to promote Western morality. Today in a more egalitarian world with a graduated income tax, more support has to come in small doses from middle class people contributing to their own churches. This support is of two kinds: financial and organizational.

As I have already remarked, businessmen do tend to be churchgoers and to make annual pledges. What may be as important, business people fill a large number of the seats on church governing bodies. They bring their management, and legal, and financial talents to keep religious institutions running. This is a good deal for all parties. The churches get professional management help and the businessmen, who like nothing better than a busman's holiday, get to discharge their religious duties by running another organization.

Business management of our churches, particularly of our Protestant churches, does raise problems from a spiritual point of view. The vestry may be more interested in bricks and mortar and in numbers than in the faith. The rector may feel constrained in his sermons to refer to wealth as a "divine trust" rather than as an awful responsibility. Given the commitment and inclinations of most churchgoers, this pragmatic emphasis is probably necessary to keep them coming.

As long as there is a dedicated band of spiritual activists in the congregation and the preacher can get at least equal time to put his own message across, a church can probably escape the danger of turning into a debating society or into a nice place to go that has bowling alleys and a good softball team. With support from the business community and from others, churches will continue to broadcast its moral messages: people are worthy of respect; there is such a thing as being decent; some things are done and some things are not done. The next step from sanctity of the individual is sanctity of property. This is the only moral climate in which the free enterprise system can continue to operate as a humane and constructive force. In fact, it is the only climate in which it will be allowed to continue at all.

In a democracy, the voters will not long permit an amoral, self-seeking, competitive economy. The only real alternative to a working morality based on religious teaching is one based on socialist ideology and implemented by new laws and by repression.

15

EDUCATION

An eager coed from Chicago
Earned thirteen degrees in a row.
She learned how to speak
In both Russian and Greek,
But she never did learn to say "no."

WHEREAS RELIGIOUS tradition influences the long-range moral tone of a nation, its educational tradition has a more immediate effect. As a rule, a country gets the schooling system it deserves. When things are running smoothly, the educational establishment complements the structure, goals, and priorities of the "real world." An effective school system is a mirror of society. If its image is faulty, if social mores or national missions change without a corresponding change in the schools, there are tensions and problems.

The obvious ties between the business world and the educational establishment are at higher levels—college and graduate school—but because of the intimate relationship between business and society we cannot completely ignore the primary and secondary levels of schooling. Before getting on to the American scene, let us take a brief look at a bit of English history for an insight into the society–schooling relationship.

THE ENGLISH EXAMPLE

From the days of Empire to at least World War II, the English school system was set up on class lines: its purpose was to provide leaders for the nation and for the Empire. Middle and upper class people sent their children (males particularly) to public (preparatory) schools, which were precisely ranked in prestige. The graduates of the top-ranked schools went to the top universities— Oxford and Cambridge ("Oxbridge")—and from there to run the nation and the Empire.

The "old school tie" was an important and valuable status symbol—not the college tie but the Eton, Harrow, or Winchester tie. This made sense. All sorts of bounders, colonials, even Americans got into Oxford and Cambridge, but the public schools stayed pure. Even today, and even in the Labour party, English leaders tend to be Eton-Oxford or Harrow-Cambridge. (The particular college at Oxbridge is also important, but the subject is too technical to go into here.)

In those days there *was* education for the children of the poor but it tended to be limited, patronizing, and taught by women. My mother taught in such schools: the feeling of the teachers really was that they were doing a nice thing. Occasionally, a bright "grammar school" student would beat the system and win a scholarship to Oxford or Cambridge. Once he was there, the British sense of fair play allowed him to be accepted as middle class.

The curriculum and customs of the English public schools were designed to create leaders. The internal school hierarchy—fags, prefects, student government—was well designed to create graduates who would assume perquisites and responsibilities as a natural right. It was a tough monastic life.[1] The curriculum, which emphasized Latin and Greek, was well suited to the purpose—not to help solve the financial problems of Poona but to discipline future leaders and give them an exclusive common heritage and, if necessary, a common language.

There seems to have been three types of students at Oxford and Cambridge in those days: (1) young gentlemen who were putting in three years of social training before entering London club life or returning to huntin' and shootin' in the counties; (2) serious students who were the intellectuals of their time and who would enter the arts or the government or even business; and (3) true intellectuals who would preserve the scholastic traditions of the universities. Teaching methods were informal enough to accommodate all three types. The dedicated scholars often stayed for the rest of their lives, moving from rank to rank: junior fellow, senior fellow, don, tutor, and so on. They formed the hard core that made these universities the envy of the world.[2]

This was a fine system for Victorian England. As the empire crumbled and Fabian ideas moved in, it became a liability. The new ethic, promoted by the socialists and by democratic thinkers from across the Atlantic, demanded that everyone have a fair shot at a decent education. This raised the problems of space, financing, and student selection—problems that are still not completely solved. In a typically English compromise, the old apparatus was retained and a new one added—new schools and new ("red brick") universities.

[1]How the boys and girls got together socially is something of a mystery. I guess some things like sex cannot be suppressed.

[2]Fiction gives the truest pictures of the students of those years. Almost any of the books by P(elham) G(renville) Wodehouse will take care of the cloth-headed contingent. *A Dance to the Music of Time* by Anthony Powell (4 vols.; Boston: Little, Brown, 1963–1976) deals with the intellectuals. The *Strangers and Brothers* series by C. P. Snow (New York: Scribner's, 1940–1970) documents the academic world.

(Some fine old ones had been around for a long time: Edinburgh, Dublin, Sheffield, Trinity.) A meritorious selection system was set up that involved such horrors (for the students and their parents) as "O-level" and "11's-plus" tests.[3] This is a fair mirror of the new society: it preserves a class system but permits mobility.

As the English educational system got out of phase with society, the students at the great universities suffered the worst strains. With the old order crumbling, their own place in the scheme of things became uncertain. Their reaction was often to reject the establishment. In the 1920s and 1930s many of them turned to the new fascism or to Russia. Some became the communists who later infiltrated the British government. When a nation's school system gets out of touch with society, bad things happen.

OTHER COUNTRIES

Evelyn Waugh said that a civilized country is one that has decent hotels. A better definition might be that it is one that has a good educational system. Remarkably few nations would qualify; offhand it is difficult to name a dozen outside of Europe. If we omit those countries over which the British flag once flew, the list is even shorter. A large part of the world, most of the United Nations members, are educational parasites that send their people abroad for higher education. It is a tremendous cultural asset for a country to have a first-class school system. Unfortunately, the building of such a structure requires a major investment in money, people, and tradition—an investment that is hard to recoup in balance of trade.

Writing from a limited knowledge base, I will consider only a few other countries that have influenced the American educational system or that compete with it.

Up to World War II, the German school system was a good

[3]Achievement tests given at certain ages to determine the academic career paths of students.

mirror of German society. It was structured and militaristic at the lower levels and hierarchical at the top. German professors were tin gods; they were also very good. The emphasis and the greatest achievements were in the sciences and mathematics. American students were parasites on the German universities until the 1930s, when the best of Germany's scholars came here as refugees and gave our higher-education system a boost. German education is still excellent; it probably always will be. Education is a cultural thing.

After the English and German, we probably owe the most to the French schools and scholarship. The French system is traditionally priest-ridden at the lower levels and elitist at the upper levels. It seems an untidy establishment to outsiders but it is rugged: it has survived revolution, occupation by invaders, and riots. It has turned out leading scholars. Like England, France has broadened its higher education since World War II but the system remains elitist. As I mentioned earlier, high-ranking government and business people are recruited almost exclusively from the *grandes écoles*.

The Japanese educational establishment has exploded in recent years. It is a bit like the English and French in that entry to the "right" schools is highly competitive and is based on tests. The competition for entrance into the best primary schools is so intense that six-year-old children have special tutors. Education is more than respected; it is revered. When a student applies to an important school (of medicine, for example), it is helpful if his family makes a handsome (nonrefundable) gift to the institution. The stress on parents and children must be severe—only a highly disciplined society could put up with it—but the system works. In fact, the Japanese now consider foreign schools inferior to their own. They used to send students to our prestigious business schools but no more; they think their own are better. They may be right.

AMERICA—LOWER LEVELS
When I went to grade and high school, public education in most of the United States still had a frontier tradition. This is a

curious statement from someone who grew up in a big city (Chicago), but it is true. In those days when people moved into a residential area they knew which school their children would attend. Where I lived it was Arlington Grade School and Morgan Park High. Away from the distant East, families sent their children to public schools, for better or worse. (The exceptions were some rich eccentrics, who often sent their sons to military school, and some religious denominations, which had their own schools.) The teachers were teachers and not candidates for administrative jobs; most of them were female and single. Discipline was absolute; we assumed that we would be struck dead if we talked back. Our principals were eight feet tall. They didn't actually beat us—not in my schools—but a note home did the job as well.

Looking back, I would say that the scholarship in those schools was mixed, probably better than we deserved and better than in most of our schools today. The emphasis was on basics; curiously, foreign languages (particularly Latin) were considered basic. Not many frills. We learned to study and we learned discipline. As only a fraction of the pupils went on to college, the goal was a high school diploma.

This pattern of primary and secondary schooling continued until after World War II, when it was shattered both from within and from without: from within by new theories of teaching and from without by forces requiring the schools to take on new sociological roles.

Teachers are now "educators" who are as concerned with the psychology of the students as with their learning. This puts an unfair burden on children. Young people are remarkable learning machines; it is a crime to have them waste their early years "interfacing" when they could be learning so much so easily. The new approach is good for the teachers: it encourages "professionalism." Their goal now is to get out of the classroom and into more important (and better-paid) jobs, such as counseling and administration. Every teacher is now expected to get a master's degree—in education, not in his or her own discipline. In our present school system the classroom teacher is the "lowest-ranking second lieutenant." A lot of them deserve combat pay.

The most violent upheavals came from the outside. Our intellectuals became concerned that black schoolchildren—who until then had been largely invisible in their own schools—were not getting a decent education. True. The accepted solution was not to improve the schools but to mix the races—to integrate. That this is a non sequitur and insulting to blacks doesn't count. The mixing is done by massive movement of school populations; the neighborhood school concept is dead.

It is hard to say which race was hurt more by integration. I, and my daughter, watched it scuttle the academic level of her high school. There *was* goodwill on the part of the white kids (and probably also on the part of the blacks), but the impact was devastating. The black kids found themselves at an academic disadvantage in a new milieu where the incumbents spoke differently, seemed snooty, and were threatening. The white kids found the newcomers to be backward academically, to use foul language (when they could understand), to be bigger and more sexually mature, and to be threatening. It was a bad year.[4]

The results of all this social engineering was predictable. From a democratic, open, and reasonably good school system (for whites) we are moving toward a class system as parents, black and white, who can afford it send their children to private schools. More and more, public schools are becoming time-serving institutions where poor children pass the most critical years of their lives under teachers who want to get out of the classroom. This is bad for society. This is bad for business.

I am not against mixing the races, but I think it should occur in a natural, relaxed atmosphere, not under compulsion or to fill

[4]For a report on the impact of these theories on higher education, see Theodore Gross, *Academic Turmoil: The Reality and the Promise of Open Education*, Garden City, N.Y.: Doubleday–Anchor, 1980.

quotas. Rather than forcing unnatural situations on our children, our social scientists might do better to study basic problems.

It is a paradigm[5] of modern anthropological theory that the capabilities of all races are identical. As Marvin Harris says, "If Hottentot babies were to be substituted at birth for English babies, their average cultural performance would not differ in any significant fashion. . . ."[6] This is a proposition that any observant ten-year-old might contest but that an academician can dispute only at his peril. When Arthur Jensen and William Shockley questioned this theory in a paper analyzing intelligence test results, they created an outcry and student protests.[7] *Scientific American* magazine felt constrained to offer a rebuttal in its lead or "editorial" article in October, 1970, and concluded that "no good case can be made for such studies on either scientific or practical grounds."[8] (*Sports Illustrated* was braver: in its January 18, 1971, issue it analyzed the anatomical superiority of black sprinters.)

This "just like us" attitude can have ludicrous manifestations. I asked my secretary one day to describe for me another department head I was going to meet. She went into great detail, which raised a question in my mind. "Is he black?" "Why, yes, come to think of it, he is."

I think we should honestly face up to the racial differences in our fellow citizens. I don't think we have to be afraid of dividing our society into identifiable "alphas" and "gammas." When blacks *have* had a shot at something approaching fair competition—in sports and in entertainment—they have been well able to take care of themselves. To understand someone is the first step to liking and respect. To judge a person by how well he fits the WASP image is the most snobbish form of racism.

[5]As the word is used by Thomas Kuhn, *The Structure of Scientific Revolutions*, Chicago: University of Chicago Press, 1970.

[6]*The Rise of Anthropological Theory*, New York: Crowell, 1968, p. 132.

[7]*Harvard Educational Review*, Winter, 1969.

[8]Walter F. Bodmer and Luigi Luca Cavalli-Sforza, "Intelligence and Race," *Scientific American*, October, 1970.

Our primary and secondary school system is in trouble. Its ills will not be cured by more money and more administrators, as our intellectuals suggest. The cure has to be in the classroom and in social tolerance.

AMERICA—HIGHER LEVELS

Our higher-education system is very good and very bad. It turns out Nobel prizewinners and graduates who are barely literate. Our educational establishment is strained by competing forces— private (elitist) versus public schooling: the idea that a diploma represents real learning versus the concept that everyone is entitled to a college degree; the battle between learning for its own sake and learning to do a job. These strains and conflicts mirror the strains in our society—and in the business world.

A problem of every personnel department is that in order to evaluate university graduates, it has to develop a confidential list of reliable schools. "We get good computer science people from Tech." This makes it tough for the student who goes to the wrong school. The academic community does not police its own work: the job is almost impossible in the face of egalitarian theory.

In those states where any high school graduate has entry into state universities, the first college year is wasted weeding our those who should not have matriculated. When there is social and political pressure not only to have the students "get through" but also to get decent grades, it is hard to maintain high standards. In some schools and in some disciplines, the granting of a Ph.D. really does require that the student make a significant contribution to his field. This can take years of dedicated and lonely effort. In other fields (particularly in education) the degree is a certificate of time served.[9]

---

[9]This brings up Meyer's inverse law: "The longer the title the more trivial the dissertation." My favorite Ph.D. thesis is *An Identification of Teaching Competencies for Teacher Coordinators of Cooperative Office Education When the Background*

Another problem is the proper use of educational plants: whether they should be used to maintain and further scholarship or should serve as high-level trade schools. The stakes are high: whether it is more important to preserve for our descendants an efficient, functional society or a humane, civilized one. It is pretty obvious that the bright accounting (or even medical) graduate is unlikely to make a lasting contribution to Western culture. It is just as obvious that a bright graduate in fine arts or philology is probably going to have trouble making a living.

The pragmatic, or philistine, trend of our curricula is accelerated by the proliferation of new departments, such as aviation, industrial arts, mechanized agriculture, and radio-television-films. These are (possibly high-level) career training departments.

Another trend is presenting courses *about* subjects instead of the subjects themselves. The field of education has been most prolific in this sort of offering (which makes work for educators). The average graduate in education has survived more hours learning *how* to teach than learning the subject to be taught.[10] (Private schools and colleges rarely ask for any education courses for their teachers.)

That our whole school system has not been converted to high-level career training and to teaching people how to teach people how to teach people is due to the perversity of some students (who *will* study Akkadian or Byzantine art); to the humanities departments that soldier on; and to the small liberal arts colleges that promote the value of a liberal education when they aren't out hustling for money.

Factors of Secondary Classroom Experience, Employment Experience in Business / Industry, and Tenured/Nontenured Status Are Considered. The mathematician Fredholm's paper, which *did* revolutionize the theory of integral equations, was called *Sur une classe d'équations fonctionnelles*.

[10]For a regional report see an article by Gene Lyons in *Texas Monthly,* September, 1979.

GRADES

The grade fetish in American education has a debilitatiog effect on our society—it tends to keep us academic adolescents. I believe in reported grades (A, B, C, or 4, 3, 2) in elementary school if only as a feedback for parents. They are less important in undergraduate years and an atavism in graduate school, where the atmosphere should be that of a community of scholars—dedicated teachers and students—and not an immature striving for a "four-point average."

The middle class American spends so many years of his life in a classroom environment that he is in danger of losing sight of the true route to learning—personal reading, study, and experimentation. It is amazing what fatuous crap mature businessmen will swallow if it is presented to them in a comforting classroom environment—particularly if the teacher is a "Ph.D." The glue that holds this liturgy together is the grade system.

Report cards and grades have an almost mystical significance. Parents brag that little Glucose is maintaining a 3.5 average, as though this had some special virtue. The impact on the student is traumatic. For at least 16 years of his life he gets regular reports telling him that he is doing well (or poorly). For many students this is their only prop and reassurance—proof that they are smart and worthwhile and that, eventually, the world is going to owe them a living. They can become addicted to these regular "fixes."

After graduation, withdrawal symptoms can be severe. Many corporations set up a regular review and evaluation system to help their people phase out.[11] The civil service does the same thing, and even the Army has regular reviews for its officers (meaningless, since only "superior" is acceptable). A lot of grown people pay good money to return to school—to get back to the womb, back to a supportive classroom environment and to reassuring grades—when a little common sense would tell them they could spend their time better in a library.

[11]This doesn't always work well. See *HIM*, Chapter 2.

This classroom ritual and grade dependence is mostly an American disease. The great English universities use a tutor system that gives the student freedom to go to lectures or not and to pursue an academic goal. An unfortunate result of our system is to enhance the status of our professors—the priests of the academic liturgy. This may be the reason our government so often turns to academics, who may have had no practical experience, when it is in trouble. The English would be much less likely to look for help from this quarter. (Keynes was an exception, but then Keynes *was* an exception.)

BUSINESS SCHOOLS

Business schools, America's gift to the academic world, are designed to turn out masters of business administration (MBAs) who can move smoothly into the business world and make a lot of money. Business schools are largely the creatures of, and are supported by, the business community. They are high-class trade schools.

Consider the following breakdown of courses offered by one of our best business schools:[12]

Accounting	6
Economics	11
Finance	15
Government (regulation)	9
Industrial relations	7
Law	2
Management	7
Management science	15
Marketing	20
Mathematics and computing	4

[12]See *HIM*, appendix to Chapter 11.

Organization	3
Personnel	5
Special (hospital management)	6
Statistics	8

Don't read too much into these data; there is no reason to get carried away making statistical tests. I made selections only by course title, not by content. I know nothing of the number of students who take them. What is significant is the categories that are not represented:

Literature	0
Political science	0
History	0
Anthropology (in personnel?)	0
Psychology (in personnel?)	0
Philosophy	0

An unkind liberal arts professor might say that these bright business students spend two years in a cultural vacuum. This is not quite fair: the students do bring scholastic baggage with them, and what they do on their own time is their own business. To an outsider it might seem scary that our future business leaders, who will have so much control over shaping our national character and destiny, are given a trade school education.

Has the century-long influx of highly trained specialists into the business world (Wharton was founded in 1881) been good for American business or, for that matter, for our way of life? It is hard to say. Certainly our nation has prospered, but how much of this was due to abundant natural resources, space, and technology and how much was due to good business management? Now that we are, for the first time, facing effective foreign competition it seems that the strength of the United States is in nonbusiness areas—farming and technology—and its weaknesses are in management and finance. Our managers have let our industrial efficiency (productivity) falter to the point where we have trouble competing in certain industries like steelmaking and automobile manufacturing even with the advantages of compact marketing areas and indigenous resources.

It is not my purpose to run down business schools: I have known too many competent, public-spirited graduates to want to do that. My point is that our business schools may be getting out of phase with the spirit of our nation and with its responsibilities. Fifty years ago our economy may have been best served by training leaders to develop our resources and accumulate wealth. Today it may be more important to consider the political and social role of the United States on the world stage. A school system that does not mirror the needs of society is in trouble.

BUSINESS AND UNIVERSITIES

There is a symbiosis between business and the higher-education establishment. One of the techniques a chamber of commerce uses to attract industry is to brag about local schools.

It is good for a university to be near an industrial complex: near a major source of financial support and, more important, near a thriving community that will help it recruit and keep good faculty. Not only business school professors but engineers, sociologists, and even English teachers find support and inspiration from a busy community. There are only a few "ivory tower" types who want to get away from it all. Most college teachers have an almost pathetic desire to be involved in the "real world," and business provides the easiest entry.

Business needs available educational institutions as a source of support for the morale of its employees; as convenient, prestigious places to train people; and as a source of specialized technical assistance.

The classroom dependence of many employees may be so strong that, for practical or psychological reasons, they do not want to work in an isolated location where they cannot continue their schooling. It is convenient for a corporation to enroll its people in short courses at a local school. The expense is less and the local college is very willing to work with management to tailor courses to special needs.

This business–academic relationship is usually a positive factor in our society. It can become negative if business is too interfering—academic freedom can be forfeited not only to government regulations but also to pragmatism. Business tends to be concerned with, and to support, only those disciplines that it considers to have practical value: business, engineering, accounting, law.

Business hires people who have career-oriented rather than liberal arts degrees. This can make for tension in academic faculties where the "real world" professors have access to both business and government support while the humanities, or "ivory tower," professors have to struggle along on their base pay.

The concept that our universities are battlegrounds of ideas—between socialist and capitalist ideologies, for example—does not seem to have been appreciated by the business community. That business does have a stake in the whole intellectual world should be obvious since the uprisings of the 1960s, the almost daily reports of student unrest in other countries, and the holding of hostages by Iranian "students." The actors in these dramas are not usually engineering or business school students.

BUSINESS SUPPORT

Business supports education through both individual contracts and across-the-board donations.

I have the annual report (a business touch) of Washington University in St. Louis on my desk. Washington University may not have the prestige of Princeton, but it is one of our best private universities. The section in the report on financial conditions is illuminating. Government support for the year was over

$49 million; private support was over $16 million; tuition was some $32 million. Our private schools are not as private as they might be!

Of the private gifts, grants, and bequests, business corporations provided 21 percent, second only to alumni gifts of 23 percent. This does not include consulting fees paid by business or the support of short courses. Alumni giving is augmented by corporate generosity. My old company will put up three dollars for every one an employee (even a retired employee) contributes to an educational institution of his choice. Such handouts are rarely questioned by shareholders or by corporate controllers. Businessmen see higher education, like motherhood and God, as a good thing, and they contribute.

Historically, the support of higher education by rich businessmen is remarkable. The names of our private universities read like a "who's who" of our industrialists: Duke, Carnegie, Rice, Stanford (the original dedication was "to the glory of Leland Stanford and God"). The names of the buildings on our campuses pretty well completes the list of our business leaders.[13]

Whether business and businessmen get their money's worth for all this generosity is a good question. There has to be frustration in the board room when students denounce the business establishment in foul language. Fear of seeing business support dry up does give college administrators incentive to cool the uprisings. What is true is that the public owes a debt to the business community and to its leaders.

[13]Collecting the names on the façades of our schools is almost as much fun as collecting American town names (Bugtussle, Texas; Waterproof, Louisiana). My favorite is the Alfred E. Packer Grill at the University of Colorado. Packer was the only American ever convicted of cannibalism.

16

ART

LOOK FOR a billboard in your town, sponsored by the local chamber of commerce, with a message something like this: "Art is good business. Support the Mudsville Symphony Orchestra." Overlooking the fact that the advice may be a non sequitur (depending on the quality of the local musicians) and that this is a screaming case of the medium not being the message, there is food here for thought. Is art good business? Should business support the fine arts? The answers to these questions are yes and it does.

CORPORATE SUPPORT

Corporations support the arts casually, as good members of the community (check the sponsorship list in the back of your little theater or symphony program); as investors, for a rate of return; and finally for prestige and image. Texaco Company, which is supposed to have the tender corporate heart of a mother-in-law, has supported the broadcasts of the Metropolitan Opera since the days of radio. Memories of my youth are haunted by the shrieking over the Philco on Saturday afternoons of sopranos in obvious pain.

Some companies have discovered that art pieces can provide a fantastic "paper" rate of return, and they clutter the lobbies of their corporate homes with statuary and their executive offices with paintings. Whether these (often good) investments are ever reflected on the corporate balance sheet I don't know. I don't even know if they are looked at very often after the initial open-house bash. I do know that such purchases help painters and sculptors and art dealers.

Where business really gets its teeth into the art scene is in the big "hardware" items—in buildings and in their furnishings. Most corporate headquarters stand as mute testimony to the fact that creativity is a lonely attribute not shared by committees. Like dictators, building committees go for the big, the tall, and the bizarre. Glass skyscrapers (or steel or copper if these are major products) give cities from Houston to Johannesburg a bad case of the "look-alikes." Old cities with charm are not immune: San Francisco, London, and even Paris are joining the brave new world. I knew a dear old Boston lady who refused to raise her gaze above the level of the façade of the old library after what big business did to Copley Square.

What the building committee starts, the interior designers finish by turning working areas into a mixture of a Ramada Inn lobby, a jungle, and the Chicago World's Fair.[1] How much all this fabric and furnishing supports the arts is hard to say—some of the money must go to real artists.

[1]Designers are as willing as committees to display key products. The walls of the elevators in one mining headquarters carry tons of textured copper sheets up and down every day.

While corporations do support the visual and the performing arts, they are not always good friends of the written word. Business has given us "businessese," to the detriment of the English language and possibly the French language (Franglaise?) and other Western tongues. English also struggles under the burdens of "legalese" and "officialese." The spoken word suffers in business-sponsored television commercials: "More importantly, these blades are 30 percent sharper."

Writers seem to be a hardy lot. They can roll with the punch and even "write down" to the new standards. Perhaps they don't need help. There may come a time when few people remember what good written English (or French, or German, or whatever) was all about.

INDIVIDUAL SUPPORT

Corporations are not the only sponsors listed in the back of your theater program. Most of the supporters are individuals, and a lot of these are business people: top executives and middle managers. Unlike support for other community efforts such as the United Fund (discussed later), which may be given because of a sense of duty, support for art groups is usually voluntary. To have a corporate headquarters move into town is good news for performing artists. They can successfully solicit top management for money, but they will also get unsolicited support.

The really handsome contributions to the arts—visual, performing, and literary—have come from individuals: often from rich industrialists and businessmen. These men and women—Carnegie, Rhodes, Gardener, Rockefeller, Cullen, to name a few—gave because they wanted to make our world a nicer place in which to live rather than to promote free enterprise. But they were (perhaps unconsciously) carrying on an old tradition.

In feudal times it was the nobles and the princes who patronized the arts and the sciences. With the rise of capitalism the new leaders took on this old reponsibility. When capitalism declines, the state takes over. Today we have Lincoln Center; yesterday we had Carnegie Hall.[2] Even the Russian communists recognized this duty. Early in the game they instituted "halls of culture" in their cities and turned palaces and churches into museums to preserve the treasures of the tsars. Just who *does* support the arts in a nation is a fairly accurate indication of who runs the economy.

WHY?

We have seen that religion and education are not only worthy of business support for their own sakes but that they also provide tangible benefits. Can we say the same for the fine arts? Apart from the rising value of the pictures on the board room walls (which will never be sold), why should business support the arts?

There are really three answers to this question. The first was implied in the last section: business supports the arts to wave the flag and to show that its heart is in the right place. If industry, rather than government, is the main cultural force in a community, it demonstrates that even though the capitalist system may be profit-oriented, it still has time for finer things. This helps legitimize business leadership in community affairs. When the government steps in to aid the arts it scores points at least for planned capitalism. When business, or businessmen, provide the support (to build a concert hall or to endow a liberal arts chair, for example), bureaucracy loses twice: in possible prestige and in allowing important money to slip through the IRS (or the Inland Revenue) sieve.

The second reason for industry to support the arts is more practical: business really does need a healthy art community in

---

[2]Governments do not like to retain the names of the original sponsors, but the public is reluctant to change. The Museum of Natural History is still the Field Museum to Chicagoans; the National Art Museum is still the Mellon Gallery to Washingtonians.

order to prosper. The goals of business are to "make" money and to support reasonably affluent employees—the middle class. If the cultural scene is barren, the acquisition of money doesn't make too much sense. An environment without esthetics is a tad mercenary. It invokes a vision of the final act: a desolate world where most of us are deservedly dead and two surviving "gold bugs" are trying to sell each other their gold bricks.

Just as prospective employees may not want to work in a city that does not have a higher-education institution, so they may be reluctant to move to, and raise children in, a cultural desert (or one that does not have parks and zoos, which we may as well include as art forms). For some reason, not explained by sociologists or anthropologists, mathematicians, chemists, and other scientists are often practicing musicians—they want to play in an ensemble. (Mathematicians may be intrigued by the permutations of fugues— but chemists?) A high-technology company that wants to attract and keep technicians had better look to its local orchestra as well as to its fringe benefits.

The final reason for industry to support the arts is straightforward and businesslike: the arts provide an effective medium for advertising.

The philosophy of modern television advertising is a sort of *quid pro quo*. Only if the advertiser provides a minimum level of entertainment will the viewer sit still for the program and ultimately for the commercials. The problem for a serious advertiser and for his agent (unless he is willing to settle for "spot" commercials, which will be shown while the viewer goes for a beer) is to find something that will stay on the air and hold an audience.

Sports have the best track record of viewer loyalty, but they tend to be tied up by "macho" industries like beer, razor blades, and automobile tires. (An exception is Cadillac's traditional sponsoring of the Masters Golf Tournament.) Business has discovered that not all viewers are flat-headed slobs; they will sit still for fine arts, for plays, for music, and for ballet. Texaco has known this for years.

Such high-class television programs give the sponsor an opportunity to establish rapport with the audience: "We will forgo the usual commercial breaks out of respect for the material. So sit back, enjoy the show, and give thanks to IBM (or Prudential, or EXXON)." This approach is particularly effective for institutional advertising. Outfits like the American Gas Association sponsor fine television series. The airways do tend to get a bit cluttered with culture and cuteness around Christmas and Easter, but this sort of advertising really is helping improve the standards of television programming.

Not all cultural promotions are televised; some involve live action, such as festivals, traveling theater groups, and competitions. The idea is to present the sponsoring company in a favorable light, preferably in a way that is popular and that may become a tradition. Braun is a sponsor of the Royal Choral Society in England; Royal Doulton sponsors the Mozart Memorial Prize.

The idea of direct participation in and support of the arts is increasing. It is often a cost-effective way to get people to think well of a company. Big companies can afford to put on a whole show, but smaller companies may get into the act in a more modest way—like buying advertising space on the outfield wall. In England, the Association for Business Sponsorship of the Arts (ABSA) coordinates the contributions of smaller corporations to do worthwhile things. ABSA's goal is to help the arts, but business must consider it a good deal, since contributions are increasing.

The biggest extravaganza of them all was the traveling King Tut exhibition, which was sponsored by industy. It gave a lot of pleasure to a lot of people.

ART AND TOP MANAGEMENT

Top management people often feel a bit uncomfortable in the presence of local artists. For one thing, artists reject the business dress code and tribal mores; they have an offhand attitude toward profits (but not toward money) and they generate feelings of inferiority by their assumption that their goals are higher and more meaningful than those of industry.

If the top man is a "good old boy," his first instinct is to turn this sort of thing over to his public relations people and hope that it isn't going to cost too much and that the stockholders aren't going to get restless.

This is unduly cautious. Business needs the arts and would like to get the artistic community on its side. The arts need business, particulary if they are having trouble getting money from the government. All of us, perhaps especially big business, need to live in a civilized and culturally stimulating world.

17

BUSINESS AND GOVERNMENT

THE TITLE of this chapter makes it sound like a rerun of Chapter 4, "Government and Business," but it isn't. The transposition of words is important. Here I am talking about the battleground, the arena, where business fights the ideological war to keep the forces of regulation and bureaucracy at bay. In Chapter 4 I discussed the necessary and actual role of government in a capitalist society as the moderator and monitor of the business world. This chapter is combat reporting; Chapter 4 was "Eyewitness News" coverage of the doings of an invasion army.

The chief battle sites we are concerned with are legislative chambers and corridors—city halls, county courthouses, state capitals, the whole city of Washington, and even Brussels, the headquarters of the Common Market.[1] The object of the battle is to let the voices of industry be heard wherever laws are made. These voices may be contradictory when one corporation's meat is another corporation's poison, but there are efforts to have whole industries or trades (such as natural gas and nonferrous metals) speak as one. At an even higher level, there are national organizations such as the Business Roundtable in the United States and the Confederation of British Industry in England that speak for all industry (except for those malcontents who drop out).

The persuasion tactics used in the battle are the same as those used in any power play between individuals: parent and child, salesman and client, guy and girl. They are instruction (appeal and reason), flattery (appeal to patriotism or morality), threat, and the promise of reward (excluding bribery, as we stick to legal methods). As far as I know, there are no other approaches. The most rational of these is appeal to reason. "Go to bed, darling; at your age you need all the sleep you can get" seems far more civilized than the alternatives: "Show Daddy what a big girl you are," "If you go now, dear, Mommy will bring you a nice glass of Ovaltine," "Get upstairs you little monster before I beat you to a jelly!"

The main carriers of corporate (and special-interest) messages are lobbyists.

LOBBYING

Lobbyists speak for others, either out of conviction or because they are paid to do so. (John Alden was the first recorded American lobbyist.) It is characteristic of Western governments that citizens have the right to petition their lawmakers, either personally or through agents, if they don't like what is going on. This "basic" right was secured by the British barons from King John (one of the few

[1]"Big Firms Step Up Lobbying in Brussels," *The Wall Street Journal*, July 16, 1980.

meaningful concessions he made) and is documented in the Magna Carta. Starting with the 25-member committee that the barons set up, government doings in Western nations have been subjected, in varying degrees, to the help, bullying, pleading, cosseting, threats, and promises of hordes of lobbyists. Today there are more registered and unregistered lobbyists in Washington than there are elected lawmakers.

Is lobbying a good thing? Does it promote participatory democracy, or does it warp the legislative process in favor of the rich, the well-organized, and the loud-mouthed? Like most human institutions it is both good and bad.[2]

The Good Word

The League of Women Voters describes lobbying as "the art of applying pressure." This is coming on a bit strong! The art of lobbying is more sophisticated than that of selling used cars or collecting bad debts. The good business lobbyist does four things: provides information to lawmakers; helps do staff work for officials (if they let him); reports back to his employers to keep them informed; and, finally, attempts direct influence or persuasion. This last duty is soft sell (we get to the hard sell later). For the most part these activities are beneficial.

A congressman, even with a large and expensive staff to brief him, cannot be an expert in all the areas in which he is expected to make important decisions. If the question concerns merchant shipping, say, the obvious thing to do is to get help from the Maritime Committee.[3] The congressman doesn't have to accept this information at face value; in fact, he should balance it against

[2]Lobbying has inspired a considerable literature. A good example is James Deakin, *The Lobbyists*, Washington, D.C.: Public Affairs, 1966. To me the best concise modern reference is *The Washington Lobby: 1979 Edition*, published by the Congressional Quarterly, Washington, D.C.

[3]I consider trade organizations, special-interest groups, corporate representatives, and unregistered lobbyists as *lobbyists*. The 1946 Lobbying Act is so vague that this is the only reasonable approach in a summary chapter like this.

information from other sources. The important point is that the lawmaker and his staff have ready access to well-presented and factual (if biased) data on almost any subject.

If a congressman has a natural and proper interest in a certain type of industry—automobiles for a Michigan representative, oil for an Oklahoman, for example—he may find it convenient to have industry people work with his staff. This is the best kind of lobbying from the business point of view, and first-class support—legal, economic, engineering—will be willingly provided. This gets industry involved in the lawmaking process, dangerously involved some may say. It is still not illegal and has the redeeming feature that usually—usually—what is good for business *is* good for the country.

The selling by most business lobbyists is low key: often they take a congressman out to eat and talk of anything but business. The goal is for both parties to get to know and respect each other so that the lawmaker will know where to go when he wants help. The registered lobbyist's assets, his stock-in-trade, are friends.

One last plus for lobbying. Every corporation above trivial size must have a listening post in Washington, in state capitals, and even in local legislatures. Lobbyists man these stations.

Before I take up the negative aspects of lobbying, I need to discuss nonbusiness lobbies, because such lobbies are more likely to get out of line.

Nonbusiness Lobbies

There are more nonbusiness lobbies in Washington than industry ones. I would like to leave them out of this business-oriented book but I can't. As far as the public is concerned lobbyists are lobbyists, and the carryings-on of the others reflect on business lobbies, whose goals usually are to promote industry efficiency and prosperity. The proliferation of special-interest lobbies has created a whole new class of people who are ultimately supported by the taxpayers.

Just to list the different types of nonbusiness Washington lobbies is quite a job. Other writers would come up with a different list, but here is mine:

- Labor—supported by unions
- Foreign
- Local government—there is a National Association of Counties and a U.S. Conference of Mayors
- Farming
- Professional—the American Medical Association is the classic
- Environmental
- Consumer
- Education
- Veterans—Legion, VFW, and so on
- Civil rights
- Women's rights
- Other special-interest groups and whatever I forgot

The old-fashioned aim of these lobbying groups is to get favors and money (usually money) from the federal government at the expense of less organized citizens and to promote favorable legislation. There is now a brighter goal: to invoke the establishment of a new regulatory agency (like the EPA) or even—total victory!—a new cabinet department. The education lobby did it.

While business lobbies usually try to persuade by providing information and by appealing to reason, the basic tool of other lobbies is arm twisting, or what I call in the next section indirect lobbying. Before discussing the *modus operandi* (MO) of legislator baiting, I had better say something about special-interest or citizen action lobbies, which are becoming increasingly popular.

Back in the 1930s, one of my college friends had an idea that was way ahead of its time. He wanted to have thousands of buttons made (this was before the age of the bumper sticker) that simply said "A Home for the Jews." He figured he would have it made. Zionists would buy and wear the buttons proudly while less noble souls who wanted to get rid of Jews would wear them aggressively. As far as I know, there was no prejudice behind my friend's little shoatlike eyes. He had independently discovered the key to creating a special-interest group and ultimately a lobby. Unfortunately, World War II interrupted his plans along with those of many another genius.

I get dozens of letters, usually with an American flag on the letterhead, from outfits that are going to do all sorts of good things: reduce the income tax, control government bureaucracy, bring back the B-1 bomber, eliminate the national debt, restore the gold standard, revive hanging. For a lousy five dollars—for ten I get a handsome lapel pin—I can get all these things done. (Presumably somewhere along the way they will also tell my own constitutionally elected representatives to drop dead.)

The trick is for the organizers to select a list of emotional goals that any reasonable person will support. (In this they are better off than the medical foundations, which have to select the most hideous unbespoke disease and hope it doesn't get cured too soon.) If enough people respond they are in business. Set up a lobby, hire some secretaries, and join the Washington Establishment. Such operations can be very profitable.

The Bad Word

An objection to lobbying is that it bypasses the democratic process. A well-organized and well-supported lobby can force through legislation that is contrary to national interest and even to the will of the majority. Historic examples are legion.

The outstanding illustration in American history was the work of the Prohibition lobby, to which hard-drinking politicians eventually caved in. A more recent example is the work of the gun lobby (the American Rifle Association). Opinion polls show that the majority of citizens want civilized control at least of hand guns. The gun lobby has managed to convince our lawmakers that such legislation would be political suicide.

Lobbies have warped our foreign policy. The old China lobby kept the greatest nation on earth behaving for 30 years as though mainland China didn't exist. Although experienced British and American China hands like General Stilwell[4] testified that Chiang Kai-shek was vain, pompous, and phony as a four-dollar bill (and his wife was unspeakable), we continued to deal with him as if he represented the Chinese people. The Israel lobby today is so powerful that any serious presidential candidate has to make a ritual trip to Tel Aviv to proclaim his loyalty (a trip that can conveniently be combined with a visit to the Pope).

How can these special-interest lobbies be so powerful? Certainly the techniques used by the business lobby don't have this sort of clout. The secret is threat—threat to withhold support for and to unseat the incumbent.

The gun lobby claims it can have 30,000 letters sent to congressmen the day after "unfriendly" legislation is proposed. The Israel lobby threatens to withhold the American Jewish vote from leaders who are not sufficiently pro-Israel. This is called indirect lobbying and its impact is devastating, because most legislators (in spite of handsome pensions) would rather be dead in a ditch in Washington than alive anywhere else. Why this is true I leave to the next section.

Corporations are not in a good position to use indirect lobbying. Their working stiffs are as apt to support the labor lobby as management's position. Middle management is concerned more with personal empire building than with national affairs. Besides their first loyalty might be to the gun lobby or to the environment. Irving Kristol suggests that corporations organize their shareholders as a constituency.[5] This is wishful thinking. As Kristol himself points out, most shareholders are speculators who have no company loyalty. His proposed methods of turning them into gung-ho

[4]B. W. Tuchman, *Stilwell and the American Experience in China*, New York: Macmillan, 1970.

[5]I. Kristol, *Two Cheers for Capitalism*, New York: Basic Books, 1978, p. 146.

supporters are illegal. More important, the largest shareholders are faceless institutions and many individual investors keep their shares under a street name. The company doesn't know who they are.

The second, unanswerable, objection to the lobbying establishment is inefficiency and cost. American taxpayers, workers, and corporations actually support *two* very expensive governments in Washington (and to a lesser extent in state capitals): our elected representatives and the larger, more expensive, "shadow" or second government of lobbists, agents, consultants, research institutes, and lawyers which we support to keep an eye on the incumbents to try to get them to do what we want. This incredible army of Congress watchers is the most ringing vote of nonconfidence in the history of representative government. Politicians often find it more expedient to placate the interest groups (the other government), usually with promises of money, than to talk to the folks back home.

Lobbying organizations can grow even faster than government bureaucracies. The National Association of Counties (a new one) has grown from an $18,000 annual budget in 1957 to one of over $5 million today—paid by county taxpayers.[6] Now a $5 million organization has a well-paid top management, as do all big lobbies. The first concern of these people can switch from the "cause" to perpetuating their soft jobs. Setting up a new lobby can be a very good deal. The leaders (like lawyers) can wind up with more in common with their opposite numbers in other pressure groups than with the people they represent.

The cost of lobbying is actually a good talking point for socialists. Under socialism the lobbists would have to fold their tents; their threats would be hollow.

THE WASHINGTON ESTABLISHMENT
Every once in a while *The New Yorker* rather petulantly allows

[6]See the "Regions" column of *The Wall Street Journal*, August 12, 1980.

as how the proper place for our national government is in New York rather than in Washington. The editors are right. A capital city like London or Rome or Paris or Tokyo is a many-dimensioned thing: concerned with industry, shipping, entertainment, *and* government. Washington is one-dimensional—government. There are no competing interests; there is no other route to power. Out of this single-minded obsession has grown the Washington Establishment.

The Washington Establishment is a structured society, as structed as an old Army post or a military retirement community. The outward ranking is based on elected position, military rank, and civil service grade. (It is spooky for an outsider to hear establishment people drop high GS numbers as names are dropped in a more civilized society.) The real ranking is based on power—influence. There is an elite class; there is a vast army of shaded degrees in the middle: there are the eager newcomers just starting up the power tree; and there are the rejects. Money is important but only as it contributes to power. Rejects are those not in the power struggle: the poor, tourists (almost any visitor for that matter), even a retired millionaire who doesn't want to participate.

At the top of the establishment are the high government figures: the President and the Vice President (of course), cabinet members, supreme court justices, department heads, important congressmen, top-ranking bureaucrats, the right types of ambassadors, and the President's men. Also included are members of the second government whose influence puts them on top: partners in prestigious law firms, some super intellectuals.

The middle group has a wider spectrum, ranging from those who have just emerged from oblivion to people who are almost ready to move up. Junior senators and representatives are in this group, along with a crowd of lobbyists, civil service workers, consultants, aides, reporters—a cast of thousands. What distinguishes these people is that they all have a pretty good idea of each other's position in the pecking order and they are all on the make.

They are paid directly or indirectly by Uncle Sam or by distant supporters, and they are doing quite nicely thank you.[7]

Washington is a beautiful city; it is a big city; it is also a daytime city. When the sun goes down the important, and the very important, people head for the hills of Maryland and Virginia.[8] As night falls, the great city seems to collapse like a wet paper bag: a black paper bag because most of the permanent residents—rejects—are black. Life and lifemanship go on, but the scene shifts from the Capitol to the cocktail circuit. To be stranded for a long weekend in downtown D.C. makes a hollow mockery of the burlesque comedian's jokes about a weekend in Philadelphia.

The Washington scene may not sound very attractive as I describe it, but this is probably a biased and certainly an abbreviated description. The fact is that the natives love it. To be so close to the source of power, even to engage in their own little power plays, seems to exhilarate them.

I have a smart young friend who, after graduating from a decent liberal arts college, got a job on the staff of a congressman. Unfortunately, his patron did not survive the next election, and he was left in the lurch. In an earlier day, we might have said that this was a good time for the young man to get an "honest" job, but not today. After some looking and using his contacts, he got a good[9] job on the staff of the brick lobby, despite the fact that he knew nothing of bricks, let alone civil engineering. He was last heard considering going to law school to get the ultimate establishment union card.

There are some points in this story that are worth a fast mull. The guy is highly intelligent (his SAT scores had to be measured on

[7]One good way to make money is to be close enough to a large cash stream to be able to skim some off the top (the Las Vegas or banker's approach). Another is to get small amounts from a large number of people (the March of Dimes approach).

[8]Exceptions are the rich people who can afford to live in Georgetown or in apartments like Watergate—that's right, Watergate.

[9]All establishment jobs are good jobs.

the Richter scale). There are a lot of sharp people in the establishment. We could have the wisest government in the world if individual intelligence were additive: unfortunately, in groups and in committees it seems to be mutually annihilating. The next point is that my friend moved easily from the elected establishment to the second government and expects someday to move back. The most important point is that he stayed in Washington. People who breathe its miasmic air get Potomac Fever; to be anywhere else is to be only half alive. This is what makes indirect lobbying so effective.

There is a character you run into in Washington, usually at a downtown hotel bar, after the locals have gone home. He is a businessman who has come to the Capitol to get redress for real or imagined wrongs. He has spent the day being given the bureaucratic runaround or has just been told that his hearing is inexplicably postponed to next week. He is a big man back in Muncie, Indiana, but here he is a reject. Like a naked colonel in a communal combat zone shower, he feels sort of unzipped and has to tell his troubles. He is last seen crying in his Cutty Sark and mumbling, "But I am a taxpayer; I pay for all this." I listen because I don't like to drink alone, but he gets no sympathy from me. Why should *he* get consideration from an establishment that chewed up and spit out the last three presidents?

The Washington Establishment is very hard for an ousider to crack—another reason companies set up resident representatives or lobbies. Sometimes a desperate loner, like our boozing businessman, tries to buy entry, much as a lonely traveler might patronize a foreign whorehouse. In Washington, influence, like sex, is for sale.

INFLUENCE

Outside the constitutional arms of government, the most influential people in the establishment are successful Washington lawyers. They are partners in powerful law firms like Covington & Burlington, Arnold & Porter, Hogan & Hartson. Their top men, often super intellectuals like Ball, Clifford, Freeman, and Califano, move smoothly from their lucrative legal jobs to executive appointments and back. For a corporation to retain one of these prestigious firms is to gain access and influence. Unfortunatey, such outfits are busy and expensive. They would hardly have time for our drinking friend. If he is going to establish a Washington legal connection, he is going to have to settle for the minor leagues.

The most effective way for anyone to influence the legislative process is to be on a first-name basis with a legislator; to be able to pick up the phone and say, "Hey, George, what are you guys trying to do? Don't you know what this means to us?" This sort of access is available only to a few business leaders. Washington law firms can provide it secondhand. What business needs are pan-industry groups in Washington whose power, prestige, and contacts will rival those of the great law firms. There are such things.

Pan-Industry Groups

Pan-industry groups have one thing in common: they claim to speak for the whole business community. Apart from this they vary greatly from large to small, from organized to ad hoc, from highly exclusive to completely open. The best known today are probably the U.S. Chamber of Commerce, the National Association of Manufacturers (NAM), the Business Roundtable, the Committee for Economic Development (CED), and, lately, the Trilateral Commission.

The most influential of these may be the Business Roundtable. Members of the group are chief executive officers (CEOs), the sort of people who do have contacts in Congress. In its published decisions, the Roundtable tries to be statesmanlike, to promote what is best for the nation rather than for any parochial industry position. The Roundtable opposed legislation to susidize the domestic merchant marine industry; recently it came out against the government bail-out of Chrysler. This is a good way to lose some friends but to gain credibility.

The biggest, best known, and best organized of the pan-industry organizations is the U.S. Chamber of Commerce. It dates back a bit. It was created in 1912 at the suggestion of President Taft to promote better business–government relations. (Times change.) Today there are thousands of chambers (and junior chambers) throughout the country. Members are both corporate and individual—anyone is welcome. The organization has over 40 standing committees of dedicated businessmen. Its headquarters are in Washington, D.C., naturally. It is the world's largest lobby.

The Chamber of Commerce, along with the NAM,[10] is recognized by members of Congress as the voice of business. High-ranking Chamber of Commerce lobbyists and committee members maintain close contacts with congressmen, may be briefed on new legislation, and are asked to testify at hearings. With some 2 million members, the Chamber is a potent indirect lobbying force. It keeps up with pending legislation and informs its people with a flood of publications: testimony, research, news, speeches, and reprints. Its best-known organs are *Nation's Business*, a monthly magazine, and *Washington Report*, a weekly newsletter. In its publications it presents the pan-industry position and suggests action—like what to write to whom. A force to be reckoned with.

While the size of the Chamber of Commerce is a source of its strength, it is also the source of some weaknesses. Since the Chamber welcomes all business and does not want to offend any, its positions have to be general rather than specific. They are usually negative: against increased regulation, against new programs and spending, and against higher taxes. This makes it a predictable outfit. Any congressman, liberal or conservative, knows beforehand

---

[10]I have slighted the NAM in interests of brevity. It is smaller than the Chamber of Commerce but in some areas, particularly manufacturing, it is just as influential. See, for example, *The Washington Lobby*, op. cit.

what position the Chamber will take on any legislation. Don't look for much innovation from the Chamber of Commerce.

In *any* organization above a certain size, there are choice management and staff jobs. The Chamber of Commerce employs over 400 people in Washington alone, working in its handsome headquarters near the White House. It is easy for an employee to lose his crusading zeal in the more immediate battle up the organization ladder.

Most writers on lobbying view the Chamber of Commerce and other business pressure groups with alarm: "They are taking over the government!" I also view them with alarm, but for different reasons: for their tremendous cost in talent and money, for their implied lack of support for elected government, and mostly for their *in*effectiveness. The Chamber of Commerce was founded in 1912. Since that time lobbying efforts have increased a couple of orders of magnitude, and although the conservatives may have won some skirmishes, they have lost every battle! Taxes have gone way up, government size and influence have ballooned, a vast regulatory apparatus has been built, and transfer payments account for almost half our tax money.

As far as providing industry with an effective voice, I have more hope in small, selective outfits like the Business Roundtable and the Committee for Economic Development than in the giants. Small groups can earn respect for statesmanlike decisions; they can act rather than react. They can be heard over the predictable background noise of the Washington Establishment.

POLITICAL ACTION

Perhaps recognizing the ineffectiveness of lobbying, pressure groups have turned to a new tactic in the legislative battlegrounds: the political action committee (PAC). The idea is simple: it is more effective to try to get and retain the right sort of incumbents than to try to convert the ones that emerge from the old-fashioned unstructured (democratic) election process. The tools are election-time propaganda and money: money given or withheld from campaigning politicians.

To decide who its friends and enemies are, each action group maintains a running tabulation of the voting records of lawmakers and converts this into a score. There is no place to hide. Those with a high score get campaign contributions; those with a low score get none. ("This little piggy got roast beef and this little piggy got none.") If someone's score is really low, a PAC may contribute to his opponent.

Although this tactic has a businesslike ring—money talks—it was a labor lobby that first used it effectively: the Committee on Political Education (COPE) of the AFL-CIO. Now almost every established lobbying group has its own PAC keeping scores. There are new outfits like the Business Industry Political Action Committee (BIPAC) whose only object is to influence elections. The Washington scene has a whole bunch of new acronyms to deal with: ACA, NCEC, SANE, and so on.

How effective are these PACs? Pretty damn effective if you are on the receiving end of a contribution or if one goes to your opponent. The proliferation of PACs does tend to blunt the impact that COPE, for example, once enjoyed. It's a pretty faceless congressman who can't find *some* outfit to support him. The new money may tend to polarize our legislators. An independent thinker who really prefers a middle-of-the-road voting position may find it expedient to lean definitely to the left or to the right to improve his score on some PAC list.

Local Government

If the preceding discussion makes the Washington battleground look tough—almost a no-win situation for business—then I have not been misinterpreted. There is a brighter side: local government at the state, country (or parish), and city level. Here the businessman or his lobbyists are among friends. Local politicians really want industries to enter, to stay, and to prosper in their jurisdictions. The key question is just how powerful these friendly local governments are compared with the central government. This is the old Federalist question that all Western nations face. In the United States it is called "states rights," a problem that has been with us since the beginning. For the benefit of any engineering majors who may be reading this, I give a little history.

The Story of States Rights

After the War of Independence, the new American nation was in a mess. The farmers were in economic bondage to the cities, paper money was almost worthless, the former colonies were in debt both to indigenous financiers and to England. The war was over but many problems were unresolved. The nation was on the brink of rebellion. What the new nation needed was an effective central government, but the old colonies weren't about to forfeit the very rights (states rights) that they had fought to get from England.

To bring order out of confusion, a convention of the nation's leaders met in Philadelphia to draw up that remarkable document, the Constitution of the United States, which defined the powers of a proposed central government. The document was only a bright hope until ratified by the state legislatures.

This was a very tough sell; it meant asking the states to give up cherished rights to a new and untried federation. All Americans owe a debt to men like Hamilton, Morris, Jay, and Madison, who propagandized the new order. Their best argument was that only in unity is there strength. Still, they probably would not have succeeded if the country had not been in such a mess (or if Jefferson had not been in France). The states came in reluctantly but they came in.

The Tenth Amendment to the Constitution haunts us to this day: "The powers not delegated to the United States . . . are reserved to the States. . . ." This is an open-ended commitment:

what the national government takes the states lose. This power struggle finally resulted in war. As far as the Confederate leaders were concerned, the War Between the States (the Civil War) was not fought over slavery but over states rights. General Lee was opposed to slavery. The Union won.

The last telling blow to states rights, or prestige, was struck by the Nixon administration (an unlikely source). It is called "revenue sharing" and is supposedly a system in which a generous government gives back to the states some of the money their people send to Washington. Actually these are state-level transfer payments taking from rich states and giving to poor ones. Each state stands meekly with its bowl extended like Oliver Twist waiting for its portion from Washington. Recently, the handouts don't even come from taxes; they come from an increase in the national debt. The victory of central government over the states is complete. Or is it?

The Rise of States

Don't drag out your Confederate money, boys. I am not talking about the *United* States. Not yet.

If the nineteenth century was the time of consolidation of states into huge blocs (including the American West), the twentieth has been the time of dissolution. The remnants of the British, French, Dutch, and even the abortive American[11] empires lie like colored shards on our maps. Germany, Korea, Vietnam, Ireland, Cyprus, and Yemen are split into competing factions. All over the world people want out. The Scots and the Welsh want to split from England, the Basques from Spain, the Kurds from Iran (who wouldn't). Even in Canada the Quebecois want out, and some of the Western provinces are making warning noises.

The new ingredient in at least some of these separatist movements is that they are founded not on nationalism or racism but on economics. The Scots were quiet as long as they were poor

[11]I am proud to have been in Manila on Philippine Independence Day, July 4, 1946. The main thing I remember is that part of the grandstand collapsed.

relations; now they wonder why they should support Westminster with *their* oil. The oil-producing provinces of Canada wonder why they should sell *their* oil—cheap—to the Easterners. The same sort of thing could happen here.

Without the restrictions from Washington, Alaska could have per capita income approaching that of Kuwait. Texas and Louisiana would be better off. Why should the Breadbasket (see Chapter 10) subsidize the rest of the nation? The rich states are looking at Washington with an increasingly critical eye, and they don't like what they see.

I know that Washington Establishment people have my best interests at heart, but I have to tell them they aren't very well liked. Irrational people like me don't like being told where their children can go to school, whether they can use saccharin, what hardware they have to buy for their cars, how fast they can drive. For the money we send with our tax return (after buying a stamp), we seem to be getting poor value. Our postal service gets worse; our armed services are supposed to be deteriorating; foreigners despise our cheap dollars; our foreign policy is a joke. For most of us, a letter bearing a D.C. imprint (sent free) is something to fear.

The only people who want to join us as a new state are the Puerto Ricans, and they don't seem to want to adopt our customs or even our language: they want to preserve their position in the welfare queue. Alaska and Hawaii must wonder why they were so eager to come aboard.

I don't think the United States is about to split up into separate nations. Like family members who know each other too well, we are still bound by shared history—too much blood has been shed. I do think that dissatisfaction with the central government and revenue sharing, which makes states look invidiously at each other, could start a new states rights movement. As the English have had to make concessions to the Scots, so our central government might have to relinquish some of its powers, which would revert (constitutionally) to the states. In spite of the fact that this would initially involve the messiest and most expensive of details, such delegation would be welcomed by the business community.

PROVINCIAL BUSINESS POWER

Provincial governments, from the city to the state level, are pale copies of the national establishment, complete with executive, legislative, and judicial branches. They have their own second governments. For corporations, these bodies provide much more friendly waters in which to swim—the corporate fish are much bigger. Seen from across the Potomac, even large corporations look like small beer: seen from the county courthouse, the same companies look like the source of constituent prosperity, the main component in the tax base, and a source of campaign contributions.

Local politicians look to local business for support. It is to provincial incumbents that businessmen can most often make those all-important phone calls; "Hey, Mac, what in the hell are you guys trying to do to us?" At their best, provincial governments and business form one big, happy family working for the same goals: to promote local prosperity, to fight the feds, and (recently) to get as much money as possible from Washington. Service organizations like Rotary Club, the League of Women Voters, and the local chamber of commerce stand tall (more on this in the next chapter). The danger is that this jolly collusion can lead to favoritism and corruption.

Corruption has been the chronic disease of American provincial governments. It is not as bad today as it was in the last century, when New York legislators routinely checked with Commodore Vanderbilt before they voted, but things are still troubled. I grew up in Chicago at a time when we expected our elected representatives to be crooks and were seldom disappointed. While I was in school in Boston, the mayor split his time between Beacon Hill and the jail (from which he was reelected). Later, working in Texas, I noted heavy traffic between the capitol and the jailhouse. My present home state, Louisiana, has had its problems.[12]

Business doesn't like municipal corruption. At times it takes drastic action. In Shreveport, where I live, the business community once got so tired of inept local government that it hand-picked a decent but unknown man, supported him, and got him elected mayor to the everlasting advantage of the citizens and industry. It has been common in the South for a group of powerful businessmen to "run" a city.[13] Until Houston got too big, a group used to run it from a room in the old Lamar Hotel. The business leaders provided a climate for explosive growth, *but* they overlooked a few things: there is no zoning in Houston; it has possibly the worst public transportation problem in the country. There is still an argument for the services of professional administrators in city hall.

Should industry promote states rights for its own good? I don't know. It is not one of the nostrums I save for the last chapter. The preferred solution would seem to be more efficient, more rational national government. If the size of the official Washington Establishment—civil service, staff, appointees, and department members—were cut in half (say) and if the second government were similarly reduced, we might have a leaner, more effective apparatus. At least it would reduce the tremendous overhead carried by industry and individual taxpayers.

Start a new special-interest group today!

[12]At the time of this writing, we are down to 4 people indicted in a Brilab case. In the last year over 30 incumbents were convicted of vote buying. Not long ago, our assistant commissioner of agriculture was sentenced for attempted bribery.

[13]The outstanding current example of business control is Dallas (see "Company Town," *The Wall Street Journal,* September 24, 1979). It works. The city is clean and prosperous, has a budget surplus, and has inspired a TV series.

18

SERVICE AND CHARITY

A young theologian named Garrity
Courted three girls from Cromarty.
He said "Faith is a dream,
And Hope is a scream,
But the greatest of these is Charity."

OUR LAST battleground of ideas is the world of service and charity. The operations we are concerned with are referred to under a lot of different names: public service organizations, private charities, voluntary action groups. Together, they are sometimes called the "third sector," a catchall term that includes religion, education, and art, three categories that I have considered separately. There is still a lot of the third sector left to talk about and it is important. Service

254

and charity work accounts for a significant part of the social activity in Western societies. The proper role of business (if any) in these doings is interesting.

By the very nature of their activities, which are based on voluntary contributions of money and time, service groups are in opposition to the concepts of a planned society. Socialists and planners have to mistrust them as well-intentioned meddlers in things that are too important to be left to amateurs. Before considering the pros and cons of service work, I had better classify the types of organizations I have in mind.

I am not going to explore the murky paths of the medical funds, such as the Heart Fund and the Easter Seal Society.[1] Apart from collection activities, these outfits are closed systems involving money, professional managers, and medical facilities. Another part of the third sector I omit are independent foundations (such as the Ford Foundation) and operating foundations (such as the Carnegie Foundation for the Advancement of Teaching).[2] Again, these organizations seem to work in worlds of their own, and in spite of the capitalist names of their founders they are as likely to support liberal causes as free enterprise. There are still plenty of loose ends lying around and I consider them under the headings of fraternal organizations, United Way organizations, company and community foundations, and special causes.

FRATERNAL ORGANIZATIONS

North America has provided the most fertile ground for the growth of fraternal organizations. Visit any old city in the United States or Canada—Bradford, Pennsylvania, is a good choice—and chances are that the most impressive building in the old town

[1] For a good treatment see Carl Bakal, *Charity USA*, New York: Times Books, 1979.

[2] See *The Foundation Directory*, New York: Columbia University Press (biannual).

(impressive, not beautiful) is the ancestral home of the Elks, or the Lions, or the Odd Fellows, or the Woodsmen of the World. These fraternities were not originally service-oriented; their mission was social and their power political. As the urbanization of America shook up old ways and as waves of immigrants threatened the power structure, the fraternal orders were looked upon as lifeboats in troubled waters. Many of them were insurance-oriented—to insure against penurious old age and to provide a decent burial.

As American life settled into new patterns, the old lifeboat philosophy lost its appeal, and the clubs turned their energies to service and charity and away from survival. This is not necessarily an irreversible process: if society becomes too unsettled or if members again feel threatened by new Americans or by ethnic groups, the old ways could return. (Worse, organizations like the American Nazis, the Ku Klux Klan, and the Black Panthers could revive.)

When the fraternal organizations did take on the problems of society, they did it in a big way with (once?) typical American zeal and optimism. They were well equipped for their new role. With affluent members, many from the business community, they had the means, the managerial skills, and the contacts. Target areas tended to be visible and rewarding—the kinds of goals business leaders, who like a decent return on investment, would pick. Possibly the best-known effort, and one only a grinch would fault, is the Shriners program for crippled children.

Shrine Hospitals

The Mystic Shrine is an elite subset of the Masons. As such, it is a worldwide organization (in those countries where Masonry is permitted). The Shrine was originally a social club—"the playground of the Masonry." In the early 1920s, after half a century of fun and games, the Shrine turned to philanthropy and established a network of hospitals to care for crippled children.

From its beginnings in 1922, the hospital program has been a success story. Today there are 18 functioning orthopedic hospitals and 3 burn clinics in the United States, Mexico, and Canada. Over 200,000 children have been helped, and the fraternity has provided over half a billion dollars for this work—money which has either been given outright or raised by the organization. (Go to the Shrine Circus!)

More impressive than the statistics is the philosophy of the program. There is no charge to patients and care is total. If a child who is in for a leg operation (say) has bad teeth, dental care is provided. Schooling, recreation, character-building activities (such as scouting), and a homelike atmosphere are all laid on. Through their contacts and reputation, the Shriners obtain the services of local doctors and of specialists (sometimes for free), and the hospitals are natural centers for research. The very presence of a Shrine hospital or burn clinic is a plus for a community. The Shriners have a right to be proud.

Service Clubs

While the Shrine is dedicated to people-to-people (particularly people-to-young-people) charities, other fraternities have an ideological leaning toward business and social problems. We have already looked at the chambers of commerce under government; another example is the Lions Club. Although the Lions are involved in charity work, their main emphasis is on good government, citizenship, and international cooperation.

The epitome of service clubs is Rotary. Borrowing a page from *Tom Sawyer* (the whitewash thing), the Rotarians make service, and the sacrifice that goes with it, an honor. Only one member is allowed from each business or profession in a community. This makes the club exclusive; it also makes businesses, which approve their corporate members, partners in the organization goal: to improve business–community relations.

The League of Women Voters long ago won its battle for female franchise, but it carries on. The new aim is to inform voters, without taking sides (usually, the League *is* for ERA), in order to improve the voting and selection process. Not a bad goal.

The most "good works" group of all may also be a women's club. The Junior League is spread across the land like a blessing, doing good works and trying to live down its aristocratic origins. Its people *are* better fixed than most of us, which gives its young members the time and means to do good things: both charity and service.

An important contribution of service clubs is providing forums for speakers to address us all. The politician, educator, social worker, or business executive may be ostensibly talking only to a select group, but his high points will be repeated on the local TV evening news.

"I Gave at the Office"—The United Way

The United Way drive—or the United Torch, or the Community Fund, or whatever name it goes under—seems always to have been with us. Actually the movement did not really get organized until 1949 as the successor of the Community Chests of "Monopoly" fame. The idea behind these drives is simple and attractive—that all worthy community service and charity projects combine their fund raising in a single effort to reduce overhead costs and make things easier for the givers. Most people and corporations consider the United Way to be a good thing—it added "We gave at the office" to our language—but like all organizations it has its little ways.

The United Way of America is a centralized, national organization, not a local charity as many contributors think. It is "big business," raising over a billion dollars a year. Its chief executive gets a six-figure salary, which may be quite proper but which seems a little out of keeping with the mission of helping the poor. (Friends of the little people—Chicago aldermen, labor leaders, fund managers—seem to do very well for themselves.) Services and charities that turn their fund raising over to the United Way (many do not wish to or are not admitted) have to accept that share of collection funds which the board deems proper. On the other hand, donors have little to say about where their money will wind up. The secret of the fund's success over the years has been its alliance with the business community.

Business likes the United Way. A single drive is more effective and "businesslike": it reduces solicitation overhead; it frees workers from the distraction of many fund drives; and, as we shall see, it gives business some control of how the money will be spent. Under the groundrules of the usually invisible hand of the national organization, the business community pretty well takes over the local effort.

In every community there is a fund drive committee that raises contributions and a budget committee that allocates the funds. These committees are usually dominated by business people: not through any devious plot but because business leaders are the ones who have the time and interest to do the work. The community fund leader is usually a high-ranking executive who is encouraged by his company to take the time off to do a good job. The committee lays on progress report luncheons and solicits volunteers to run the drive—often the middle management equivalent of the "lowest-ranking second lieutenant." Most important for the success of the drive, corporations mobilize their own employees with meetings (on company time), pledge cards, and "fair share" guidelines. The crowning touch is that contributions are collected as painlessly as possible through payroll deductions. Corporations do put pressure on their employees to contribute, sometimes excessive pressure, but usually no more than is implied by the unwritten employee–employer covenant we discussed in Chapter 6.

In addition to all this support, many companies make direct corporation contributions to the fund. To me this seems uncalled for, out of keeping with the original intent of the United Way, and perhaps even improper (more on this later). Bakal considers the amount of corporate giving to be mean; this is based on the idea that corporations are sort of super citizens.[3] (He does not add administra-

[3]Carl Bakal, *Charity USA*, op. cit.

tive costs and managers' time into corporate giving, but he does include them in fund overhead. This may be good investigative reporting but it is bad double-entry accounting.)

Business support is crucial. Fund raisers know that the private sector—medical, legal, small business—will probably fail to meet its modest goals and that success depends on the support of industry and civil service (and the military if there is a military base in the community). In most communities the fund's goals are met. Where does the money go?

The Services

A local United Way will typically help support about 30 agencies. These include well-known outfits like the Red Cross, the YMCA and YWCA, the Boy Scouts and Girl Scouts, the Salvation Army, and also rather special local services such as day care centers; alcoholics and family counseling; dental, sight, and hearing clinics; Goodwill Industries; and Meals on Wheels. One supported agency is always the United Way itself (whose request is honored).

I have sat on a budget committee whose duty it was to distribute the money. It is a difficult and soul-searching job—*every* charity seems so worthy. It is hard to drop an organization; it is hard to add a new one. The natural tendency is to use last year's allocation as a guide, which at least gives the supported agencies a chance to plan. Each outfit presents its case along with audited books to show how the money will be spent.

Budget committee members, usually business leaders, like to get something tangible for "their" money: so many summer campers, so many eyeglasses provided, a record of past success. They are wary of action-oriented programs or civil rights projects that peddle concepts rather than things. The only intangible that is generally accepted is the promotion of "good citizenship," usually through youth groups.

A rather large share of United Way money does go to youth and recreation projects—scouting and YMCAs are conspicuous examples.[4] This may also be a business bias. Business leaders know that they will be expected—required by the Fair Employment Practice Commission (FEPC)—to hire these young people when they grow up. Money spent on improving their "character and citizenship" seems like a good investment.

The leaning of the budget committee toward tangible, goal-oriented organizations and character-building services makes the United Way suspect in the eyes of liberals—the eternal conflict between the concepts of free enterprise and personal responsibility on the one hand and "social justice" on the other. Before tackling this central issue, I had better tidy up the listing by considering some other services and charities.

FOUNDATIONS

There are two kinds of foundations that concern us: "community" foundations and "corporate" or company-sponsored foundations. While not as well known as the Mellon Foundation, for example, these organizations are growing in size and influence. They may offer an alternative to the United Way to consolidate individual gifts, corporate gifts, and local government support.

Community foundations operate as sort of municipal slush funds—like the rector's discretionary fund—which can be quickly mobilized to satisfy special community and social needs beyond those handled by the welfare state. Examples include grants to restore historic buildings, to aid struggling artists, to provide expensive medical treatments and scholarships, to support youth work in inner cities, and to support libraries and zoos. The grants are characterized by service to the community and flexibility, and are often oriented to cultural activities.

[4]Some large youth organizations such as the Future Farmers of America and 4-H are not supported by the United Way—4-H is supported by the Department of Agriculture! This raises some questions. If 4-H, why not scouting? Why should tax money support such an organization anyway?

Community foundations are a community asset. Since they are supported by government and by gifts from individuals and from corporations, this pretty well confines them to large cities. (The New York Community Trust is the largest.)

Although donors *can* specify how their money is to be spent (this is not irrevocable, as conditions change), most giving is unrestricted; money is given directly to the foundation, which decides how to spend it. The governing bodies of community foundations are supposed to be representative of the community and include public officials, educators, and clergymen. Business does not have the control of spending that it does of United Way funds. Banks voluntarily take on the job of trust management.

Community foundations make a lot of sense, particularly if one assumes that minimal community welfare services are already available and that the best use of voluntary (rather than tax) contributions is to improve the way of life.

There are so many requests for corporate contributions that big companies have been forced to set up a new staff department (here we go again) to process requests and make grants. At least this gets the corporate officers out of the charity business and leaves them free to run the company.

With money coming in and going out, it is just good business for the new departments to maintain working funds so that they don't have to go to the treasurer every time they give money—the genesis of company-sponsored foundations. Such funds make good sense: they provide a corporate tax break; they allow corporate contributions to the funds to vary with prosperity (lean years and fat years).

Some of these company foundations are large.[5] In a few cases the grants amount to no more than the interest on capital, which makes the foundations self-perpetuating. The spectrum of grants may be quite similar to that of the community foundation. It may

[5]About $75 million in assets for the General Motors Fund and $100 million for the Alcoa Foundation. See *The Foundation Directory*, op. cit.

not. In any event, distribution is under control of the sponsoring company. Not surprisingly, companies tend to spend their money near home for visible, well-defined projects. The grantee knows for sure just who the local fairy godmother is.

SPECIAL CAUSES

In any progressive community with a healthy middle class (see the next chapter), a multitude of private service and charitable organizations will spring up to deal with special problems. They may be church-oriented—to help refugees, for example—or they may just represent the collective conscience or civic pride of like-thinking people.

A lot of these groups are concerned with "bricks and mortar" projects—to save the Strand Theater or to restore the Highland neighborhood. Others are ecology-oriented—to save the redwoods or to leave the Buffalo River "wild." Most of these organizations are long on enthusiasm and short on funds. For money they can turn to community funds, to corporate funds, or, if they are fortunate, to government.

What happens to these ad hoc organizations? Some give up, but others do not. Some complete their project and honorably fold (unlike the March of Dimes); others, particularly ecology types, have their projects usurped by government agencies or by professional nature boys. Some become permanent and achieve the ultimate respectability of being a United Way agency.

ADVANTAGES OF PRIVATE SERVICE AND CHARITY

While it is hard for us to imagine a society without these privately funded services, it is obvious that a nation can do without them—there is no Junior League in Russia or Cuba or China. Although a lot of private money does go into charity, it is small compared with government welfare spending. (If the working stiff who is pressured to give to the United Way knew that 45 percent of his tax dollars are used for transfer payments to others, he might wonder what all the fuss was about.) The advantages of service and charity organizations seem to come under the headings of efficiency, local pride, and civic conscience.

Efficiency

Although they have less to spend, private services are much more efficient than their public opposite numbers. This is because they do not (cannot) pay their professionals the salaries of civil service workers; because they operate with much less red tape and overhead; and, most significantly, because they mobilize armies of volunteers.

Consider the Girl Scouts as an example.[6] The Pelican Council of the Girl Scouts of the United States of America serves nine parishes in northwestern Louisiana—an area of 6,814 square miles, which includes towns, rural areas, and a lot of piney woods. There are about 3,500 girl scouts and brownies in the council program, organized in troops in the various neighborhoods. The council maintains camping areas and one large established camp (Camp Wawbansee).

To run this operation there are five professional scouters, four clerks, and one caretaker—all underpaid by civil service (or even by business) standards. These people answer to a management group of 24 volunteers. There are, in all, some 750 volunteer helpers in the council whose contributed time depends on their jobs: troop leaders, neighborhood chairmen, trainers. The council office is in Shreveport, housed in temporary quarters and partially subsidized by the landlords—a far cry from the classy, underutilized United Way building. The office does have its own transportation: two Ford stationwagons, vintage 1963 and 1973.

[6] I shall use them as examples here and later. This is because (1) I am lazy and (2) I know the organization, since my wife was a council president. Almost any United Way organization could serve as an example of efficiency.

Critics may object to the mission of the Girl Scouts, but nobody can object that donated money is not efficiently spent. It would be an interesting exercise to compare the existing organization and costs with those of a corresponding civil service operation.

Local Pride

I can't really claim that as a citizen of Shreveport I feel a warm glow of pride and say "We take care of our own." We don't. The government spends a lot more on welfare here than does the private sector. Still, the things I am apt to point out to a visitor are the results of private donations and efforts: museums, theater, conservatory, the work being done to restore old historic buildings and run-down areas, the new Goodwill Industries workshop.

It is these outward, visible signs of collective generosity and effort that give a community character and provide a source of civic pride. Local support for charity and services and for religion, education, and the arts helps make a city "a good place to live in" and creates a good climate for business. All these things *could* be financed by government grants, but local citizens might have difficulty identifying with the projects. It may shrivel a community's spirit (if there is such a thing), as much as that of an individual, to sit around and see what the government is going to do for it this year.

Civic Conscience

Private charity and service operations, particularly the special-cause kind, can serve as a civic conscience and goad the rest of us into doing things, or putting a stop to things, we would rather ignore.

It is remarkable what a small group of angry or motivated citizens can get done in a reasonable free society. It was small groups of Victorian ladies who had the courage to go into the London slums and expose the plight of the poor. It is concerned citizens who finally say "e-bloody-nough" to developers, who chain themselves to trees, or who lie down in the paths of bulldozers.

(Why do people usually look ridiculous when they try to do something good?) It is citizens groups that alert the rest of us to the spreading concrete jungle, and they can be effective. In several cities—San Francisco and New Orleans come to mind—there are freeways that end in space rather than slashing through old and historic neighborhoods. In my own town the building of a highway bridge on uncertain foundations over the city water supply lake has been kept on "hold" status for years.

As long as there are such spontaneous action groups, we have a civic conscience to alert us to the possibly well-meaning mistakes of our planners—at least until such groups get absorbed by professional nature boys.

DISADVANTAGES OF PRIVATE SERVICE AND CHARITY

To planners, the works of private charities and service organizations are hopelessly unstructured and amateurish. Harold Lasky, the British socialist, said (I quote from Bakal, I hope he got it right) that such groups should operate ". . . without the intervention of gracious ladies, or benevolent busybodies, or stockbrokers to whom a hospital is a hobby, or snobs who see in charity a ladder. . . ." From the union's point of view, volunteers take jobs away from paid workers. (One chapter in Bakal's book is aptly titled "The Volunteer: Saint or Scab?") Another objection is that private services are elitist and provide for so-called middle class rather than for more socially relevant needs.

There is truth in these charges. It is obviously a waste of taxpayers' money, and poor planning, to leave super highways suspended in the air. Without Gray Ladies and Candy Stripers, our hospitals would have to increase their paid staff—and hospital costs would go up. The volunteer problem may take care of itself. As more and more women in middle income families have to work rather than accept a lower standard of life, the supply of (female) volunteers is drying up. Women's liberation organizations such as

NOW (National Organization for Women) object to voluntarism as demeaning.

It is private charities and service organizations such as scouting that compete with (and foul up, from the socialists' point of view) government welfare programs like the Job Corps and CETA.[7] Bureaucracy fights back.

Years ago my mother was the volunteer manager of the Sarah Hackett Stevenson Home for Women in Chicago. The purpose of the charity was to provide a temporary refuge for women from broken homes who had young children; to give them a chance to put the pieces together and become self-supporting. The Cook County welfare professionals hated this operation. They considered it elitist (the young ladies did tend to be white and middle class, and to get on their feet rather quickly) and a threat to the even-handed distribution of largess. As long as the home paid its own way and fulfilled the mission of its founder, it was safe. As the building grew old and failed to meet stringent safety codes, it could be, and was, shut down.

The best government weapons against private services and charities are tax laws and the FEPC. To classify a charity as being ineligible for tax-exempt status is to shoot it down (it will, of course, be dropped by the United Way). Organizations have to be careful to stay out of partisan politics and to take "affirmative action" both in the hiring of people and in the make-up of the people they help. Let us see how this has affected scouting.

Girl Scouts Again

Scouting is often criticized as a creature of the affluent middle class. This was probably true once—when I was young—but it is not a fair charge today. Both the Boy Scouts and the Girl Scouts are trying desperately to expand their programs to minority groups and across economic boundaries. This is a very tough change to make.

[7]The conflict is ideological, not overt. CETA (Comprehensive Employment and Training Act) workers, for example, now work for the Girl Scouts.

Lord Baden-Powell founded the Boy Scouts in England in 1908 after his experiences in the Boer War had shown him that the average soldier was poorly prepared for field life. (When I was in the Boy Scouts of America it still had military overtones: we did close-order drill, for example.) Scouting appealed to middle class boys: for fun and friendship and for patriotic reasons (perhaps they were *Chums* readers). The Boy Scouts of America was based on the English model. The Girl Scouts was based on the Boy Scouts.

As recently as a generation ago, scouting was considered as normal a part of growing up—in the right circles—as going to confirmation class or playing in the school band. The natural home of scouting was the neighborhood school. The troops may not have *met* there—more likely they met in the basement of the First Methodist Church—but this is where the recruiting took place. The neighborhood school is now dying, if not dead. The old scout hut is probably vandalized. Private schools are poor bases for scouting—the population is too volatile or scattered. Losing its natural habitat is only part of scouting's problems.

Partly through social awareness and partly to keep from being dropped as a United Way agency, scouting tries to reach the minorities and to change its goals to be more "relevant." The Girl Scouts actively recruit in black and minority schools and have revised their manuals[8] for easier reading and translated some into Spanish. A big problem is getting leaders. The natural leaders, former Girl Scouts, either are working or are uncomfortable in the new order. Besides, the professionals found that they had to have minority leaders for successful minority troops. Such leaders are hard to find and hard to keep, and require training and close supervision.

This may be scouting's finest hour—bringing young people into social contact before their prejudices are fixed. It may be the last gasp of an outmoded idea.

[8]It is doubtful if many scouts could, or would, read the manuals of 50 years ago.

The Shrine Program

I said earlier that only a grinch could fault the Shrine hospitals for crippled children. Well, pucker up and get ready to hiss, kiddos, because here I go.

Patients for the hospitals are selected on the basis of recommendations by Shriners. For every child selected by this random method, there are hundreds who are doomed to live with their suffering. One thing sure in this world of uncertainty is that poor people in North and Central America can turn out handicapped children faster than the Shriners can build hospitals.

Although the hospitals do provide total care while the patient is resident, eventually the child has to go home. Having tasted the fruits of the WASP world, he or she has to go back to a poor, backward, and perhaps hostile environment.

In theological terms, this makes the Shriners guilty of the sin of playing God—the same charge that can be made against Save the Children, CARE, and all other charities that try to solve global problems by helping selected people. The money might be better spent on improving birth control or pediatrics in the home country.

Hiss! Boo!

The Shriners' best answer to this reasoning is the "one-child argument." "If just one child is rescued from misery to lead a happy, productive life, the whole program is worthwhile." A tough act to follow.

A PARABLE

Is private charity outmoded, or does it still have a place in the welfare state? I can't answer this question, even though my own prejudices are lying all over these pages in dead and dying clauses. The best I can do is recite a parable—not even a proper parable because it is true.

Years ago when I was in basic training I was turned into a soldier largely through the efforts of two sergeants. They were both good soldiers, both good instructors—keep this in mind—but they had different approaches to training.

The first sergeant stood in front of our miserable platoon one day and hollered (I have cleaned up the language): "Some of you guys have the makings of good soldiers and some of you are goof-offs. I only got one life; I only got a few weeks to do a miracle—make soldiers out of this mob. As far as you goof-offs are concerned, you can wind up in the stockade for all I care. It's going to take real soldiers to beat Hitler,[9] and I am going to spend my time with the men who came to fight."

The other sergeant addressed us under similar circumstances but in these terms: "Some of you guys are coming along all right and some of you ain't worth a damn. I'm supposed to make soldiers out of all of you. I am going to spend my time climbing all over the backs of the goldbricks and sad sacks who think this is some sort of CCC camp. The good men will make it all right without my help."

THE RIGHT TO HELP

Do corporations have the right to give money to charity? The money they give is not management's money: it rightly belongs to the shareholders or to the workers if they are underpaid.

This question has been kicked around for at least a hundred years. In the United States it was partially resolved by the New Jersey Supreme Court in the 1953 test case of *P. P. Smith Company* v. *Barlow*. The court ruled that corporate giving is "essential to public welfare, and therefor, of necessity, to corporate welfare." The learned justices may be in favor of someone giving away someone else's money, but a curiously mixed bag of our intellectuals (super and standard) are not. This may be the one issue on which Ralph Nader, John Kenneth Galbraith, and Milton Friedman are agreed.

Friedman is opposed to corporate gifts for classical reasons: the

[9]Good propaganda but not applicable. We came along too late for the Wehrmächt ever to be aware that we were in the fight.

money is not management's to give. The only duty of management is to increase profits.

Nader's objections are socially oriented: business giving supports, or favors, the wrong people. Educational grants, for example, go to affluent white universities rather than to struggling black ones.[10]

Galbraith condemns corporate giving because it gives business too much power to shape society to its own selfish ends. Right on, John! At least this ought to raise a laugh in corporate board rooms from directors who have been having trouble shaping their own companies, let alone society, since about the time of the Coolidge administration.

The strong feelings of widely different ideological types at least indicate that the support of private charities and service organizations is a legitimate battleground between social planners and supporters of free enterprise. Although American corporations do give a lot—over $2 billion dollars in 1979, or 1 percent of profits—the question of corporate giving may be more emotional and academic than significant. The amount corporations give (or even *could* give) is small compared with the generosity of the welfare state. Why do companies hand over all this money and risk the restlessness of their shareholders? Mostly, I think, they just want to be good neighbors.

The most important contribution that industry can make to help preserve a prosperous and livable society is not money at all: it is *people*, the right sort of people. Which brings us to a new section of this book—the score, the payoff, the sort of world we want for ourselves and for our children.

[10]This may sound weird to a foreign reader. The fact is that after years of integration we still have predominately black and white colleges, often serving the same regions and teaching the same courses. We turn a blind eye on this anomaly because the black schools enable students to get degrees that they probably couldn't get otherwise.

PART FOUR

The Score

19

THE MIDDLE CLASS

THE MOST IMPORTANT products of the business community are not things but people—members of the middle class. The term "middle class" has all but lost its meaning. Secure in the knowledge that we as readers and writers are members of this class, we all use the term without definition. It really deserves a closer look, if only because the presence of an effective middle class is (sometimes grudgingly) acknowledged by intellectuals and even by pragmatic dictators as the basis of a successful society. Tracking the health and effectiveness of the middle class is probably the single best way of keeping a running score on how well a nation is doing.

Before getting on to a eulogy of the middle class (writing as a partisan), I had better clear up some misconceptions. I begin by listing what the middle class is *not*, even though it might like to be.

The middle class does not necessarily have the best critical taste—the Elizabethan grunts who flocked to Shakespeare's plays showed better taste than the Victorian ladies (the very model of the middle class) who supported Gilbert and Sullivan. The middle class is not necessarily the most literate. The Russians—you can't have a *middle* class in a one-class society—are probably the most discriminating and prolific readers in the world. The middle class is not necessarily richer than (say) the working class; it is not always well-to-do. This notion is a holdover from earlier days, but it is not true today—not when a brickmason gets $15 an hour and a substitute special-education teacher with a master's degree gets $20 a day. Members of the middle class are not necessarily on the side of free enterprise or capitalism. The success of the Scandinavian social democracies is due to the continuing existence of a stable and respected middle class—the requirement for a stable society with any economic and political philosophy short of dictatorship and repression.

The Middle Class Mystique

Members of the middle class are usually identified by vocation: doctor, engineer, store manager, and so forth. This is only part of the story; one we can take as read. Just as important for the well-being and stability of society are the behavioral characteristics of middle class members.

Middleclassmanship[1] is a state of mind. It is not even a pragmatic state of mind, as it involves doing a lot of things for little or no monetary return. The middle class mystique is understudied.[2]

---

[1]Following the example of Steven Potter in, for example, *Gamesmanship* (New York: Henry Holt, n.d.) I use the convenient neologisms "middleclassmanship" and "middleclassman."

[2]There *is* a good bit of literature on the middle class, mostly with titles like "The Emergence of the Middle Class in _____" and "_____ in Middle Class Society." The characteristics of the class are assumed known. An exception is John Raynor, *The Middle Class*, London: Longmans, 1969.

Our sociologists prefer to document the life styles of Puerto Rican mothers on welfare with nine children of unknown parentage. This may be due to the "taking for granted" I mentioned earlier and also because the middle class is assumed to be tough—it can take care of itself (possibly a dangerous assumption, as we shall see). Intellectuals may not even like the middle class. Socialists consider it a necessary evil at best.

"We" and "They"

The heart of middle class philosophy is revealed in two pronouns: "we" and "they" (or "them" and "us"). Members of other classes say, "This road is terrible! Why don't *they* do something about it?" A middleclassman says, "This road is terrible! *We* have got to get it fixed." And, by golly, he raises a stink and gets something done.

This feeling of responsibility leads a member of the middle class to do strange things, things which do little for him personally, which take up his time, and for which he will receive little thanks. He sits on boring committees, attends PTA meetings, is a member of a service club, leads a scout troop, and fights his church's battles as a member of the vestry. He is a good neighbor: he is concerned about zoning and keeps his own yard tidy. His wife, a middleclasswoman, collects from her neighbors for the Heart Fund. They both vote regularly.

This is a partial list which can be extended. Together these efforts go a long way to shape and support a decent society. What sort of recognition does the middleclassman get? Precious little. We have a Labor Day but we don't have a Middle Class Day. He has been derided and ridiculed in print from the days of *Babbitt* to the writing of modern columnists and is considered a "square" by his own children. He is a perfect taxpayer: usually salaried, he pays the government its money before he gets his own check. He has available few tax "loopholes" or "gimmicks": when he gets a raise, the government receives more of it than he does. He makes few demands on the exchequer. As a group, the middle class gives more and takes less than other classes (which I define later).

Why?

People willingly stay in the middle class and new people join the ranks (some drop out, as we shall see). Considering the obvious disadvantages of membership, this seems irrational. Why would anyone be a middleclassman? The incentives are buried deep in Western society (the middle class is almost exclusively a Western phenomenon). A proper discussion of the anomaly would have to be made by a philosopher or a psychologist or both. The following analysis is based on a layman's, an amateur's, understanding.

Reasons for membership seem to come under the categories of decency, snobbery, and tradition. Most often the middle class is something we are born into, like being a member of the Presbyterian church. The decency reason does stem from the morality of Western religion. The middleclassman is not necessarily a church member (although most Protestant churchmen are middleclassmen), but he respects and accepts the moral teaching of other people's churches and temples. Decency, respect for others, fair play—these are the unexciting concepts that help keep a person in the group. He knows he is a bit of a fool to stay but he is stuck. There are some things which are "not done" and some which are "done." The middleclassman does not look for free handouts (the work ethic?) or take advantage of or look down on fellow citizens. He does try to do his best to improve things, even to the extent of volunteering for military service in times of danger.

My mother was a snob. She was proud of the fact that we were middle class (she called it *upper* middle class, whatever that means). Snobbery is not very nice but it has its uses. For me it meant that there were certain children, probably good kids, who I couldn't play with. It made me learn a rather elaborate code of Victorian table manners that I will use until I die. On the other hand, "maintaining her position" prompted my mother to donate countless hours of her time to service causes—causes which were good and which helped others.

Snobbery is probably the greatest incentive for outsiders to move "up" to the middle class. The ultimate goal for an immigrant or a minority group member is to be accepted by the middle class— the "mainstream of America." The outsider's children may not share his enthusiasm and in moving up he may turn his back on his old friends, his old religion, and even his relatives—but no matter; we have a new recruit and we need all the bodies we can get.

Novelists, who may be better psychologists than most psychologists, have been preoccupied with class distinctions. This is particularly true of English writers: Margery Sharpe is a felicitous example. In *The Flowering Thorn*,[3] her heroine, Leslie, is wakened in the middle of the night:

> She is conscious, for the first time in her life, of being one of the gentry. The gentry, on whom people still at a pinch depended: who were still, it seemed, expected to rise out of their beds and career through a thunderstorm whenever an incontinent young woman saw fit to have a baby.

This is the tradition aspect of the middle class mystique. The middle class is the inheritor of the duties of the gentry, the squires and such, just below the nobility, who mixed with and took care of the people. These traditional duties, whose roots are lost in the mists of time, can recur surprisingly in times of stress. In a disaster, people look desperately for a leader. In wartime, as a young junior officer, I was shocked to have my men, older and stronger than I, huddle around me in a sticky situation (they should have spread out). Our middle class may be carrying psychological baggage that is older than our nation.

I have tried to define the middle class mystique, and perhaps made the class look silly, but I haven't pointed out why it is necessary. (The good things it does could obviously be done by

[3]Boston: Little, Brown, 1934.

government agencies.) Before tackling this question, I had better define the other classes in Western society.

OTHER CLASSES

In the old days things were simple: there was a working class, a middle class (upper and lower?), and the aristocracy. Things are more complicated today. My list of other classes is parasitic, working, shyster, vested, intellectual, social and jet set, and ruling. The proliferation of types is largely due to the workings of modern governments and social theories.

Parasitic Class

The parasitic class is composed of people who take more from society than they give—not just to meet emergencies but as a way of life. The members of this class are usually isolated as minorities in identifiable communities[4] for economic and social (often language) reasons. They are not necessarily ethnic minorities; certainly second- and third-generation white welfare communities in Appalachia qualify.

The goal of *individuals* in the parasitic class may be to move to the working class, but the *class* goal is to get more money from the government. The procedure for doing this involves a numbers game—two numbers games.

The first numbers game is to have children. For middle class couples, children are a heavy responsibility and a financial burden; for the parasitic class the opposite is true. The size of the welfare check, the number of food stamps, depends on the number of dependent children. There is often talk of changing this—in China people are actually penalized for having too many children—but in the Western world it seems unlikely. Our welfare policies are based, after all, on middle class morality.

The second numbers game involves ethnic minorities. The idea

---

[4]Not "ghettos"—the word is often misused.

is to show that *your* minority is more numerous than other minorities. The logic is obscure: that the larger group is more deserving? that block voting will promote an unequal distribution of funds?[5] In order to help the minorities play this numbers game, the 1980 U.S. Census asked the citizen to identify himself as black, Eskimo, Indian, Samoan, or one of *five* types of Hispanic. Only the whites are considered to be a homogeneous group.

Working Class

The working class is an old, familiar classification, not as well defined today as in the days of the "cloth-capped vulgarians" but still identifiable by the way its members make a living and by their attitudes.

Working class people are not parasites; they pay their taxes and by their labors make the system work. Whether they are "noble" or not I don't know, but I do know that they don't share all the mores of the middle class. Workers tend to be inward looking; not that they are mean or greedy but that their generosity is confined to home and family rather than to society at large. Interests run to sports, spectator and participatory, and to informal socializing. Politics are pragmatic—to vote for whoever is, or seems to be, on the side of the working man with little concern for national or international policies. As far as most workers are concerned, nothing is so bad that it can't be cured by a pay raise.

The working class and the middle class can work productively together as long as the workers have respect for the middleclassman. Why the hell should they have respect? I have already noted that the middle class is not necessarily smarter or more tasteful: it is hard to respect someone for his assumed morality. Middle class managers and engineers *do* make the decisions. When two groups

[5]Most parasitic class members do not vote unless organized or bribed. In any case, votes are not bought by government largess, since gratitude is the rarest of human traits. Votes are got by *promises*, not by *performance*. Some of our politicians know this; others do not and persist, futilely, in trying to "buy" votes.

work together without an established pecking order, they work as adversaries. The antidote to bitterness, such as there often is in England, is free class mobility or at least the absence of inherited class membership.

Shyster Class

The shyster[6] class obviously includes the crooks and crime figures we have discussed. It embraces many more—all people, in fact, who bend the law and who take from society more than they return. The list is long and varied: croupiers and cocktail waitresses who don't report their earnings; people who cheat on paying their income taxes, who use tax shelters, or who deal mostly in un-money; bankers who "launder" dirty money; shady land speculators and developers; anyone who makes or markets shoddy goods; lawyers who make their living from trumped-up damage, malpractice, and class action suits; quacks and prostitutes. The list can go on. In some countries almost the whole business community could be included.

Dealing with this class is the job of law enforcement agencies. Shysters are enemies of capitalism, of business, of the middle class— of everyone who does his job, pays his taxes, and tries to do the decent thing.

Vested Class

This is a growing class. It is composed of people who look like middleclassmen but who have abandoned the activist part of the middle class mystique—they are "they" people rather than "we" people. Like the working class, they look inward. Their concern is to preserve vested interests.

The most obvious members of the vested class are retirees. Once hardworking members of the middle class, they decide to take a break, collect their Social Security and pension checks, and hang

---

[6]"Person without professional honor" (Concise Oxford Dictionary).

on. In some cases they retire to enclaves with fences and guards to shut out the world. Sometimes they move to retirement cities, such as Green Valley, Arizona, which exclude untidyness like young people and children (dogs are okay). What they talk about I don't know: past glories, I guess, or the stupidity of "them" on the outside.

Unfortunately, more young people are moving into the vested class. The prototype is a civil service worker who realizes that he is never going to set the world on fire, that he will get regular modest promotions, and that he will retire on a comfortable (indexed) pension. He never was a party to the businessman's unwritten convenant we talked about in Chapter 6. Even military officers often opt for vested class membership. Officers used to be middle class (or aristocracy, in the days when commissions were bought), but no more. We haven't had a fighting war for many years, and anyway most service jobs do not anticipate combat. The big subject of conversation at officers' club bars is retirement plans.

Business unwittingly fosters vested class membership. The emphasis on fringe benefits and tenure, along with the proliferation of staff rather than operational jobs, encourages a "civil service" attitude.

The vested man is the norm in the socialist blueprint; he is the citizen of planned capitalism.

Intellectual Class

The intellectual class is not a large one but I have to include it to take care of people who don't fit anywhere else. Most of the "intellectuals" I discussed earlier belong in other classes: in the middle class or in the vested class, particularly if they have tenure. The real mark of the intellectual class is that its members put their own discipline and studies ahead of social concerns or even, in some cases, their nation.

The "true intellectuals" obviously belong in this class: the "super intellectuals" probably don't (we return to them later). There are others, people whose work is their life, who can be conveniently included: musicians, artists, poets, and those writers who don't care who reads their work.

Social and Jet Set Class

I consider these two together to save space. I classify them as separate sets out of consideration for the fact that the two groups instinctively hate each other's guts. The thing they have in common is money: old money and new money: Palm Beach and Palm Springs.

The social set is dedicated to preserving tradition, privilege, property, and propriety; the jet set to having a good time and to conspicuous consumption. To make it into the social set, money is not enough—one must have "family."[7] All it takes for men to get into the jet set is money, stamina, and a strong stomach. Women need to be young and beautiful, and to have more cleavage than Matt Dillon.

The monied classes really aren't too important to our story. They aren't middle class and they don't threaten the middle class. Few rich businessmen have any inclination to join the jet or social set (which they probably could not get into anyway).

Society people do make handsome contributions to culture and to education which help us all. The jet set spends money, a lot of which winds up in the hands of business.

Ruling Class

The aristocracy is gone but there is a ruling class in Western nations. This class exists almost exclusively at the national level. In the United States its members are concentrated in Washington with a very few outlanders in the statehouses of large states (and possibly in the mayor's mansion in New York City). Some of these leaders are elected; some are not.

[7]See Cleveland Amory, *Who Killed Society?* New York: Harper Brothers, 1960. Nobody, really; it is still doing fine.

Family names like Churchill, Lodge, and Stevenson are always with us. New names, a lot of them of super intellectuals, keep coming and going. The frequency of change is a measure of the democracy of a society. Before World War II, France under the Third Republic had many governments, all headed by permutations of the same few names.[8]

The existence of a ruling class seems to be a condition of an ongoing society. This may be good or bad: good in that government is led by dedicated people who know the rules; bad in that the ruling class may lose touch with the rest of us, particularly with the middle class. The middle class, and business, should try to move people up to the ruling class to make itself heard.

Well, those are my identified classes. The list is probably not exhaustive (invent your own).[9] Certainly the classes are not mutually exclusive. It is possible to be a member of more than one class. A successful operator, for example, may be a legitimate member of both the shyster class and the jet set. All classes, with the possible exception of the social set, compete with the middle class for money, bodies, and prestige. Not class warfare as Marx used the term but confrontations of a different sort. Before looking at these struggles, let us consider the value of the middle class as a stabilizing element in society.

VALUE OF THE MIDDLE CLASS

After the flattering image I have presented, it hardly seems necessary to justify the middle class. I do have the feeling that some of my readers are figuratively standing up and waving their hands to get equal time. From the Marxist point of view, the "virtues" I describe are hardly virtues at all.

[8]See William L. Shirer, *The Collapse of the Third Republic*, New York: Simon & Schuster, 1969.

[9]There must be a student class—people who are too old to be classified with their parents but too young to know where to go.

The service activities of the middle class can be interpreted as organized busybodying, contributing to the repression of better-planned alternatives. Care of the elderly and disadvantaged, the running of scout troops, and care of crippled children may better be handled by government agencies that will disperse services with more justice and equity. The "we" in the "we or they" antithesis can be seen as a defense of property and privilege. Even the remarkable efficiency of mixed professional and volunteer projects (See Chapter 18) compared with the civil service run of alternatives is a mixed blessing—volunteer work takes jobs and money away from properly trained and organized people.

I don't buy these arguments but I have to admit their propriety when seen from the side of the social planners, to whom the middle class is an impediment to socialist goals. As a basically conservative group, the middle class usually does support free enterprise, if that is the existing system.

There is one value of the middle class which I refuse to concede: its role as the model of a nation's personality. When people write or speak (usually derisively) of the American character or of Americans in general, they are referring to middle America. To others, even to ourselves, the middle class *is* America. A nation without an effective middle class has a split personality: to most Americans, a Mexican is either a peon or stinking rich. Like any good superego, the middle class is also the conscience of a Western nation—it retains these roles by means of communication.

Communications

My local daily paper publishes the articles of many columnists: Bishop, Buchwald, Buckley, Goodman, Kilpatrick, Kraft, Rowan. As a middleclassman I read them all. These writers have different leanings and priorities. They have one thing (apart from writing well) in common: they all address the middle class reader as though no other class existed. This makes sense: most of their readers are members of the middle class.

Books and periodicals and "highbrow" television programs are directed by the middle class to the middle class. The intellectual class writes to (or at) the middle class—intellectuals write to each other in different media.[10] Literary contributions by other classes (except for trashy, sexy best sellers) are minimal.

The reasons for this concentration on one target class are obvious. As a writer I know that the middle class is my natural market: it is the one which will pay for the privilege of reading and which will follow, but not necessarily agree with, my arguments. Most important, it is the middle class reader who may do something to support his convictions (the "we" syndrome). He will put pressure on the powers, form committees, vote (even for tax increases), discuss with his fellows, and write letters to the *Times*. This is the communication and action system (feedback loop if you prefer) that controls and shapes national image and purpose. It is individual members of the middle class who serve as the neurons of a nation's nervous system.

Emerging Nations

Without a viable and effective middle class a nation is either a tribal battleground or a more or less secure dictatorship. The first need of an emerging country is not to build steel mills or to establish a national airline; it is to develop an effective middle class. Since middle class attitudes have a long cultural history, this is a difficult job. It can be done. After World War II, Japan was a shambles: physically, economically, spiritually. With a certain amount of American prodding and leadership, the Japanese created an economic and political climate that encouraged the growth of a middle class.[11] This was a remarkable achievement. The middle class does

---

[10]While the middleclassman reads *Time* or *U.S. News and World Report* or *Scientific American*, the intellectual reads *Foreign Affairs* or *Commentary* or the *Physical Review*.

[11]Ezra Vogel, *Japan's New Middle Class*, Berkeley: University of California Press, 1963.

not "emerge" spontaneously, like athlete's foot. It has to be encouraged and protected by government policy. The Japanese are smart enough to know this; preserving the middle class is still a high priority of the Japanese government.

A look at the African continent is interesting. The islands of stability are South Africa and Kenya, which have functional middle classes. Most other countries are in a mess.[12] When the colonizers left, the local equivalent of a middle class went too. Rhodesia is an interesting case; after fighting the whites for years, the new black president (a Marxist) made an immediate appeal for them to stay. The country needs the old middle class for its skills—banking, engineering, management, and so on. It just may need the middle class even more to preserve a national identity.

There are two bad ways for a developing nation to try to create a middle class overnight. One is to import it; the other is to build a large civil service with presumably middle class managers. Civil service people become members of the vested class (or even of the jet set if their pay is high enough, as in some OPEC nations). A "middle class" of mercenaries can provide technical skills but will not identify with or give character to the host country.

The Ivory Coast, a former French colony, is prospering (hotel rates in Abidjan are comparable to those in Paris!).[13] Since its independence in 1960, it has had only one ruler: Houphouet-Baigny. The nation is rich largely because it has exploited (plundered) its equatorial hardwood forests. The economy works because Houphouet-Baigny not only encouraged the old French managers and technicians to stay but has encouraged other Westerners (and Lebanese) to come in and run the country, at higher pay than the natives receive. Foreigners (including farm workers from poor African neighbors) make up a third of the population. The local

---

[12]René Dumont, *False Start in Africa*, London: Deutsch, 1966.

[13]See a series of articles by Jean-Claude Pomonti, originally published in *Le Monde* and translated in the *Manchester Guardian Weekly*, February 24 and March 2, 1980.

people must be frustrated. It is unlikely that the nation could survive an economic slump with a "middle class" that is really a vested class and that has its heart in France.

The Shah of Iran tried to create a middle class, to keep up with the modernization of his country, by sending students abroad for training. It didn't work. Iran today has no recognizable character. It takes more than education to develop a middle class mystique. Mexico wants to develop a middle class to match its new oil wealth. Saudi Arabia is trying to develop a middle class by granting free loans (or even gifts) to its own businessmen. The success of this policy will ultimately determine the stability of the regime. It may determine the stability of the Western world.

THREATS TO THE MIDDLE CLASS

The main threat to the middle class in Western nations is that the economic, political, and social climate will become so unfriendly or difficult for middleclassmen that they will opt out and join other classes. People can switch rather than fight. Most writing on the "decline of the middle class" assumes that the class itself is going to the dogs. A lot of this criticism is unfair.

From the writings of Dickens (*Martin Chuzzlewit*) to today's letters to the London *Times*, it has been a popular foreign indoor sport to ridicule middle class Americans as grasping, materialistic, and flat-headed. Our own intellectuals have taken up the cry.

In a recent bestseller, Christopher Lasch charges us with galloping narcissism (handy definition: "Love rejected turns back to the self as hatred").[14] Narcissism is very big today. It explains everything, even our nasty sexual habits. If you go to a shrink, narcissism will likely be his diagnosis. Since Lasch's conclusions are based on clinical sessions, they can hardly be laid at the door of the middle class (the cringing buyers of the book). Few middleclassmen have either the time or the money for psychoanalysis.

[14]C. Lasch, *The Culture of Narcissism*, New York: Warner, 1979, p. 78.

An unfairness of much criticism is that it reproves us for not being what we never claimed to be. The middle class is not intellectual or particularly cultured (remember Joe Dalton); its strong points are service, decency, and some common sense.

Intellectual writers assume that things used to be better—that we are a dying society. Lasch says that Americans no longer know how to bring up their children. Did we ever know? I guess my parents succeeded in raising my sister and my brother and me: we managed to stay (pretty much) out of jails and whorehouses and to become contributing citizens, but I would never use my parents as models. To be less "narcissistic," I refer readers to the relationship between Mr. and Mrs. Shofield and Penrod, the early years of Nancy Mitford, or even the youth of Winston Churchill.

Late in the book, Lasch does say that "there are still traditions of localism, self-help, and community action that only need a vision of a new society to give them vigor." Now he is talking about the middle class. Thanks a lot.

There is one more enemy of the middle class—a new one—celebrity worship. Under this doctrine (promoted by television and by slick magazines), only a few—the rich, the famous, the power-ful—are *people*. The rest of us, including most of the middle class, are, well, un-people.

Switching

It can become too difficult or too humiliating for people to want to stay in or to get into the middle class. To be a good middleclass-man requires minimums of money, time, and respect.

Middleclassmen are not greedy (if they were they would switch to the shyster class). They do need to make enough money (or to be left enough by the government) to be reasonably secure and not to be despised. Middleclassmen are willing to make financial sacrifices. Following the example of his English opposite number, the American skimps to be able to send his children to private schools. In order to make ends meet, his wife may work too. As this drastically reduces free time, the couple may be forced out of the middle class.

It takes optional time to do middle class things: to sit on committees, to lead scout troops, to badger elected leaders, even to write letters, to read, and to telephone. Taxation and inflation can force a middle class couple to become reluctant members of the vested class.

Business tries to keep its middleclassmen affluent, but its options are limited. The working class is able to exert increasing pressure to get an ever larger share of available money. Time—lack of time—is the greatest threat to an effective middle class, as anyone knows who has tried to round up volunteers for a project.

Some people have an open option of class membership. This is particularly true of rich people, such as sports figures, entertainers, and celebrities. A baseball star may elect, by his good works, to join the middle class; he may stay comfortably in the working class and go coon hunting with his buddies in the off-season; if he is a swinger, he may join the jet set. Itzhak Perlman, the violinist, works for handicapped children. He chose the middle class.

Respect

The middle class is a minority in its own land (with the possible exception of Israel). It can set the tone and character of its country only if the other classes respect it as capable and deserving. This is a reasonable concession. As long as the middle class is willing to do the dirty work, the others are free to pursue their own goals: money, security, power, or learning. The middle class will lose this respect if it is too small, too splintered, too ridiculed, or too poor.

General acceptance of the (possibly simplistic) middle class values of decency, dedication, and patriotism can make a nation tough. It was middle class morality that enabled the English to survive their ordeal in World War II; on the other side, the same morality (few Germans knew what bastards their leaders were) enabled the Germans to put up a magnificent fight. The French middle class was discredited before the war—splintered into left and right factions, with both houses derided by the workers and the communists. The French middle class could not play a leading and stiffening role.

THE CLASS APPROACH

As a sometime mathematician, I know that there are many routes to solutions but that some are more "elegant" than others. The choice of an appropriate coordinate system, for example, can dramatically simplify an applied problem. The class approach clarifies (for me) the cardinal questions: What makes a decent, effective society? What is the role of business in this process?[15]

The proper role of business is to support the middle class. This gives meaning to all the preceding chapters (with the exception of those on elementary economics). It explains the attitude of business toward its employees, the importance of cultural tradition, and the significance of the battlegrounds: education, religion, services, government, and the arts.

The presence of a viable middle class does not guarantee a free enterprise economy. It does imply that whatever the system is, it will have a good chance of working in a humane way. The innate conservatism of the middle class will tend to preserve and improve the existing order. If this be a capitalist system, the middle class is both its best defender and the reasonable target of socialists who try to discredit it.

The only remaining piece of business (and the reason I don't stop here) is to present my reasons for preferring free enterprise. This has to be a subjective argument outside the scope of class analysis.

[15]These are problems not neatly dealt with by most academic disciplines. Economists are obsessed with money, numbers, and equations; sociologists with (preferably) depressed minorities and questionnaires; anthropologists (the best bet) with exotic cultures and with attacking each other; political scientists with governing systems.

20

FREEDOM AND DEMOCRACY

THE CHOICE BETWEEN capitalism (market economy) and socialism (planned economy) may ultimately depend on what sort of freedom one prefers. Socialism does promise freedom of a sort, but it is quite a different thing from that of nineteenth-century liberalism. Democracy is something else. It is possible to have tyranny under a democratic form if that is what the people want and to have individual freedom under an enlightened dictatorship or colonial administration. On the other hand, a democratic selection and rejection process seems essential to maintain individual liberty.

THE WAVE OF THE FUTURE

If it were possible to graph the character of Western economies as time moves on, the curves for each nation would look something

293

like the diagram above. The economic climate oscillates; it moves toward total planning until a reaction sets in and then moves back toward a market economy without ever going all the way either way. Why can't nations make up their minds?

The fact is that economic systems, like all human creations, carry the seeds of their own destruction. As Marx pointed out, laissez-faire capitalism is self-destructive: as businesses get too big and powerful, a reaction sets in among a democratic (or revolutionary) people. What Marx did *not* recognize is that socialism also destroys itself. As the inefficiency of a planned economy becomes apparent, the leaders—even Russian leaders—turn desperately to the profit motive to give it a boost.[1] There is also a psychological reason. People are restless; whatever the prevailing system, they want to try something different (particularly in bad times). In most countries there is an "out" political party—Democratic, Republican, Labour, Conservative—standing by to accommodate them.

As mathematicians know, there are only two things that can happen to an oscillating function (a wiggly line). It can zero in, like the business end of a gimlet (the tool, not the drink) on a single

[1]For any Marxists who may still be reading, this is not a dialectical approach. I refuse to use a term I don't understand, even after reading Heilbroner (*Marxism for and Against*, New York: Norton, 1980). He claims that only a dialectical analysis takes *changes* into account. This is not true—not since Newton and Leibnitz invented calculus. One modern method of analysis, systems dynamics, is based almost entirely on change and "contradiction." See Jay Forrester, *Principles of Systems*, Cambridge, Mass.: Wright-Allen, 1968. See also *HIM*, Chapter 11.

concentration point, or it can keep on wiggling. If the single point is predicted to be on the planned economic boundary, it is gleefully referred to by socialists as "the wave of the future." (Not since the 1920s have there been many "wave of the future" capitalists.) Unfortunately for us free enterprise types, the dice are loaded in favor of the planners or collectivists.

The reason for this bias is statutory. When the "liberals" are in power, they fortify their position by legal means: they legislate new departments and government regulation. By their very nature, conservatives resist making new laws to perpetuate their position (Proposition 13 is an exception), and they usually lack the wit or the time to undo the apparatus their predecessors have created. We still have some anachronistic departments left over from New Deal days.

The economy may or may not prosper as the political climate moves from the "right" to the "left" on our sketch. What *does* change is the concept of freedom: from individual freedom (liberty) to collective freedom (security).

FREEDOM[2]

There are three key planks in the conservative creed: (1) individual freedom or liberty cannot exist without economic freedom; (2) the system of private property is the most important guarantee of freedom not only for those who have it but also for those who don't; and (3) the right to do one's own thing is the final defense against collectivism—against a planned society. These are strong propositions and nothing to be ashamed of. From an objective viewpoint, there is more empirical evidence that they are true than there is for any of the claimed benefits of socialism.

The converse of economic freedom is a planned society. While

---

[2]In this section and in the remainder of this chapter, I lean on two references: Schumpeter, *CSD*, and F. A. Hayek, *The Road to Serfdom*, Chicago: University of Chicago Press, 1944. I will not clutter the text with specific references.

the planners may approach their task with high ideals and even with the intent of allowing some individual discretion, they soon find out that they can no more put up with back talk than can a first sergeant. Only under a free enterprise system, with its terrific diversity of autonomous entities, goals, missions, and hierarchical structures, can management afford to—and does it have to—listen to the worker with a beef. Unless egalitarian socialism is the goal of the planners,[3] the value and the remuneration of each worker will be set by a faceless planning board. As Leon Trotsky said (1937), "The old principle: who does not work shall not eat, has been replaced by a new one: who does not obey shall not eat." Actually, the worker may not even have the option of starvation. He may be allowed neither to quit nor to disobey.

The private property banner is the flag that makes socialists see red: the very symbol of inequality and discrimination. The capitalist is apt to argue for private property as the only reasonable reward of success, the only reason to take the economic risks that keep a society viable and competitive. True. But there is a more fundamental argument for private property. With property goes power. The factory owners (probably shareholders in today's world) have the power to provide jobs, to support the arts and learning, even to advertise. If all property were owned by the state, the state would be all-powerful. Only it could confer benefits and remuneration. Individual power, or freedom, would be that granted by the planners on the basis of their own value system.

The right to do one's own thing is obviously contradictory to collectivism. Who has this kind of license anyway? We don't have complete freedom to go our own way: we can't (shouldn't) hold up a bank or even run a red light. The liberal definition of individual freedom demands only that there be known, published groundrules within which a person is free to operate. More important, the

---

[3]This is the only logically consistent form of socialism, since only it eliminates "antisocialist" value judgments.

person has the assurance that these rules will not be retroactively changed even in the name of justice or of common sense. The principle that provides this freedom is the Rule of Law.

THERE OUGHT TO BE A LAW

In Western countries the role of laws is to set limits on individual freedom and to define the rules under which individuals and corporations may safely operate. The Rule of Law is not arbitrarily or retroactively changed even to serve the "public interest" or to correct "obvious injustices." True liberal tradition calls for laws to be as few and as simple as possible to still ensure an ordered society.

We pay a high price, in both frustration and humiliation, by sticking to the Rule of Law. This frustration is usually voiced in the cry "There ought to be a Law."

There ought to be a law against income tax loopholes which encourage ads in *The Wall Street Journal* aimed at wealthy readers: "Pay zero taxes! Your accountant can help, but *you* must make the decisions."

There ought to be a law to take care of the president of a Miami bank whose principal business is to handle money from drug trafficking. When he tells the interviewer on the evening TV news, "I am a banker. I don't ask where the money comes from; I operate within the law," he is safe and he knows it. He may be a new American but he knows more about the Rule of Law than most of us.

There ought to be a law that supports the President of the United States when he says he wants to send Iranian students back home. Even foreigners are protected by the Rule of Law when they are on our territory.

We pay a price for the Rule of Law, but the price paid by a planned society for *its* form of law may be higher. Under socialism, law is used to tell people and organizations what they must do rather than what they may not do. (Regulation is a step in this direction.) It is also used, often retroactively, in the public interest, to correct antisocial behavior. Any business that made too much money would probably have it taken away. (The "windfall" profits tax on the oil industry exemplified this sort of punitive legislation. At least it wasn't retroactive.) Anyone who got out of line or who got rich could expect to wind up before a "people's court" and eventually be the star turn in a jolly public flogging, mutilation, or execution.

SOCIALIST FREEDOM

Socialists and planners do offer freedom. They offer freedom from want and insecurity and—what may be a better recruiting slogan—freedom from being looked down on or despised by other classes or groups that are getting a bigger cut of the communal pie.[4] These freedoms can be appealing (remember Dieter and Anneliese in Chapter 3), but they must oppose and replace individual freedom or liberty. In order to justify this exchange of one set of freedoms for another, socialists, from Marx to the present, have had to postulate a special kind of citizen.[5]

The new man is a social or communal person, an enlightened comrade who puts social gains ahead of his own welfare. To Marx, people were the product of society rather than the other way around. There *are* such communal citizens. In the early days of the Russian experiment there were some who asked only to be given a shovel to help dig the Moscow subway. The real question is, are there enough of them—are they a majority? This is the dubious basic principle on which the socialist platform rests. Early socialists

---

[4] If I were pushing socialism, I would pass out the *Texas Monthly* rather than the *Daily Worker*—not because of the text (which *is* good) but because of the advertisements. From a conspicuous consumption point of view, they make *The New Yorker* look like a Sears catalog.

[5] "Freedom does not necessarily diminish as a whole, even if we curtail or surrender property rights in labor, provided we esteem more highly freedoms gained. . . ." R. L. Heilbroner, *Marxism for and Against*, New York: Norton, 1980, p. 157.

looked for social, politically sophisticated followers in the working class. They were disappointed. The average worker turned out to be just as greedy and self-centered as the rest of us or, at best, a half-baked sloganeer like Peter Sellers in *I'm All Right, Jack* and nowhere near as funny.

So much for freedom. You pays your money and you takes your choice. You can have collective freedom or you can have individual freedom. You can't have both. I suppose if a majority wanted the collective brand, old reactionaries like me would be interned or shot. A neat democratic solution.

DEMOCRACY

The working democracy of Western nations is not the classical democracy of our propaganda. Classical or abstract democracy is the creature of the Fourth of July speaker: the claim that all decisions are, or should be, made by majority vote. It is the democracy of the town meeting, where all decisions, down to putting a new culvert under Church Street, are decided by vote—and almost half the people go home mad.

Decisions at the national, state, county, or city level just aren't made this way; they are made by professional politicians. Even though many of these decisions are highly unpopular with the electorate (check at your local bar), the procedure is accepted as democratic and proper. In those rare cases where a national question, like the entry of Britain into the Common Market, *is* turned over to the people to decide in a referendum, it is looked upon by the voters as a sign of government weakness.

Government by professionals is a far cry from participatory democracy, but this is the way it has to be. We can't have referendums every Thursday.[6] Very few of us have the time or the

[6]There is enough of this in Louisiana! As a citizen of Shreveport, in the northern part of the state, I used to vote on the carryings-on of the levee board in New Orleans.

knowledge to make policy decisions. We have to turn the job over to professionals. This does not make the voter impotent or useless; he still has the ultimate responsibility. Like the shareholders of a corporation, he has to elect competent management and reject bad. This is not an easy job.

The voter (or corporation) must follow the legislative process at least partially objectively. It is not enough for the voter to denounce dumb decisions and applaud only those he finds suitable. He should have some idea of why these moves were made and of the political philosophy of the makers. He must—and this is hard—realize that what is good for him is not necessarily good for the nation; that his own congressman has more to do than serve his constituents. The voter should have some confidence in the elected leaders: most of them are reasonably intelligent, dedicated people. At least they are trying. He should be patient and give the leader a chance before condemning him. Good decisions take time; policy formulation takes longer.

The voter should not unduly bug his congressman; nor (worse) should he join a pressure group whose purpose is to do so. This sounds un-American—"write your congressman"—but is just common sense. If we identify ourselves as special cases and put too much pressure on our representatives to do the same, our legislative bodies become untidy assemblies of Greek-Americans, oil company-Americans, Mexican-Americans, farmer-Americans, Israeli-Americans, and so on, rather than of the American-Americans we need to run the country. The voter can serve his nation better by studying the records of incumbents and candidates and by trying to get good ones in and bad ones out. To badger the politician in office is like choosing a doctor and then arguing about the medicine he prescribes. If you don't like the doctor, look for a new one.

Let me take a shot at another sacred cow—the admonition to "get out and vote." The charge should be to "vote if you know what or who you are voting for." When I encounter a list of names that I know nothing about (school board members, for example), I leave the choice to someone else.

Working democracy is clumsy, expensive, and time-consuming and a far cry from the participatory democracy taught in civics class. It can become a tyranny of the majority or, worse, a tyranny of the best-organized pressure groups. It is still the only known way to run a country and keep the wiggly line of its economic character from going all the way to either boundary. We can still "throw the rascals out." What happens to democracy if we move all the way to a planned economy?

SOCIALISM AND DEMOCRACY

It might seem that socialism and democracy are not entirely incompatible—there are people's democracies all over the place. Marxists have been so concerned with economic matters that whole areas of social and political life are poorly defined in their new order: civil rights, education, the media, the election and removal of judges and civil servants, cultural activities, even foreign policy and the organization of the armed forces. Some of these are conveniently dismissed by Marxists as being the province of elected representatives in a "participatory democracy." A picture emerges of a socialist planning board, sort of a super conglomerate, controlling industry, while a democratically elected government does the other chores. The picture is out of focus.

As the power of the planning board increases, it *cannot* leave the other aspects of government to elected politicians. Education must be controlled to provide the proper numbers and types of skilled workers. The law, as we have already seen, must become an enforcing arm. Welfare payments cannot be too generous and old-age benefits must be tied to workers' salaries. The military has to be part of the plan, if only because it competes for manpower. Foreign policy is the outward, visible sign of inward socialist grace.

This doesn't leave much for the elected representatives to do, but it does leave room for elections. The people can be periodically rounded up to vote for candidates to fill all sorts of important-sounding jobs. The people of the USSR elect deputies and members of the Supreme Soviet, who elect the president. Sounds great. It would be if the people had a multiple choice and if the Communist party, the planners, didn't have its *own* government, which really runs things.

Who is the president of the USSR?

The Wave of the Future Again

Is socialism the wave of the future? Will we sacrifice all individual freedom in the name of economic freedom? I don't think so. I think the economic worm will continue to wiggle somewhere between the boundaries of communism and a market economy.

Having just blown my punchline—the opportunity to scare the hell out of the reader—I had better raise some warnings. I think we will muddle on with varing degrees of a free and of a regulated economy *if* the voters are sufficiently informed and interested to elect and support good politicians and reject bad ones; *if* people look upon their legislatures as governments and not as the source of all security and favors; and *if* the majority of the voters continue to think of themselves as citizens of the nation and not as members of special, deserving minority groups.

It is the special interest of business to keep the moving finger as close to free enterprise as it can—as close as the rest of the nation will let it. This is the subject of the next (and last) chapter.

21

SHOW AND TELL

THIS CHAPTER is not essential reading. But some sort of summary chapter, in which the economist writer, for example, presents the solutions to all our problems, is expected. Omission of the peroration is frowned on by reviewers: "After a long and tedious book, the author could at least have had the decency to summarize his conclusions." Actually, there is nothing new here, no recommendations to the business world that have not been explicitly or inferentially made in the preceding chapters. More important, there are no suggested business strategies that have not been proposed or tried by business at one time or another.[1]

[1] A concise summary, which is not incompatible with my ideas, is M. L. Weidenbaum, *Strategies for Business Survival in a World of Government Intervention*. Available from the Center for the Study of American Business at Washington University in St. Louis.

I can't rewrite the book. About all I can do is emphasize some points which seem to merit a final review. Some things I accept as given: that prosperity in a nation requires a healthy business community and a reasonably fair distribution of the fruits of production; that business is most effective in a free enterprise environment; that it is to the advantage of business to oppose "creeping socialism," excessive regulation, and ultimately the establishment of a socialist state. Some questions I ignore as being too controversial or poorly defined: the proper level of charitable contributions by industry is an example. Areas that do seem to be worth one more rehash are preserving or enhancing the business image; establishing better working relations with government; taking political stands; and preserving business integrity.

The ideas are not presented in any priority order. Nor is the reader required to agree with any of them. In fact, the "old contemptibles" who have followed me from the beginning should be quite capable of writing their own "show and tell" chapter if they don't like mine.

IMAGE

The image of a corporation—how it is perceived by outsiders, and by the insiders who work for it—is created from relatively few impressions. Is the mission of the corporation worthwhile? Does the company treat its employees fairly? Does it turn out an honest product at a reasonable price? Does it foul the environment? Is it a good neighbor? Does management exploit the corporation to enrich itself?

These are the "gut" issues by which a company is judged. Others, such as dedication to long-range planning, may be equally important but they are not obvious to outsiders—or to many insiders. Industries that have failed (fairly or unfairly) in one or more of these categories have image problems. In America today it is the automobile makers and Big Oil that are despised. Yesterday it was the railroads and Con Ed.

I can't take a stand on mission. If a company prints porno-graphic literature, that is its business. The environmental question is now a three-cornered battle between the nature boys, govern-ment, and industry. I leave the honest product question to a later section on integrity. Fairness to employees and management remuneration are largely questions of money. Money is something business has some control over, and here I want to get in my two cents' worth.

Wages

Business should fight against higher wages (except, possibly, as they cover inflation). Management usually does this and often loses. The reason it *should* fight is not well understood. It is not greed. It is working for the best interests of society, for its own survival, and ultimately for the well-being of the workers. Money saved in wage contracts does not go into the pockets of management or even those of the shareholders; it is usually spent to reduce the amount of needed borrowing and to update plant—it is the price of survival.

As I pointed out in Chapter 6, the rank-and-file employees of big business (or of government) are well compensated, both in money and in fringe benefits. They may not *feel* that they make enough money (there is no such thing as "enough" money), but in comparison to workers for small business, service people, and craftsmen trying to make it on their own—the groups I call the "outies"—they do very well indeed. In fact, a large company that builds a plant in a nonindustrial town can upset the social and pay structure of the community. Labor leaders have never accepted this.

It is part of labor's doctrine that every worker should get more (real) money every year for doing the same job. This may be part of the American dream, but it is bad economics. Increased prod-uctivity may make it possible to escalate wages, but doing so makes little sense. The result of this "upward and onward" doctrine is that when a company finds itself in a relatively stagnant situation (or in a recession), its unit costs continue to go up and it becomes uncompetitive. It may go out of business, like the U.S. Merchant Marine, or it may have to move to a new location (or fly a flag of convenience) and train new workers who have less seniority.

Labor wants to be represented on the board of directors. Management opposes the idea because it breaks the "old boy" pattern. I think it is a good idea. At least it might be a start toward social responsibility by labor leaders.

Top Management Compensation

Top management salaries are too high. Six- and even seven-figure salaries hurt the business image; they make industry leaders look grasping to outsiders and set a bad example to labor. I am not against handsome rewards for top management if they are deserved, but I don't think they should be laid on like company water.

The criterion for big reward should be big risk. The highly paid basketball player takes a long chance on his ability (for every NBA player on the roster there are hundreds who didn't make it). The wildcatter may get rich with a discovery well (but nine out of ten exploratory wells are dry). It should be the same in business. The swinger who creates a new company (and lots of new jobs), the leader who turns a losing corporation around, the entrepreneur who merges moribund companies into a viable conglomerate, even the manager who is willing to take chances on new ideas deserve to be rewarded. The reward should be provided through share options or incentive pay, *not* through higher base salary or programmed bonuses.

Many top-level jobs in industry are not prone to risk. They are caretaker jobs, like that of (say) a lieutenant general in peacetime, and the salaries should be comparable. Formula bonuses based on profits are not only bad for corporate image; they discourage risk taking. In retrospect, there is something obscene about the managers of the American automobile industry paying themselves millions in bonuses in the years when their cautious policies were ruining the competitive position of the industry and hurting all of us.

Top management should restrain its impulse to flaunt its perquisites. The only thing surer than that special parking places will have to be provided at the Super Bowl city to accommodate company jets is that there will be a television cameraman waiting on the apron to take pictures of industry's leaders staggering down the ladders with drinks in hand.

I must sound mean: put a lid on the wages to the troops, take away goodies from the top brass. My own position may be irrelevant. Industries in all Western countries have to tighten their belts in any event. American business, like American government, may not be paying its way. In recent years our total corporate debt has run about four times our national debt.[2] We spend a lower percentage of our GNP to modernize and upgrade industry than do other Western nations (even less than Britain, which many Americans think is settling happily back into the Stone Age). These are mortgages against the future that will have to be paid eventually. We are now paying for a generation of neglect of railroad rights-of-way in higher freight rates and dangerous roadbeds. An earlier administration built our interstate highways, which we are now hard put to maintain. The Romans had a similar problem with their freeways.

Public Relations (PR)

Most corporate and industry PR efforts are ineffective. Institutional TV advertising[3] is almost a disaster. Inane Madison Avenue catchphrases like "We are working to keep your trust" (it doesn't take much of a wit to point out that you can't keep what you haven't got) don't help, but mostly the problem is that Americans don't trust commercials. With the exception of the Lite Beer skits, most of us

[2]See the *Survey of Current Business*, U.S. Department of Commerce. The figures are reported annually in the August issue.
[3]See *HIM*, Chapter 1.

use the commercial break to get another drink or go the john—
pretty much in that order. Before "truth in advertising" we were fed
a lot of malarky. Now we are fed trivia: Who needs to get "100
percent of his daily vitamin requirements" in a single bowl of
breakfast cereal?

The best PR is people to people; the next best is corporations to
people. The answers to the questions "Who do you work for?" and
"What kind of outfit is it?" are more important PR-wise than canned
messages. Business must try to run a happy ship and hire and
encourage the right kind of people—middle class people. Corporations have to hire specialists and technologists for exacting jobs but
they might take chances on other types of people—even historians
and English majors—for other positions. This could create a more
interesting business personality and, incidentally, promote liberal
education.

Corporations-to-people relationships usually involve handouts
or favors, either through the United Way or directly from the
"angels" in the PR department. To make these contacts more
effective, a corporation might consider using a Corporate Fund
rather than the United Way for distribution. The company is going
to do the organizing and solicitation anyway; it may as well give its
own people, down to low levels,[4] a chance to say how the money will
be spent. At least it can strike one agency off its list—the United
Way.

REGULATION

Government regulation of industry has been a theme of this
book. It is the cutting edge in the battle between the ideology of a
planned economy versus that of economic freedom. Regulation is
based on laws. Business cannot oppose existing laws except through

---

[4]There is a Freudian risk here for the Red Cross. Most veterans have it in for this
worthy organization because it charged soldiers a nickel for donuts. This is silly.
Money, particularly small change, was the most expendable and unspendable thing
in the combat zone. The real beef is that the Red Cross girls dated only officers.

the long-term process of trying to get them changed—a political response that I reserve for the next section. Business can do things to better live with existing rules: it can strive for clarifying decisions in order to at least define the usual murky regulations and the powers of the regulatory bodies; it can fight against unnecessary harassment.

Business can fight back. Without violating the spirit of the law it can object to trivial demands and to contradictory demands by different agencies. Too often, managers adopt the position that "you can't fight city hall" and try to honor redundant and irrational requests. I think they should at least object. The following form letter might be used as a start.

To: Government Agency
From: Corporation Vice President
Subject: Your Request for Information

I received your request of _____ for a new report on _____.

I am happy to report that you, and other government agencies, already have the information you want. It is contained in the following reports:

Report	Agency	Date
•	•	•
•	•	•
•	•	•

For your convenience, I have attached copies of pages of these reports with the information you want highlighted.

I feel sure that you will agree with me that it is more efficient and cheaper, both for taxpayers and for consumers, to eliminate the expense of preparing, filing, and processing a new report.

The pertinent information we have previously submitted is true to the best of our knowledge. It came from our records, which are available for inspection.

Thank you for your continuing interest in our operations and policies.

Would such a letter do any good? I doubt it, but it might serve notice that the worm is trying to turn. As a student friend of mine once complained, "In the face of organized stupidity, a man is helpless." (He was referring to the upper levels of the Harvard English department, which did seem a bit unfair.)

POLITICS

In Chapter 17 I discussed the continuing battle waged by business to make itself heard in legislative halls. This tactical in-fighting must go on. Another important aspect to business political influence is the strategic or long-range effort to get right-thinking people (from the business point of view) in high places. There are two parts to this mission. First, industry must know what sorts of laws it wants—laws that are good not only for business but also for society. Second, it must take a more active part in the selection and election process.

Industry leaders are often parochial in their legislative inter-ests. The health of the market economy is not just a function of labor, tax, and regulatory law; it is an integral part of society, so much so that *every* issue, from foreign policy to farm policy, can affect the industrial complex. Business cannot afford to take an automatic conservative stand on issues or to peremptorily eliminate some issues as somebody else's concern. The following two exam-ples may make my point.

"Socialized" Medicine

American businessmen instinctively reject national health plans. Doctors are good guys—our sort of people. Health plans are creeping socialism. The whole thing is too expensive.

During the 1980 election campaign, President Carter claimed that a proposed health plan would cost some $70 billion. Senator Kennedy disagreed, saying it would cost a mere $20 billion. They were both wrong. It would have cost nothing! That's right, nothing. Unless the quality of service, medical salaries, corruption, and

administrative costs go up, which seems unlikely, nationaliz
medicine will only change the way in which we pay for what we a
already paying for. People do not die in our streets; they get medica
care.

Under the present system, unless a person is already on
welfare or is highly insured, he must pauperize himself before the
government takes over. There is one possible saving in this rather
mixed system. A reasonably well-fixed person, finding that he had
an expensive terminal disease, might perfer to do himself in rather
than waste his estate and be a burden on his children.

Under the existing system, business picks up rather more than
its share of medical costs through taxes and fringe benefits to
employees (increasingly noncontributory). The nationalized
medicine fight would seem to be something best left to the
American Medical Association and the liberals. No point in business
making new enemies over the issue.

Immigration

National immigration policy and enforcement might not seem
to be a concern of industry, but it is. There are two popular schools
of thought which lead to opposite conclusions.[5] One theory is that
the new immigrants—such as Haitians and Cubans—will provide a
needed labor pool for the next century. The other theory is that
most of these new Americans will join the parasitic (or shyster) class
and be a new burden for business, which will soon have revised
hiring quotas and, later, quotas for the executive suite.

Since either of these outcomes would have important implica-
tions for industry, business should make up its mind and take a
stand on immigration policy. There has to be a better way of
selecting new citizens than picking them out of the sea.

[5]There are other positions that are less businesslike—for example, the idea that
new Americans enrich our society (the Mexican restaurant position). Another is my
argument in Chapter 13 that cultural diversity undermines national identity. There is
also the position that the best thing we can do for posterity is to preserve our own
environment and way of life by keeping population in bounds.

*d
e
l

tely chose the preceding examples because they
kinds of political doings that management does not
ider. There should be some sort of forum within a
where the inmates can. talk about which current
are important to business and what positions (if any) the
on wants to take.

uggest a resident political scientist as a floating staff member.
ecessarily a rabid conservative, but an intelligent, personable
or woman who keeps up with both domestic and foreign affairs,
stays in touch with the lobbying effort, and who can lead
scussions.

This is only a first step. It doesn't help much for management to
reach consensus on issues if there is no way to influence national
policy.

Political Action

The efforts of lobbyists and political action committees (PACs)
were described in Chapter 17: these efforts may not be enough to
protect business viability. Lobbying is usually a short-term, tactical
response to "Oh my God" situations: "Oh my God, what are they
trying to do to us now?" PAC efforts are usually aimed at retaining
or unseating incumbents on the basis of their voting records. Until
industry makes effective moves to get business-oriented people into
national government (as we have seen, it sometimes does at local
levels), it is destined to be governed by lawyers.

The obvious answer is to get good business people to run for
high office. Corporations do try. They give leaves of absence for
political campaigning. Unfortunately, few business school graduates
aspire to political office. They aren't about to take even a paid leave
and give their peers a chance to move up on them. Their idea of
success is a (corporate) vice presidency. Business needs people
whose idea of success is a seat in Congress. There are such people.

In any election there are more losers than winners. If these losers are truly motivated political animals, their instinct is to lick their wounds, recover their finances, and try again. This presents an opportunity for business. It can hire the best of the losers and put them on some sort of "fast track" to learn about corporate life and people. The goal is not brainwashing; it is not even to gain long-term employees. The dedicated politician will be around only until the next election. Of course there is a risk: political recruits may like the business world so much that they decide to stay. You can't lose them all.

INTEGRITY

My last item of "show and tell" involves business integrity—a nice high plane on which to close this book. There are two kinds of business integrity: people integrity—the morality thing; and product integrity—giving the consumer a fair shake for his money. They are both critical to society's toleration of the business establishment and of a market economy.

Morality

Industry probably has a higher moral code than any other major institution in Western society. If I ever check my bank statement (I don't), it is to look for mistakes, not fraud; when I give my broker an order, it is done; if a manufactured item has a warranty, it will be honored.

Corporations do not often sell jobs; they do not (in the Western world) bribe customers. There *is* hugga-mugga, but it is the exception rather than the rule. It is apt to involve small business and government contracts. Industry must protect its image: it must try to be purer than Caesar's wife.

There is still a lot of so-called white-collar crime—embezzling and misuse of funds and materiel by employees. This does not usually affect customers (except as it raises overhead and prices). Corporations "swallow" the loss and keep the incident quiet. Worse, their usual reaction is just to fire the wrongdoer and close his personnel file. This seems like the decent, humane thing to do, but I think it is a mistake.

Corporations should publicize employee crime—after all, country clubs list delinquents on their bulletin boards. Unless the amount involved is trivial, they should prosecute. I don't like white-collar criminals. I can more easily forgive a man with a hungry family who robs a store than an overpaid employee who steals from the company that supports him—who steals from me too, and from you, since we will pay for it in increased prices. Companies keep such incidents quiet to preserve their image. I think this is a delusion: outsiders will have more confidence in a company that is not afraid to police its own operations.

Product Integrity

Just as important as business morality for public toleration of the capitalist industrial complex is product integrity. This implies a lot more than "truth in advertising," which is a minimal and almost insulting condition imposed by consumer groups. At the national level, it gives buyers confidence that goods marked "Made in USA" (or Made in _____) are the best possible compromise between quality and price. A corollary to this is that when you pay more for an item, a vacuum cleaner, say, you actually get a better sweeper than if you had bought a cheaper model. This is honest pricing; honest fabrication is more subtle.

Every engineer knows of hundreds of ways in which a product can be made more cheaply, will look just as good, and will still probably survive the warranty period. A cheap paint job on an automobile will look as good, for at least a year, as a proper job. A washing machine with copper rather than silver relay points will perform just as well for a while. Sleeve bearings are just as good as ball bearings until they wear out. The customer is helpless to know whether a product is honestly built or not—even an engineer would have to disassemble it. *Consumer Reports* does do product testing for buyers, but even it can't make the ultimate test: How is the thing going to look after five years of service?

In the Automotive Museum at the Indianapolis Speedway, there is a 1929 Packard touring car owned by the late Colonel Roscoe Turner: it has 351,000 miles on the odometer. To me it looks better than a modern car: the finish and the brightwork are solid and immaculate; the whole thing reeks of craftsmanship. It looks ready to go another 100,000 miles (at ten miles to the gallon). Such a monster is obsolete today—OK, I'll buy that—but is the workmanship, the product integrity, also obsolete?

Before World War II, things were simple. Mostly, Americans bought American goods (and British bought British) because there was little option. With the Common Market and new levels of industrialization, the whole world is now the marketing area. Check the British humor magazine *Punch,* which caters to the affluent middle class. The majority of the advertising space, particularly the premium space, is not bought by English manufacturers (or even by Scotch whiskey distillers). The advertising corporations represent all the industrial nations and even some others (Jamaica Airlines usually has a nice spread). Someone out there is watching us. Product integrity is now more than just decency; it is essential for survival. The following translation from the Japanese may make the point better than I can. (The translation is to Pidgin English, an international language that seems more appropriate than American businessee.)

The locale is the board room of a Japanese corporation. The Honorable Board Members (HBMs) have gathered to hear a report from an Honorable International Industrial Intelligence Agent (HIIIA) back from the States.

HIIIA:
> Him big fellow honorable suburbanite.
> Plenty big fellow grass chop-chop machine belong him.
> Him big fellow plenty pully-pully along rope topside chop-chop machine.

Alla same he go CLANG, BANG, WOOF.
He no go t-pocketa, t-pocketa.
He say E-Z START along topside.
Plenty swearing along him big fellow—plenty hernia.

HBMS:

Ah so.

The rest is, or will be, history.[6] The Japanese make and export a lawn mower that can be started by a ten-year-old child, has prompt and easy maintainance, is competitively priced, does a great job, and gets 67 miles to the gallon. Red-blooded, round-eyed, all-American boys fight and claw to get in line to buy them. "Get out of my way, buster!"

The reader may have gathered that I am, or rather was, an engineer. I drive a foreign car. I want my next car to be American, but I demand that it not put me in debtor's prison and that it be one I can brag about. I want to follow the old American custom of showing it off to my (preferably jealous) neighbors. I may even condescend to raise the hood and let them see the guts of the lovely thing. I will go further.

I would like my next camera, shirt, typewriter, tennis racquet, even my next lawn mower to be Made in USA. I want to ride on American planes and ships and trains (on a decent roadbed), *but* I refuse to pay a premium for the privilege. I want these things to be manufactured in a free enterprise economy in which competitive forces will protect my investment.

I think a lot of people feel the same way.

[6]This was written before I heard that Honda is now marketing lawn mowers in this country.

INDEX